Parliament and the People
The Reality and the Public Perception

Philip Laundy

LONDON AND NEW YORK

First published 1997 by Ashgate Publishing

Reissued 2018 by Routledge
2 Park Square, Milton Park, Abingdon, Oxon, OX14 4RN
711 Third Avenue, New York, NY 10017

Routledge is an imprint of the Taylor & Francis Group, an informa business

Copyright © Philip Laundy 1997

All rights reserved. No part of this book may be reprinted or reproduced or utilised in any form or by any electronic, mechanical, or other means, now known or hereafter invented, including photocopying and recording, or in any information storage or retrieval system, without permission in writing from the publishers.

Notice:
Product or corporate names may be trademarks or registered trademarks, and are used only for identification and explanation without intent to infringe.

Publisher's Note
The publisher has gone to great lengths to ensure the quality of this reprint but points out that some imperfections in the original copies may be apparent.

Disclaimer
The publisher has made every effort to trace copyright holders and welcomes correspondence from those they have been unable to contact.

A Library of Congress record exists under LC control number: 97015772

Typeset by Manton Typesetters, 5-7 Eastfield Road, Louth, Lincolnshire, United Kingdom.

ISBN 13: 978-1-138-32789-4 (hbk)
ISBN 13: 978-1-138-32791-7 (pbk)
ISBN 13: 978-0-429-44900-0 (ebk)

Contents

Introduction vii

1	Setting the Scene	1
2	The Eroding Sovereignty of Legislators	11
3	Enhancing Professionalism through the Work of Parliamentary Associations	17
4	Changing the Public Perception	25
5	Political Reporting	35
6	Ensuring Ethical Standards in Public Life	41
7	The Role of Political Parties	53
8	The Evolving Civil Service	61
9	Direct Democracy: The Way Forward?	69
10	Who do Politicians Really Represent?	77
11	Conclusion	81

Appendices

1	Standards in Public Life	91
2	Rebuilding Trust	171
3	Committee Systems	217
4	Making Laws Make Sense	221

Index 225

Introduction

From 24 to 27 February 1995 the Commonwealth Parliamentary Association, in association with Wilton Park, the conference organizers, sponsored a conference at Wiston House in Sussex on the theme 'Parliament and the People: Making Democratic Institutions More Representative, Responsible and Relevant'.

The conference was attended by delegates from various countries of the Commonwealth, Europe, the United States and elsewhere. Most of them were parliamentarians, some were public servants and parliamentary officers, but also present were others having a direct interest in the subjects under discussion. This study is an attempt to summarize and evaluate the discussions in as objective a manner as possible. However, since it was a condition of the conference that all comments made were non-attributable, it will only be possible to identify speakers where special permission has been obtained.

The title chosen for this study does not exactly repeat the stated theme of the conference because, underlying all the discussions which took place, was the question of how the public perceives parliamentary institutions, and the extent to which public opinion reflects the reality of political life. There is no doubt that, in many of the countries of the world, the public hold their representative institutions and those they elect in very low esteem. Cases of corruption, impropriety, conflict of interest, influence-peddling, and crimes and misdemeanours in general receive wide exposure in any country which enjoys press freedom – and the taint of the guilty readily attaches itself to politicians in general. In fact, as one delegate remarked, the very word 'politician' has a pejorative connotation in his country.

The very fact that this conference was called demonstrated that a serious situation existed in public life, which needed to be confronted. In some countries it has led to an investigation into standards of conduct, a notable example being the appointment by the British Prime Minister, Mr John Major, of the Committee on Standards of Conduct in Public Life under the chairmanship of a judge, Lord Nolan. While a very important session of the conference was devoted to this issue, the broader mandate was directed to the improvement of the effectiveness of parliamentary institutions and the political system in general, 'Making democratic institutions more representative, responsible and relevant' being the issue in question. The terms 'representativeness' and 'responsibility' are clear enough. But what of relevance? If something is to be relevant, it has to be relevant to something else. Are we talking about relevance to the needs of a changing society, to the problems confronting a country, to the demands of the people, to the fair distribution of limited resources – bearing in mind that there is usually a wide gap between what the people want and what their governments are able to deliver? What emerged during the conference touched on all these aspects. Indeed, there was no difficulty in identifying the issues and the problems. Identifying the solutions proved much more challenging.

1 Setting the Scene

The introductory presentation was made by Mr Colin Shepherd, MP, Chairman of the Executive Committee of the Commonwealth Parliamentary Association (CPA). He stated that there were 184 countries in the world today (another delegate subsequently claimed that there were 190), of which 51 were members of the Commonwealth. At the time of writing, 48 of these countries have elected representative institutions, parliamentary government being currently suspended in The Gambia, Nigeria and Uganda, and recently restored in Sierra Leone. The CPA alone has a membership of some 11 000 elected parliamentarians and, when one considers the number of representative institutions throughout the world at the national, federal, state, provincial, regional, municipal and local levels, it is clear that countless thousands, or more probably millions, of elected people are entrusted with the governance, interests and welfare of the populations they represent.

While most, if not all, pay lip service to the principles of democracy, many fall short of the ideals to which they claim to be committed. Not only are they regarded with cynicism and distrust by those they represent, but there is frequently a lack of understanding on the part of the people as to the true role of their political institutions, the way they operate, the duties of elected representatives and of what they do, as well as what they are supposed to do.

A starting point in evaluating what is required if the political process is to be improved is perhaps the identification of the criteria necessary for a model democracy. Even this is not as straightforward as it may sound, given the widespread variations among systems of government, national traditions and culture, and other differences which render each country unique. The fundamental *raison d'être* of any elected assembly is, of course, that it be representative. But representation must be a reality and not simply a concept. Those affected by the policies and decisions of government must have an input into the process. They must understand how it works, and be aware of the avenues open to them for direct participation. The right to vote is at the root of the representative system, but a democracy must take account of the fact that the views held by people are many and varied, that their interests do not necessarily coincide, and that not everyone is going to be happy with an election result. Minorities fear that they may be subject to the so-called 'tyranny of the majority', which commands the voting strength. Yet there can be situations where the tyranny of the minority holds sway, as was the case in South Africa during the long years of the apartheid regime. No voting system, by itself, can take account of all these problems, but at the very least it must be fair, it must be seen to be fair, and elections must take place at regular intervals.

Among the most important of modern political institutions are political parties, and they are a fundamental element in the system of representation. Some political parties have a long historic tradition behind them, some derive from ideologies, and some were formed in response to social and economic pressures. Some parties are broadly-based and designed to attract a wide spectrum of opinion; others are more narrowly-based, including the so-called 'single-issue' parties. In some countries, tribal or community loyalties are an important factor in determining the support enjoyed by a particular party.

The voting system has also been a crucial influence in the formation and development of political parties. There are many different voting systems, the most simple being the plurality or 'first-past-the-post' system, whereby the candidate receiving more votes than his nearest rival wins the seat, even though his share of the popular vote may be well below 50 per cent. This system is used for congressional elections in the USA and for parliamentary elections in both the UK and many Commonwealth countries. A variation of this system is the preferential vote, as used for elections to the Australian House of Representatives, whereby the voter ranks the candidates in order of preference. If the top candidate fails to obtain an overall majority, the bottom candidate is eliminated and his or her votes are distributed according to the preferences indicated, the process continuing until one candidate emerges with an overall majority. A further variation is the two-ballot system, as used in France, under which a second ballot is held in any constituency in which the leading candidate has failed to obtain an absolute majority, the second ballot being decisive regardless of the size of the majority.

Most other systems are based on proportional representation, of which there are various forms. Some countries, including Germany, use a mixed system, the elector having two votes: one being cast for an individual candidate under the 'first-past-the-post' system, the other being for a party list, the list seats being allocated to the parties by a proportional system.

The 'first-past-the-post' system is the least likely to produce a representative result, since a winning party can, and frequently does, win a substantial majority of parliamentary seats with considerably less than 50 per cent of the popular vote. There are even occasions when the winning party's share of the popular vote is less than that of its nearest rival. Under this system smaller parties are unlikely to win many seats unless their votes are concentrated in certain regions. The argument in favour of the system is that it is simple to operate and that it makes for stable government. It also encourages the formation of broadly-based parties which are themselves coalitions of opinion, rather than parties seeking a separate identity in order to underline adherence to a narrower political platform.

Many countries of the world employ a system of proportional representation, one of the newest converts being New Zealand which recently adopted a system based on the German model. Most of the countries with a proportional representation system have a tradition of coalition government, since it is virtually impossible for one party to win an outright majority at an election. With such a system the party strengths reflect the party preferences of the people more accurately, and the spoils of office are not monopolized by a single party.

It is not proposed to consider in detail the various systems of proportional representation which operate throughout the world. Suffice it to say that the experiences of those countries having a proportional electoral system have varied considerably. It seems to have worked well in Switzerland where power-sharing is rooted in the political system. It has not led to instability in the Scandinavian countries, whose systems are designed to reflect voter opinion with a fine degree of accuracy. By contrast, Italy, where the electoral system was recently changed, has experienced great difficulty in maintaining the stability of its system of government since the Second World War. In Israel, where electors vote not for individual candidates but for a party list, the small religious parties exercise an influence out of all proportion to their popular support. Malta, where boundary manipulation once had the effect of distorting an election result, amended its electoral law in 1986 to provide that if a party won 50 per cent or more of the popular vote but not a majority of the seats, it was entitled to an increase in the number of its members in order to provide it with a majority.

There is clearly no ideal electoral system, but if proportional representation is preferred it should be designed to produce a genuinely representative result. If a simpler system is favoured, it is less likely to reflect voter opinion accurately but should at the very least, be consistent with democratic principles. Perhaps precautions should be built into the system to avoid the kind of result which occurred in the Canadian province of New Brunswick in 1987, when the winning party won all the seats in the legislature with 60 per cent of the popular vote, while the opposition, having polled 40 per cent, won no seats at all.

In his presentation Mr Colin Shepherd suggested a number of questions which needed to be addressed in relation to the electoral process. Should the elector be voting for an individual candidate, an individual as the representative of a party, or simply a party? Should it be apparent to the elector just what or who he is voting for? If the voter votes only for a party, is there not a tendency for the representative to respond to party pressure rather than the wider interests of the electorate? How should the balance of power lie between the elected member, the party and the electorate at large?

One of the disadvantages of proportional representation is that it depends on multi-member constituencies, which reduces the personal contact between the member and his or her electorate. In Israel the entire country is a single constituency for electoral purposes and, since electors vote only for a party list, the representative nature of the system is bound to be less personal. In countries with a 'first-past-the-post' electoral system, members usually represent a single constituency, which makes it easier for them to look after constituency interests and assist individual electors with their problems. With this system there is a direct relationship between the member and those he or she represents, and the electors themselves know whom to approach when in need of help or advice. This aspect of a member's duties is quite distinct from his or her duties as a legislator and party member, and has given rise to the term 'a good constituency member' when describing a politician who devotes more time to looking after the community than to participating in parliamentary debates. Party is a strong influence in the political system, and the member who stands firmly behind the party's policies and gives the whips no trouble has greater flexibility for constituency activities.

In countries operating the British parliamentary system, party discipline is strong and can even be rigid. MPs have only limited scope for independent action if they wish to retain the favour of their parties. The party system has become inseparable from modern government, to the extent that, provided the government has a majority, the powers of parliament have in effect become the powers of government. Not surprisingly, MPs have come to be regarded as 'lobby fodder', often hardly knowing what they are voting for and circumscribed in the exercise of any initiative. In some countries 'crossing the floor', or even failing to vote as instructed by the party whip, can result in expulsion from parliament – hence the frequently heard call for more independence for backbenchers and more free votes as a means of improving the system and making members more individually responsible. The truth is that MPs, in countries where they face no legal sanctions, are already free to assert themselves in this way if they are prepared to take the political risks involved. But it is too much to ask for a guarantee that there would be no penalty to pay.

If our political institutions are not truly representative of, and responsible to, those who elect them, then clearly they are failing us. However, some of the issues involved are far from clear-cut, and this complicates the matter of defining in precise and unqualified terms the criteria required for a model democracy. Edmund Burke, to whom more than one reference was made in the course of the conference, held that an elected member was not a delegate but a representative, and that he owed his electors his judgement and not his blind obedience. By this criterion an MP is no less a genuine representative when acting contrary to the wishes of his or her constituents. This is a logical view since no single representative can respond to the widely varying opinions of all his or her constituents and act in such a way as to please all of them. There are issues on which a member and the majority of his or her constituents may be at variance; in which case what should the member do? Vote according to the wishes of the majority or according to the member's own conscience? Cynics might say that the dictates of party override both when important policy issues are at stake. Of course, political conditions have changed radically since Burke's day and the party factor cannot be ignored. Nevertheless, members certainly owe their constituents their integrity, their accountability and, as stated by Burke, their honest judgement.

Most governments are elected on party platforms – policies and general principles to which their supporters adhere. Once elected, they are responsible for delivering the goods but there are usually limits to what they can deliver, and promises frequently have to be broken in the light of changing economic conditions. Whatever the system in place, responsible government is usually held to be accountable government; it is accountable to the people through an elected assembly, with effective checks and balances to ensure the fair and open operation of the system as a whole and regular elections which give the people the opportunity to pass judgement. How well do our governmental institutions measure up to the requirement of responsibility in terms of informing the people, explaining and justifying government action, providing honest and open government, and respecting these and other criteria which may be said to meet the requirements of a model democracy?

So far, we have set out certain considerations concerning representativeness and responsibility. There still remains, however, the question of relevance which, as indicated earlier, needs to be considered in the context of a specific relationship. Mr Shepherd proposed to tackle the question from two standpoints: the relevance of political institutions to those elected to them and to those affected by them. Do all citizens have a full opportunity to participate in the process, and to seek to be elected should they so wish? Do all those who are elected have access to the necessary facilities to enable them to perform their functions effectively? He suggested that the two questions were not unrelated.

Referring to the concepts of 'affirmative action' and 'positive discrimination', Mr Shepherd questioned whether these initiatives should, or should not, be invoked in order to ensure the fair representation of women and ethnic and religious minorities. There are very few, if any, parliaments in which women are represented in proportion to their numbers, and the fair representation of ethnic and religious minorities is also a vexing question. The action required to correct these undoubted shortcomings is not easy to determine: It is easier to tackle some of the fundamental principles which have to be guaranteed if representative institutions are to be relevant to the needs of those they serve and the requirements of a modern society.

First and foremost there must be full opportunity for all qualified people to vote, free from obstruction or intimidation. Effective safeguards are required to prevent multiple voting, impersonation, the stuffing of ballot boxes, and any other method of falsifying election results. There should be an equitable division of electoral districts or constituencies, allocating as far as possible an equal number of electors to each, while taking account of community of interest and the special circumstances which need to be addressed in sparsely populated regions. Constituency boundaries should be regularly reviewed and redistributed as necessary by an independent body free of political influence. The officials conducting an election must be independent and unbiased, and every reasonable facility provided for scrutiny of the count by candidates and their agents. All parties and candidates should have equal access to the media during an election campaign and those restrictions which might pertain (for example, the right to a certain number of unpaid broadcasts) should be applied in a fair and justifiable manner. There should be a limit to electoral expenses – a condition not imposed in all countries – and a full disclosure of their sources. If the people are to believe in the system, the honest operation of these principles must be transparent.

Equally transparent must be the fairness of the operation of the institution itself. It has often been stated that the majority must have its way but the minority must have its say, and the rules and procedures of the institution must guarantee freedom of debate and safeguard the rights of all members. The presiding officer plays a crucial role in this area, as it is he or she who ensures fair play, interprets the rules and procedures and has a traditional responsibility for the protection of minorities. Not all presiding officers detach themselves from their political parties – in fact, in most countries they do not – but members must have confidence in their impartiality while in the chair if the institution is to function effectively. Also essential is a continuous review of the rules and procedures to make sure that they are adapted to changing circumstances: an effective parliament is not a static institution, and rules can become archaic if they are not regularly reviewed. The institution must be accessible to the public and the media and its debates and proceedings published and made readily available. Nowadays, many parliaments broadcast their proceedings by radio and television, which has greatly extended the public's opportunities to follow the debates. In addition, all the proceedings of parliament and its committees should take place in public unless there are strong and valid reasons for meeting *in camera*.

Representative institutions must also be relevant to the needs of the representatives themselves. They require the tools they need to do their job – tools which Mr Colin Shepherd defined as information, communication and finance. Information services, principal among which is the parliamentary library which should have a comprehensive range of research and reference facilities, are indispensable to modern parliamentarians. There was a time when the responsibilities of government were largely limited to the conduct of foreign affairs, the promotion of trade, the defence of the realm and the administration of justice. Over the years, these responsibilities have increased with the result that our legislative institutions have become involved in virtually every area of public activity, including health, education, agriculture, transport, industrial relations, social welfare, environment, energy, and a wide range of other issues relating to the economy, the arts and the sciences. Without access to information, members cannot expect to be properly informed on all the matters which come to their attention. Furthermore, unprocessed information is often more calculated to confuse rather than to enlighten. Anyone familiar with a government's estimates of expenditure will know how easy it is to present a multitude of facts without conveying a great deal of information. The facilities provided should therefore include research assistance provided by officers qualified in various disciplines, who can prepare the required information in concise and comprehensible form consistent with the member's needs. While these services are available in the parliaments of developed countries, often in very sophisticated form, they are grievously lacking in the parliaments of most Third World countries, and this can severely restrict the effectiveness of the elected representatives.

Another of a parliamentarian's basic needs is the necessary means of communication with individual constituents, with the electorate collectively, with government ministers and with the bureaucracy. Postal and telephone communication should be unlimited and therefore assisted by franking privileges and a free telephone service. Reasonable transport allowances should be provided to enable members to travel between the seat of parliament and their constituencies. Ideally, members should be provided with the necessary office accommodation, equipment and staff – including a constituency office – to meet their communication needs. Contacts with ministers and government departments should be made easy, unhindered by any obstacle which would make it difficult for a member to seek legitimate information from government sources.

There was a time when membership of parliament was an unpaid occupation. This would be untenable today, particularly as membership of parliament is a full-time occupation in many countries. No doubt some elected representatives are independently wealthy, but it would be unacceptable in a modern democracy to exclude those without independent resources from seeking election. The right to do so must be open to all. Therefore salaries and allowances must be paid and they must be adequate. Remuneration of MPs is a sensitive area. To quote one comment made during the conference, 'by accepting remuneration for our efforts we sup with the devil'. The public perception seems to be that politicians are only in the business for what they can get out of it. This ignores the fact that most people need to earn a living and that, in politics, not only is there no security of tenure but re-entry into a profession or previous vocation, following a defeat, is not always easy. Nevertheless, a fine line needs to be drawn to ensure that remuneration is sufficient but not excessive. Everything concerning MPs' remuneration and benefits must be in the public domain, nor should MPs be entrusted with the voting of their own salaries, which should be determined and periodically reviewed by an independent review board. Measures must also be taken to counter the ever-present public suspicion of conflict of interest since no institution can operate effectively without public trust.

Another factor which cannot be overlooked is voter education. If the institution is to be relevant to the needs of the people, they have to understand its functions and what it is supposed to do for them. Education is an ongoing process, but the logical place for it to begin is at school. Our children should grow up to understand the basics of how we are governed and continuing education can fill in the details. Civics – in other words, 'how government works' – should therefore be formally taught at the high school level. This is not political education in the partisan sense, although political parties are an important element of the system and their role cannot be ignored. In this educational process the elected representatives have a crucial role to play in informing their electors. Visits to parliament should be regularly organized both for children and for adults, and material should be made available to schools to instruct not only the children but also the teachers. Each parliament should have an education officer and a public information department to provide the required services, and the institution itself should be readily accessible. Its functioning should not be shrouded in mystery; its procedures need to be explained. Public expectations should be geared to what the system can deliver and, only through education, can the public tailor their expectations to a realistic level. Money spent on this process is surely an investment rather than an expense.

In the course of the discussion following the initial presentation a number of points were made. The question of non-elected institutions was raised, and various participants expressed the view that non-elected legislative chambers – often the so-called upper houses in bicameral parliaments – were either useless or inappropriate. Parliamentary democracy, it was suggested, was best served by people who were elected. What, enquired one participant, constitutes a representative institution? Elected persons, interposed another, represent more than those who voted, and the political system should reflect this. Various institutions underpin a democratic society, including the judiciary, the unions, the chambers of commerce, the media, the Church and numerous other non-government organizations. Should the parliamentary committee system be adapted to admit representatives of these organizations? The fact that an electoral system does not necessarily produce a representative parliament was one of the points pursued. Should an absolute majority always be required for the formation of a government, or is there a case for a 'negative ballot box' allowing voters to register disapproval of the candidates to counter the danger of a 'brute majority'? This last point was never clarified, and it is difficult to envisage how a negative electoral system would work. Presumably, if a majority of electors in a constituency indicated that none of the candidates was acceptable, another election with new candidates would have to take place. If this were the result in a majority of constituencies, such a system might well lead to chaos.

A suggestion that political parties are representative institutions in themselves, led to the question as to whether they are organized democratically. In new democracies, parliament alone cannot ensure democracy and, according to one delegate, local government institutions were criticised as being a disaster in his country. Not only was reform required at all levels of government but the media were anxious to set the agenda and were competing with the politicians for attention. Another representative of a small country raised the question of whether members were full-time or part-time representatives and queried how much time they were prepared to devote to their parliamentary duties.

A number of delegates pursued the matter of voter education which, it was agreed, was very important. While, according to Edmund Burke's famous definition, a member is a representative and not a delegate, many electors expect their members to be delegates and do as their constituents tell them. Democracy requires the understanding of the people, but it is not always easy to involve them in less developed countries which have low rates of literacy. The role of the media in the process of voter education was discussed. In countries which enjoy a free press the media tended to see themselves in an adversarial relationship with the elected politicians. They concentrated on single issues, on scandals, on sensation, and were frequently selective in their use of facts. The media have a duty to act responsibly, and those who rely on the media for their information cannot form a rational opinion unless this duty is recognized.

One participant suggested that the media could not be blamed for everything. Parliamentarians themselves were not sufficiently self-critical, and the public could be forgiven for asking whether the politicians deserved what they were being paid. Promises are made which are not honoured, members vote for measures with which they do not necessarily agree, with the result that parliament is not independent and does not really hold the government to account. Another participant suggested that governments should be more responsive to their own supporters, and that constitutional reform might be required to force them to respond to public pressure. Party domination can result in the people being not properly represented. The comment of another delegate that oppositions are not necessarily effective reflected this line of argument. Politicians have fallen into disrepute because the people do not see the issues which they regard as meaningful to them being properly addressed.

One delegate noted that the nature of democracy had changed with the acceptance of the need for greater involvement by the people. This had led to an increasing demand for information by both the people and their representatives, to the point where there was a flood which threatened to overwhelm its usefulness. Accessibility of information was not the problem; the problem was to make it manageable, which underlined the need of parliamentarians for library and research services. In contrast, another delegate, from a small country, stated that he had never felt overwhelmed with information, but advocated access to information legislation to ensure that people were not denied information to which they were entitled. The accessibility of information cannot be taken for granted in all countries.

The views expressed above reflected the divergent backgrounds of the delegates and their home countries. It was recognized that parliament was not the only political institution to be considered and that the input of other institutions into the process should perhaps be more than advisory. Where the public were once uninformed it was suggested that they now risked being ill-informed, and that it was difficult to persuade the average voter to place the national interest before his own. On this note, the scene was set for the ensuing sessions of the conference.

2 The Eroding Sovereignty of Legislators

This issue was considered in the context of the European Union and the surrender of a measure of national sovereignty required of the member states. The governing institutions of the community are: the European Parliament, an elected body with limited powers; the Council of Ministers on which each member state is represented by its foreign minister; and the European Commission which is elected by the European Parliament and which initiates legislative proposals. The powers of the European Parliament are largely consultative, but it shares control of the budget with the Council and has the right to adopt or reject it; it has limited legislative authority and can influence approximately one-third of the legislation presented to it; and it has a right of veto over international treaties and the admission of new members. The Council of Ministers is nevertheless the more powerful body as the Parliament cannot amend legislation against the Council's will and it cannot force the Council to compromise, although the legality of the Council's acts can be reviewed by the European Court of Justice. The powers of the European Parliament do not therefore compare with those of the national parliaments of the Union's member states. For their part, the national parliaments have no authority over European legislation, although they try to subject it to scrutiny. The problem is that it is so complex and so prolific – over 2000 items poured forth between 1989 and 1995 – that adequate scrutiny is impossible.

The presenter, Mr Julian Priestley, Head of the Private Office of the President of the European Parliament, acknowledged that the structure of the European Union and its complex procedures did not facilitate effective parliamentary control and accountability. As a result, the European Parliament is not regarded by the public as a 'real parliament' and voter turn-out for Euro-elections in the member states has been very low. Another problem was that a large proportion of European legislation is of a highly technical and detailed nature – of a kind more likely to be dealt with by administrative regulation in the member states. The debates in the Parliament, conducted as they are in 11 languages, are not of a kind to inspire interest since the necessity for extensive translation stultifies debate. As Mr Priestley commented:

> Any new member of the Parliament is always told by more experienced colleagues, 'never tell a joke'. By the time the Greek witticism has been interpreted into Finnish the strength of the punch line will be somewhat diminished.

The Maastricht Treaty has nevertheless enhanced the powers of the Parliament, not only in the legislative domain, but in terms of its increased control over the appointment of the Commission. In July 1994 parliamentary committees held public hearings and all the candidates were interrogated. This exercise which, avoided the probing into the candidates' personal backgrounds that characterizes the hearings of the United States Senate on the confirmation of presidential appointments, was judged to be a success. The Parliament voted to endorse the Commission as a whole, except for the President of the Commission, who was the subject of a separate vote.

In the future, further reforms of the Union's institutions will be called for and will require the unanimous agreement of the member states, ratification by their parliaments and, in some states, approval by national referendum. Dispelling public apathy and cynicism will be an important factor in the future development of the European Union. An intergovernmental conference convened in 1996 is considering what future steps need to be taken and a Reflection Group of representatives of the member states and the European Parliament was already engaged on preparatory work for this event. Certain proposals for reform have already been aired. Some decisions of the Council of Ministers require unanimity while others require a qualified majority, and it has been suggested that all issues be decided by qualified majority. It has also been proposed that no legislation should be subject to ministerial veto. These are the kind of measures required if public opinion is to be turned around and the institutions of the community are to be seen to have democratic legitimacy.

Another important question to be addressed is whether national parliaments can be given any meaningful input into the European decision-making process. Although the European Parliament should be a partner, and not a competitor, of the national parliaments, there are serious practical problems when it comes to sharing control. First, national parliaments could not possibly cope with the proliferation of European legislation in addition to their own national workloads. Second, there would also be a problem of accountability. Given the likely extension of qualified majority voting in the Council of Ministers – an inevitable development if the community is to avoid paralysis – responsible ministers of national governments could always plead that they were outvoted and thus avoid being called to account. As regards the budget, the chaos which would result if it had to be approved by the parliament of each member state can only be imagined.

Given the workload, and the diversity of parliamentary practice and tradition among the national parliaments of the member states, it is easier to highlight the difficulties of extending control over European legislation than to devise means of giving the national parliaments greater influence. The national parliaments have introduced their own review procedures in order to keep themselves informed and maintain a degree of oversight. In the UK both Houses of Parliament appoint a Select Committee on European Legislation, their function being to examine draft legislative proposals and the explanatory memoranda prepared by the government, and report to their respective Houses. Both committees sit in public, may call witnesses and are assisted by counsel. The government is obliged to find time for debating a report whenever either committee so recommends and before the instrument concerned comes up for final adoption by the Council. The Danish parliament appoints a European Committee comprising a small number of members responsible for scrutinizing new legislation. In the German Bundestag any item of EU business is subject to debate, but only a very small percentage receives any consideration.

So what can be done to simplify procedures and improve accountability? While the volume of European legislation is unlikely to decline, it is hoped to reach agreement both on distinguishing between legislation requiring the full authority of the Council of Ministers and the European Parliament and on technical implementing measures which could be dealt with more expeditiously. It was pointed out that when the European Commission presents legislative proposals it usually does so at the request of a national government, and that the system is complicated by the fact that all national governments have to be consulted and any changes proposed taken into account. The presenter dismissed the idea of bringing together representatives of the national parliaments in a European 'second chamber', pointing out that not only would it be impractical to give such a body any effective power, it would also merely increase the workload of its members with no worthwhile results. The member states are already represented in the Council of Ministers and the intrusion of a third legislative body into the process would lead to confusion, delay and raise various questions concerning the role of each of the three institutions which would not be easy to resolve.

Nonetheless, the national parliaments need to develop a more meaningful role in the European Union, and the proposed institution of a conference consisting of the European and the national parliaments, which would meet as necessary and be consulted on the 'main features' of the Union, is a step in the right direction. This conference would hear from the President of the European Council and the President of the Commission, and the former has suggested that the first task of such a conference might be to examine the work of the Reflection Group which prepared the ground for the Intergovernmental Conference in 1996. Further duties could include debating new treaties and the admission of new member states – a logical development since major decisions affecting the structure and powers of the Union require the ratification of the national parliaments. What was not made clear in the course of the discussions on this item was how the term 'main features' would be defined and the number of members of which the proposed conference would consist. It is hardly conceivable that it would consist of all the members of all the parliaments, which leaves open the question of how the various parliaments would be represented.

Declaration no. 13 of the Maastricht Treaty calls for the setting up of information exchange and contacts between members of the European Parliament and the national parliaments, and apparently a large number of joint hearings are already taking place. It has been suggested that such a hearing should be called to deal with the problem of budgetary fraud, since most of the fraud takes place at the point of disbursement of community funds in member states. Given the poor public perception of parliaments in general, the existence of this problem is far from reassuring, and one wonders to what extent such fraud is being practised. It is clearly a matter which calls for strong and immediate action.

Whatever remedies may be sought in order to improve parliamentary control and public accountability, the key to the attainment of this goal lies with the European Parliament itself. Bearing in mind that it is democratically elected, there is a strong case for strengthening its powers. Unfortunately, Euro-elections are seen within the member states as referenda on the popularity of their national governments and, even on this basis, voter turnout is poor. The European Parliament needs to be perceived as a legitimate legislative and representative body protecting the interests of its widespread electorate. It also needs to be seen as the European-level instrument of parliamentary control. Finally, it needs to reform its own procedures, eliminating waste and extravagance, delegating more technical work to committees, and introducing more accountability into the process – particularly the accountability of the Commission to the Parliament by means of a new code of conduct agreed by the two institutions.

In the view of the presenter 'the missing dimension in the European Parliament is the party one'. Although political groupings have been formed within the Parliament itself, they are not recognized by the voters as political parties like those operating within the national framework of each member state. People voting in European elections do not vote for candidates representing European parties as such: they vote for candidates representing national parties. As a result, the coalitions based on common interest which form within the Parliament itself are more like internal political clubs. Fortunately, no such group is ever likely to have an overall majority. The better organization of these groups and the development of their own programmes were seen by the presenter as the road to the democratic legitimacy of the European Parliament. By this means they would become *bona fide* political parties and hopefully gain recognition as such by the voters who elect them.

The basic conclusion of the ensuing discussion was that no nation is fully sovereign, and a number of points were made in discussing the pros and cons of closer union. A number of speakers felt that the pooling of sovereignty led to greater benefits for all concerned. Lesser control at the national level was compensated for by greater control at the international level and the strength which results from joining forces with allies for the common good. The sacrifice of sovereignty could be well worth the economic and other advantages gained. There were areas, such as the environment and human rights, where international control was likely to be more effective than control at the national level alone. One participant criticized those who complained about sacrificing sovereignty, pointing out that sacrifices were always necessary when aiming for a higher goal. He favoured a United States of Europe – meaning, presumably, closer integration on the basis of federalism – and regretted that there were too many politicians and too few statesmen.

A critic of the European Union made the point that national parliaments compromised their sovereignty when they adopted the legislation by which they became members, and suggested they were already being eclipsed as legislatures. National laws may not be inconsistent with European laws; there are certain areas in which national parliaments can be directed to legislate, and serious erosion of national legislative competence has taken place even in economic and fiscal areas. He suggested that the adoption of a single currency would amount to a total surrender of control over monetary and fiscal policy, interest rates, inflation and all the levers of economic activity. The counterargument was that the European Union had created a much wider internal market, and that those favouring a common currency saw it as a means of overcoming speculation in the money markets and improving export prospects.

Among other observations, it was pointed out that closer union was not the only factor which had eroded the sovereignty of national parliaments; that federal and regional institutions showed many examples of the benefits they can confer; and that the sovereignty of nations was recognized in international organizations where each country was represented in its own right. In one impassioned contribution, a delegate from a developing country posed the question: whose sovereignty are we talking about? Certainly not the sovereignty of the people, he suggested, as their rights were often completely excluded. Because developing countries are subject to the economic conditions imposed by the World Bank and the International Monetary Fund the concept of national sovereignty in these circumstances is only a myth. He asked what should be the objective of countries accepting closer integration: was it political, economic or cultural union and if it should be all three, which should take priority? When governments negotiate these matters, parliaments usually had no idea what was going on. In other words what, in fact, is sovereignty, and how do you define it?

In closing the discussion the presenter agreed that concepts of national sovereignty needed to be reconsidered in the light of globalization. With regard to the European Union he feared that if the right to opt out of certain provisions of the Maastricht Treaty were taken too far, the whole system could break down. The European Parliament needed to assume more responsibility to compensate for what the national parliaments had surrendered, and there were certain legislative functions it was better equipped to perform than the national parliaments. For example, in the European Parliament because there is no party discipline nor whipping system, its members have greater independence and are more successful in amending and improving legislation. To be fully effective, it needs full powers of co-decision with the Council of Ministers on all legislation.

While one seeks to be optimistic, the debate on this issue underlined how difficult it is to ensure that representative institutions are truly democratic. The EU institutions, including a fully elected parliament, are undoubtedly representative, but their operation is not entirely consistent with the criteria which we associate with effective parliamentary control and genuine accountability. They form another level of government more remote from the people than national institutions. Few people understand how they work, and their complexity compounds the difficulty of comprehension and threatens any efforts to democratize them. Even if it proves practical to invest the European Parliament with the powers it needs to conform to the norms of a democratically elected institution, would this change the public perception? Even if European political parties were to evolve in the manner suggested, would this be sufficient to stimulate the interest of voters, bearing in mind that European elections do not determine the nature of any government? At the national level, the erosion of power is likely to continue as further powers and functions are assumed by the European Union. The hope is that the greater good which will result will make the sacrifice worthwhile.

3 Enhancing Professionalism through the Work of Parliamentary Associations

The discussion of this item was led by representatives of the world's two oldest parliamentary associations, the Inter-Parliamentary Union (IPU), founded in 1889, and the Commonwealth Parliamentary Association, inaugurated in 1911 as the Empire Parliamentary Association. The Secretary-General of the CPA, Mr Arthur Donahoe, spoke on behalf of the latter; he was followed by the Deputy Secretary-General of the IPU, Mr Anders Johnsson, speaking on behalf of the former.

Both speakers described the aims and activities of their respective organizations and, while they share a great deal of common ground, there are differences of orientation. Both are dedicated to the principles of democratic government, the strengthening of parliamentary institutions, the rule of law and the rights and freedoms of individuals irrespective of gender, race, religion or culture. The CPA, under s. 1 of its constitution, exists to 'promote knowledge of the constitutional, legislative, economic, social and cultural aspects of parliamentary democracy'. The IPU has declared that 'the principle of the representation of the people by freely elected parliamentarians is at the very foundation of the work of the Union'. Both organizations pursue their aims through the holding of regular conferences, the organization of seminars and study groups, the encouragement of exchange visits between parliamentarians of different countries, direct assistance to individual parliaments, and the issuing of regular publications.

At its London headquarters the CPA maintains a Parliamentary Information and Reference Centre which provides comparative information on how parliamentary business is conducted in Commonwealth parliaments. It responds to requests from the public as well as from parliamentarians and government officials. The IPU has a well stocked library at its Geneva headquarters, which provides an information service complemented by a database called PARLINE – a project which was launched in 1993 and which is expected to be completed by the turn of the century. It also keeps files of unpublished material which offer a unique source of parliamentary information from countries around the world.

Branches of the CPA have been formed in almost every parliament and legislature in the Commonwealth, not only at the national level, but at the state and provincial level in the case of federal countries, and in the legislatures of self-governing dependencies of the Crown and colonial territories. At the time of writing, these branches number 126. They fall within eight geographical regions, and most of them hold regional conferences, organized independently of the annual international conferences which are held in a different Commonwealth country each year, and to which every branch sends a delegation.

The IPU is a global association of national parliaments only, every country with a representative assembly being eligible for membership. The criteria for what constitutes a representative assembly are not rigidly defined. At the time of writing, 178 of the world's 190 sovereign states have what the presenter described as 'a national parliament with legislative powers and an oversight function', and of these 131 are members of the IPU. Two international conferences are held every year in various countries of the world. Most of the members of the CPA are also members of the IPU.

Immediately prior to each plenary conference the CPA holds a special two-day conference of parliamentarians from the Commonwealth's smallest jurisdictions – those with populations of fewer than 400 000. Members from approximately 30 such jurisdictions take part, representing a mix of national parliaments and legislatures of smaller states or provinces of federal countries, self-governing dependencies and colonial territories. The inauguration of this conference represented a recognition of the fact that small states have problems of their own which could be submerged or overlooked during the larger conference. This opportunity to discuss political, constitutional and procedural issues as they relate to the smaller political entities is greatly prized by the jurisdictions concerned and has proved of real value.

The IPU, which has a long-standing record of concern for women's political rights, holds a conference of women parliamentarians prior to each international conference. The Union's analytical studies and statistical compilations have consistently shown that the representation of women in parliaments worldwide is very small in relation to their numbers in the general population, and it recently adopted a 'Plan of Action to correct the present imbalances in the participation of women in political life' by which it hopes to promote the conditions necessary for giving greater substance to women's political rights. This involves the encouragement of greater political awareness among women, and emphasizing the responsibility of political parties to give a lead in promoting the political equality of women.

A Commonwealth Women Parliamentarians Group with similar aims has also been formed within the CPA.

Both organizations attach great significance to the study of electoral systems. The CPA devotes its efforts to election monitoring and observation and claims to have developed a very effective process which recognizes the importance of having an ongoing monitoring presence in place well before the election itself takes place. In 1994 it organized a conference on the electoral process, also at Wiston Park, which led to the publication of an *Election Observation Handbook*, a definitive text on electoral law, practice and monitoring, designed as a pocket guide for election observers. The IPU, for its part, has produced in-depth studies, including a comparative study of electoral systems, and another which led to a declaration which set out the criteria for free and fair elections. These criteria provide standards for voting and election rights, candidature, party and campaign rights and responsibilities, and the rights and responsibilities of states.

The IPU is very active in the area of human rights, including the rights of parliamentarians, and this absorbs a considerable proportion of its budget. It takes a special interest in elected members who are victims of political persecution, calling for intervention on their behalf. There is, unfortunately, no shortage of countries where opposition politicians have been imprisoned and it was pointed out, in the course of the discussions, that Turkey had recently imprisoned eight opposition members.

Both organizations devote much of their activities to assisting newly elected parliaments in countries which have replaced one-party with multi-party systems, or have thrown off totalitarian regimes and are emerging as new democracies. Such parliaments face special difficulties since they operate in an unfamiliar political environment and many of their elected representatives have little or no parliamentary experience. The CPA assists such parliaments through the organization of seminars conducted by experienced parliamentarians and parliamentary staff, to which the entire membership of the parliament concerned is invited. Such seminars have been held in recent years in Zambia, Ghana, Kenya, Malawi, Lesotho, the Seychelles and Grenada. Much of the assistance offered by the IPU takes the form of sending expert missions to the parliaments concerned. The experts, working with the parliamentary authorities, assess the parliament's needs and prepare a technical assistance project with recommendations for the training of staff, the provision of facilities for members, the development of library, research and information services, the supply of equipment, or any other form of aid which is called for. The next step is to identify those elements which can be financed from existing domestic resources and those which require external financial provision. The IPU contacts potential donors, such as the United Nations Development Programme, when seeking external financial support which is usually required for staff training. This is carried out either by sending the selected officers on attachment to another parliament, or by sending an expert, from its roster, to assist in the training of staff on the spot. Parliaments which have been assisted in recent years include those of the Baltic states, Mongolia, Cambodia, Vietnam, Haiti, Burkina Faso, Tanzania and Malawi. International conferences and seminars are also organized by the IPU.

Enhancing professionalism is a fundamental *raison d'être* of both associations and is an ongoing challenge. What qualifications does a parliamentarian require? The short and blunt answer is the ability to get elected. The truth is that a parliamentarian requires no formal qualifications; there are no university courses or diplomas designed for parliamentarians, no professional associations such as there are for doctors, lawyers, accountants or engineers – nothing but the experience that comes from doing the job. Yet the responsibilities of elected members are various and often difficult. They are expected to be knowledgeable and yet they cannot be experts on all of the many issues which come before their attention. The best that a new member can hope for is an induction course designed to explain the operation of the parliament, its procedures and administration, the facilities available and the duties, rights and benefits that go with the job. Some parliaments offer these courses on an in-house basis. The CPA holds seminars on parliamentary practice and procedure on a Commonwealth-wide and a regional basis, in addition to those referred to earlier, but participation is necessarily limited. Practising politicians are also at a disadvantage in attending parliamentary conferences and seminars because, given their poor public image, such activities are usually seen as junketeering. It was pointed out that doctors, engineers and other professionals who attend conferences related to their specialized fields are not criticized, whereas parliamentarians who do likewise are accused of taking holidays at public expense. Only one delegate declared that his constituents approved of his attendance at parliamentary conferences.

Politics, it may be argued, is the profession with the greatest impact on society, yet one which calls for no formal training, and no perceived need for professional development. Can the public be persuaded that politicians' faults and failures might be avoided or corrected if they are exposed to the learning experiences afforded by contacts with parliamentarians from other countries; if they have the opportunity to attend conferences and seminars in various parts of the world; if they are allowed to educate themselves by visiting other countries? No doubt a few individuals may abuse opportunities, but the serious parliamentarian is kept hard at work on these occasions.

It has to be acknowledged that the countries represented in the CPA and, to a somewhat greater extent in the IPU, are not all models of democracy and do not all measure up to the ideals professed by the associations themselves. Both associations recognize this and hope that they are able to exert a positive influence through their adherence to these ideals. The CPA maintains contacts with those Commonwealth countries where parliamentary government has been suspended, hoping that one day they can be welcomed back into the fold. In the words of Arthur Donahoe, the CPA seeks to help 'the Commonwealth's established democracies to revitalize themselves' and to assist 'the new democracies to operate effectively by adapting established parliamentary practices and introducing their own methods'. Commonwealth countries share a certain common denominator in that their systems of government evolved from the Westminster model and, although there are significant divergences, most share certain characteristics. In the case of the IPU the differences between member countries are far more wide-ranging, and it includes among its members a considerable number whose systems of government are far from democratic.

Much of the good work accomplished by both associations lies outside the formal international conferences which are regularly convened. Indeed, the observer might sometimes be tempted to wonder how much is really achieved in the debates on the conference floor. They have become political arenas in which disputes between countries frequently rise to the surface, where set speeches – sometimes amounting to diatribes – are delivered, and where it is easy to anticipate the preordained positions which certain delegates are going to adopt. Much of the frank discussion takes place outside the conference hall, where delegates are not circumscribed with regard to what they can say, and where social contacts may lead to greater understanding among the representatives of widely disparate nations.

It is an inescapable fact that, even in democratic countries, the executive is likely to play a dominant role to the detriment of the parliament. Speaking on behalf of the IPU, Anders Johnsson lamented the fact that donors tended to direct their aid to branches of government other than the parliament, so that lack of funding was a key obstacle to the promotion of the professionalism of parliamentarians. He hoped that the parliamentary community would do its best to influence their respective governments and, through them, the donor community, to give increased attention to the needs of the parliamentary institution. Pressure of this kind might hopefully lead to some success, although there may well be great reluctance on the part of some governments to do anything which would make parliament a more potent force. Of course, the efforts of the parliamentary associations, underfunded though they are, take on even greater importance in these circumstances.

The question of what constitutes professionalism was raised in the subsequent discussion. In the parliamentary context, is a professional a person of calibre or one who is professionally qualified? One delegate suggested that professionalism should not be overemphasized, as the primary role of members should be to represent the people and understand the needs of their communities. Another delegate asked how long it might take to become a professional parliamentarian, and whether they should all be qualified in law to ensure that laws are not enacted by unprofessional people. Replying to this point, a speaker said that in many parliaments there was an abundance of lawyers and that he was not persuaded it was necessary for elected representatives to be professionals. Professionalism was required at the level of the support services – professionals should be the advisers not the decision-makers. This argument was supported by another delegate who pointed out that, in Germany, 2300 people served 623 parliamentarians and that these support services were indispensable.

The consensus was that professionalism in parliamentary terms did not mean that members should necessarily be drawn from specific professions, as this could lead to a negation of democracy. Parliament should consist of the true representatives of the people, not a meritocracy. The only screening process for candidates was a political one; there was no screening process relating to specific skills. Many members represent interest groups and it is important that members should come from diverse backgrounds. The question of who should be responsible for the education of new members was raised. Is it the responsibility of parliament or the political parties? There was a great deal to learn and new members were often totally lost. Another issue raised was that of members' outside interests and their compatibility with parliamentary duties. This was considered a matter of particular importance in a small parliament where membership was usually a part-time occupation.

One delegate questioned whether the money spent on international parliamentary activities was justified. Pointing out that the media had virtually ignored the conference activities, he suggested that the money spent on a recent conference might have been better spent on digging a well in an African country. Constituents had to be convinced of the importance of these events if they were not to be cynical about them. He also felt that the associations should be doing more for Third World countries.

At the outset of his presentation, Arthur Donahoe quoted from a speech by Edmund Burke attacking the political corruption of the day. Burke spoke of the need for reform, and in particular the need to take a cool approach in order to improve without destroying. Reforms made over time will endure and can be built upon. Reforms imposed in the heat of passion will 'pull down the house.' Mr Donahoe concluded that the CPA's duty was to promote the strengthening of parliamentary institutions by cooperating with those working towards temperate reforms, and calming the temper of those who, in Burke's words, would 'pull down the house.' In this way, it may be hoped, the public perception may be turned around.

Both associations take very seriously their responsibility to promote professionalism, not only among parliamentarians, but also among those who serve them. A professional association of parliamentary officers is attached to each organization – the Society of Clerks-at-the-Table in Commonwealth Parliaments in the case of the CPA, and the Association of Secretaries-General of Parliaments in the case of the IPU. They both hold their meetings coincidentally with the conferences of the parent bodies, but are completely independent in the conduct of their proceedings. Within the CPA, regional conferences of parliamentary officers are also held, some being held jointly with the presiding officers of the parliaments concerned. Membership of the Society of Clerks-at-the-Table is open to all who serve as Table Officers in the chambers of their respective parliaments. Membership of the Association of Secretaries-General is restricted to two officers from each legislative chamber of the member parliaments – that is, four in the case of a bicameral Parliament – and these would normally be the two most senior officers. Substitutes are, however, allowed to take the place of the officers registered as members.

As was emphasized during the discussions, the professionalism of parliamentarians depends quite extensively on the professionalism of those who support them in their work, who in turn benefit from opportunities to promote their own professional development.

4 Changing the Public Perception

A session on 'Enhancing Public Perception and Understanding of Parliament and the Legislative Process' was led by the Honourable Billie Miller, Deputy Prime Minister and Minister of Foreign Affairs of Barbados, and Mr Karl Kurtz, Director of State Services of the National Conference of State Legislatures of the United States. While both acknowledged that the public perception of their respective institutions of government left much to be desired, each approached the problem from a different perspective. There is, of course, a radical difference between the parliamentary system of government, as practised in Barbados, and the congressional system which operates at both the federal and state levels in the United States. Problems and solutions are not viewed in an identical context, and it would therefore be best to review the presentations separately.

Billie Miller made the point that Westminster-style parliamentary government risks placing absolute power in the hands of the executive as long as the government controls a majority in the elected House. A proper system of accountability to the people becomes, in these circumstances, all the more important:

> I would argue that the manifesto with which government secures the confidence of the nation in an election is a commitment to the people. They should rightly expect the implementation, execution and shrewd management of the policies of that manifesto, that government should articulate, explain and justify those policies in office and consult the people when they cannot, for whatever reason, implement some of them.

She painted a dangerous scenario of what might occur if a government, whose popular base had collapsed, attempted to retain power. When a government knows it has lost the confidence of the people, its only option is to face the electorate and allow a peaceful change of government to take place, otherwise the people might take matters into their own hands and a violent situation would arise. 'We are the guardians of democracy and its exemplars. The tenure of political power is the will of the people.'

In her opinion, a shortcoming of many democracies is the failure to inform the people. An essential component in keeping people informed is freedom of access to information. Another is government initiative in consulting the public on legislation and issues of policy, preferably in advance of final decisions being taken, so that the people know what the government proposes to do. Seeking the advice of relevant interest groups can lead to the formulating of better legislation. Inviting public cooperation may encourage useful initiatives to emanate from the people themselves. The politician's slogan should be 'trust the people'. She suggested that policy and legislation should be taken to the people by way of referendum. This is an interesting point to argue; it was dealt with at a later session of the Conference and will be considered later in this book.

The public service also has a responsibility to be less secretive. Considerable power is vested in the executive through its authority to issue regulations – often described as delegated legislation – which are issued under the authority of statutes conferring the power on a particular minister or on the executive as a whole. They have the same force of law as Acts of Parliament and, in many countries, this method of legislating has become increasingly extensive. Few parliaments have devised a totally effective monitoring system, and the very proliferation of such regulations, covering as they do a vast range of public activity, makes control extremely difficult. The dangers of this significant accretion of executive power was addressed by Lord Hewart in his book *The New Despotism*, published in 1929, and little has occurred to curb this power in the years which have ensued. The executive therefore has a bounden duty to ensure that it does not exceed the powers granted to it by statute, and openness on the part of the bureaucracy is one of the means of meeting this responsibility. In the words of Billie Miller, it 'should be active in sponsoring the provision and dissemination of information', and, one might add, in explaining the effect of the regulations which it pours forth.

To quote the Prime Minister of Barbados, Mr Owen Arthur, speaking at a Retreat on Public Sector Reform in January 1995, 'we must infuse the public sector with the dynamism which has grown out of the revolution in information and organisational technologies which are so much a part of our times'. Billie Miller also quoted from a document entitled *The Civil Service: Continuity and Change* (Cmd. Paper 2627), presented to the British House of Commons in July 1994, which recommended that the civil service should promote greater transparency in government by:

> Handling information in a way which promotes informed policy making and debate, and efficient service delivery; providing timely and accessible informa-

tion to the citizen to explain government policies, actions and decisions; and restricting access to information only when there are good reasons for doing so.

Billie Miller then went on to deal with the responsibilities of the media, pointing out that they, too, have a duty to properly inform the public. In order to discharge this duty journalists themselves need to be well informed. 'Accurate reporting requires appropriate knowledge. Reporting which is critical but fair requires analysis and appreciation of the subject by the reporter.' Unfortunately, much reporting tends to be superficial – the attention-grabbing headline or the 30-second 'sound-bite' often dominate parliamentary reporting in the print and broadcast media respectively. It is a regrettable fact of political life that the obscure backbencher who wants to get into the news is more likely to do so by throwing an egg at the prime minister than by making a constructive speech.

Emphasizing her support for the televising of parliamentary proceedings, the presenter regarded the broadcast media as a very important channel of public education, enabling the people to see and hear parliament at work not only on the floor of the House but also in committees. A potent argument in favour of the televising of parliament has always been that, if parliament excludes the cameras, it places itself at a disadvantage against those who report and comment on its proceedings since the latter, who are responsible to no electorate, are free to place their own construction on the proceedings. By allowing people to see parliament as it really is, 'warts and all', at least they will receive an accurate picture and be able to form their own judgement. Billie Miller lamented the fact that televised parliamentary debates had to compete with test matches and soap operas and that, in her country, little interest was shown by the media. She felt that those who work for the media should be educated in the work of parliament and that the CPA could make a contribution by inviting representatives of the media to attend CPA conferences.

A necessary concomitant to the televising of parliamentary proceedings, in the view of the presenter, is the reform of parliamentary procedure to remove its archaic elements. The rules should be kept under constant review and the public should be given explanations as to how they work. She suggested that the CPA might have a role to play in the standardization of standing orders in Commonwealth parliaments, although I would argue that this is not a realistic proposal given their variations in size, traditions and political environments. Although most Commonwealth parliaments have drawn their inspiration from the Westminster model, their procedures have evolved independently and have been adapted to their own particular circumstances.

Parliamentarians work under tremendous pressure, and the demands of their constituents continue to grow. Their duties call for a full-time commitment to both their constituencies and their parliamentary work and without the right facilities they cannot operate efficiently. This was a recurring theme during the conference, although it was accompanied by a realization that the granting of benefits to parliamentarians does not improve the public perception. If the system is to shed its poor public image it is essential that the public understands what members of parliament have to do and what they need in order to do it. Most of the participants would agree with Billie Miller that 'a constituency office, adequate staff, information and communication services are prerequisites' for their work. It is a fact, nevertheless, that not all parliamentarians enjoy these facilities. Sophisticated research services such as those available in the parliaments of the developed countries are likely to be an unaffordable luxury in those of the developing world. Even so, a small but dedicated staff, possessing initiative and imagination, is capable of providing impressive services with limited resources, as many parliamentary jurisdictions have shown. The key lies in cooperation with the private sector, to which Billie Miller alluded, and with public institutions as well. With regard to the provision of information, the important factor is knowing where to obtain it. This is where staff initiative is crucial in making contact with outside institutions – universities, public and specialist libraries, the media, research establishments, professional associations, private companies and, of course, government departments.

The private sector, as Billie Miller said, should be seen as an ally and not as an opponent. Collaboration with private institutions promotes the cause of good government, can assist in producing good legislation, and offers the mutual benefit of consultation and the exchange of information.

The presenter dealt with the importance of public education, particularly the education of the youth, in the merits of the system of government under which they live. Young people should be encouraged to participate in the process, their concerns should be listened to, and their aspirations should not be circumscribed 'by the wishes of elders basking often solely in the merits of age deemed to be experience'. A reminder, perhaps, that there is no fool like an old fool! Parliamentary staff also need training beyond the areas of their own specific skills, through liaison with members to identify their needs and with the media to broaden their perspective of parliament. The broader vision may be lacking in the specialist working in a specialized field, and staff should be 'providers of training, expertise and total awareness of the work of parliament'.

Ms Miller spoke of the importance of attracting good candidates into parliament and of assuring them a fair remuneration. Political parties had a responsibility to ensure that the candidates nominated were of high calibre. For their part, parliamentarians must avoid conflict-of-interest situations, be fully accountable to their constituents (who include not only those who supported them but also those who voted against them), and be prepared to devote all the time that is necessary to fulfil their parliamentary and constituency duties. They must also be prepared to serve on committees (often regarded as an added burden), where much of the most important parliamentary business takes place. These are the arenas where detailed scrutiny and analysis take place, and also the level at which the public can make a direct input as witnesses. The presenter felt that the committee stage could well replace the second reading as the centre of debate on a bill, and that the rules of procedure might well be revised with this in mind.

Finally, she made a plea for what she termed the 'appropriate physical plant for a parliament'. Members had the right to comfortable accommodation and a good working environment – 'It is time that parliamentary buildings should be given the high level of priority they have always deserved' – since outward symbols reflect the dignity of the institution. She concluded with the following words:

> Disaffection with parliament and the legislature is widespread. The cure lies in the hands of its practitioners, with the help of the public. The perception and understanding, the mirror image of the institution, may not be totally wrong. What is totally clear is wherein lies the fault.

Mr Karl Kurtz dealt with the subject in the context of the USA, where the separation of powers is a factor in determining public attitudes to government institutions. The public image of the legislative branch of government tends to be separate from that of the executive branch in that the president might be popular at a time when the Congress was unpopular, and vice versa. In general there has been a decline in public confidence in all the country's institutions – in business, the churches, the police, as well as in legislatures and executive bodies. Legislators themselves are among the most severe critics of the institutions to which they belonged, because electoral campaigns focus on the candidates themselves rather than political parties. Party discipline as practised in countries with a Westminster-style system of government plays no part in American politics, and therefore party loyalty is not a factor in the electoral process, either on the part of the voters or of the candidates themselves. Candidates are able to distance themselves from the targets of criticism and join in the voices of censure as a means of seeking personal support.

Mr Kurtz provided charts based on public opinion polls which indicated how the legislatures of certain states had been evaluated. No national poll of all state and governmental institutions had ever been conducted because of the prohibitive cost of drawing a sample large enough to produce valid results. The selective polls nevertheless revealed a steady decline in public perception since 1987. Prior to 1987, polls taken in Florida and New Jersey had indicated a support level of almost 50 per cent. Steep declines were recorded in New Mexico in 1986 and in Florida in 1987, explained in the former case by political scandal and in the latter by the introduction of a tax on services. By 1992 public approval of the legislature of Illinois had fallen below 15 per cent. The lowest rating for any state was recorded in West Virginia in 1988 at 8 per cent, following a scandal which led to the imprisonment of several legislative leaders.

Mr Kurtz dealt with the question of what legislatures could do to improve their public image under five headings: performance, ethics, campaign finance, public information and civics education. On the matter of performance, it has to be accepted that legislators have tough decisions to make. While the public in general favour reduced taxes together with increased services, this is clearly not a practical proposition, and legislatures have to reach their decisions in a manner conducive to the greater public good. Priorities have to be determined, the claims of worthy projects and causes balanced on a realistic basis, and the public educated to the reality that you cannot please all of the people all of the time. The media, which invariably place themselves in an adversarial relationship to the legislature, must be met with openness and honesty. Any suspicion of concealment or deviousness will always be exploited by journalists, and criticism is less damaging when directed against the frank acknowledgment of the necessity for an unpopular measure. Echoing a point made by Billie Miller, Mr Kurtz said that efficient and effective legislative operations should be promoted by procedural reforms and the removal of archaic practices. The more the public understands how the legislature works, the better the prospects for an improved public image. Practices tending to waste time and money should be eliminated and legislators must avoid abusing their rights and privileges if they are to gain respect. It is also important to anticipate problems rather than avoid confronting them. Where issues of public policy are concerned, the chances of resolving problems are much better if they are tackled before the moment when action can no longer be delayed.

The question of ethics, which is allied to performance, is an area which has given rise to cynical public attitudes because of the activities of the few who spoil the image of the many. Codes of ethics and conflict of interest laws need strengthening. Financial disclosure, limitations on the acceptance of gifts, and the registration and regulation of lobbyists are among the important safeguards which need to be imposed in order to ensure openness and integrity. These are all matters which were considered at other sessions of the conference and to which we shall return. It is also important to educate legislators about ethical standards and promote professional conduct. In fact, some states require their members to attend ethics training programmes.

The financing of electoral campaigns is a very controversial area, described by the presenter as 'the Achilles heel of American politics'. 'Money', declared Mr Kurtz, 'is the mother's milk of politics'. He referred to contribution limits, the use of campaign funds, the public financing of electoral campaigns and disclosure as having figured among recent reforms. However, the limits imposed on electoral expenses in some countries stand in stark contrast to the lack of restriction in the USA. Consequently, only very rich candidates or those with the backing of very wealthy interests have any great hope of success in American political life.

The need to inform the public was one of the underlying themes of the conference, and Mr Kurtz stressed the importance of teaching legislators and their staff communication skills. Every possible use should be made of modern technology, and the legislature should act independently to ensure that the media are not the only source of public information. Unless the legislature is respected as an institution the public's perception will not improve. It must be seen as a strong and effective body, dedicated to the interests of those it represents, and it should publicize its activities with this in mind.

To inform is to educate, and civics education plays a crucial role in the moulding of public attitudes. As stated previously, civics education should start in school and teachers have just as much need of this form of education as pupils. The school curriculum should therefore include courses on government and the legislative process; and, in Mr Kurtz's opinion, internships and mock legislative sessions, where pupils play the parts of legislators are among the projects which should be promoted to stimulate greater awareness of the value of the system and how it works.

There is considerable diversity among the state legislatures of the USA. According to Mr Kurtz, about 12 are full-time legislatures in that they sit throughout the year and require the full-time participation of their members. He made the distinction between 'professionalized' and 'citizen' or 'traditional' legislatures, the latter consisting mainly of part-time representatives with outside professional interests, as opposed to the professional politicians who devote more of their time to their duties as legislators. The laws and regulations concerned with ethics and conflict of interest tend to be stricter in the states with 'professionalized' legislatures. Polls seem to show that the more highly a person is educated the lower is likely to be his or her regard for the legislature. In addition, the better educated pay more attention to the media which generally attack the legislature, and he viewed this as a disturbing trend.

During the discussions which followed the two presentations, more questions were posed than solutions offered. The fundamental question might be summed up as: how do we get the system back on the rails? One delegate saw the root of the problem as too much government, which in the UK context had become an elective dictatorship. Even non-governmental organizations did not necessarily reduce the power of government as many of them consisted of government appointees. He saw a danger of violence in the role of direct action, pointing out that many protesters did not take to the streets out of conviction but were paid demonstrators. Parliament needed to modernize, and make greater use of green papers (policy statements offered as a basis for discussion) and draft bills on which the public could be consulted. In this delegate's view, standing committees (which in the UK House of Commons are legislative committees) and select committees (investigative subject committees) could profitably be merged.

Another participant wondered how the perception of the politician is formed. Is a parliamentarian primarily a legislator or the representative of his or her constituency? Is a politician necessarily a good parliamentarian? Electors are usually preoccupied with their social and economic needs, and the parliamentarian cannot be all things to all people. The perception of national institutions is also influenced by global developments which cannot be influenced by ordinary members of parliament, although they may be blamed for their adverse consequences. The expectations of the people exceed what their elected representatives are able to deliver. The problem to be tackled is how to rebuild the house which is in the process of falling down.

In pursuing these arguments several further points were made. A delegate from Africa maintained that perception was determined by the social work performed by the member, and questioned whether membership of parliament was a vocation or a career. He asked whether there was a conflict between the job a legislator was supposed to do and what the public wanted him or her to do. Who, he asked, is responsible for the question of perception? Billie Miller was quick to respond that the responsibility for perception belonged to the member, and it was the responsibility of the members to make the institution work. Mr Kurtz intervened to add that members themselves were obsessed with public opinion, which inhibited leadership.

According to one delegate, the weakness of the system lay in the process of policy formation. In his country the opposition was starved of information – usually deliberately – and the executive was far too dominant. Members should have easy access to the public service and independent sources of information. Committees also required independent support services and should work independently of the party caucuses. The practice whereby committee members reported back to their party caucuses before determining their position on the issue before the committee was a negation of independence. If committees operated free from party inhibitions, they would perform far more constructive work.

This interesting and thought-provoking session, while reaching no optimistic conclusions, laid bare the challenges faced by parliaments if they were to succeed in changing the public perception. The malaise was not underestimated, and it was explored in a forceful and penetrating way. The obstacles to curing it were exposed as formidable but, hopefully, not insurmountable.

5 Political Reporting

The presenter at this session was Mr Inder Jit, a former journalist and at the time of writing a member of Lok Sabha, the lower House of the Parliament of India. His presentation centred on two aspects: the importance of a free press and the vital role it plays in a democratic society; and the extent to which the press has failed to meet its responsibilities in recent years. He described the press as the principal link of communication between parliament and the people and essential to the success of a parliamentary democracy. Ideally, it might be seen as an extension, or an ally, of the parliament, each complementing and supplementing the other in protecting essential freedoms. 'Each would be a lame duck without the other, as shown by India's experience during the emergency of 1975–77 when all fundamental rights, including the right to life and the freedom of expression, were suspended.' During this period the press were forbidden to report parliamentary proceedings without government approval. He himself was denied access to the press gallery and only pro-government journalists were accredited.

The press should be the watchdog of the people's interests, informing the public of what is happening in parliament, and also providing it with information which helps it to oversee the activities of the executive. Much of the material on which parliamentary questions, motions and debates are based comes from information provided by the press. Parliament without the press, in Mr Jit's view, is meaningless.

It is fair to comment at this point that parliament and the press need each other, as members are always seeking press coverage and the press is always looking for copy which will sell newspapers. However, the concept of the press as an ally of parliament needs to be modified by the reality that, in a free society, the press is frequently in an adversarial relationship with parliament. The function of the press is to criticize and expose rather than to praise. As Mr Jit pointed out, press disclosures have uncovered scandals, forced the resignation of ministers and even caused governments to fall.

Having elaborated on the role of the press when it fulfils its functions honourably, Mr Jit deplored the decline in standards which had taken place, declaring that facts were frequently fabricated and that 'comment' had become licence: 'In the battle for circulation, newspapers are now stooping lower and lower, ignoring healthy, time-honoured conventions.' Poor reporting had also, in his opinion, led to the decline of parliament itself. In India the fair and objective reporting of proceedings had given way to sensation-seeking, the focus being on the half-hour devoted each day to matters of national concern, known as 'Zero Hour', when members can raise any question they choose. The press shows no interest in any other proceedings and vanishes after Zero Hour, and this inadequate coverage of their proceedings had caused members themselves to lose interest.

Mr Jit did concede that the press in India today could report parliamentary proceedings without fear and defended its rights to investigate the private lives of people in public service, quoting Mahatma Gandhi, who said: 'A man's public life could not be clean if his private life was not clean.' He also used further quotations in defence of press freedom.

> Liberty of speech means that it is unassailed even when the speech hurts. (Mahatma Gandhi)

> There is not a crime, there is not a vice which does not live by secrecy. Get these things out in the open, attack them, ridicule them in the press and sooner or later public opinion will sweep them away. (Joseph Pulitzer)

> I would rather have a completely free press with all the dangers in the wrong use of that freedom than a suppressed and regulated press. (Jawaharal Nehru)

It is perhaps ironic that it was his own daughter who, as Prime Minister, revoked this freedom.

Perhaps there is one further citation which could legitimately be added to those quoted by Mr Jit. Speaking in the British House of Commons in 1810, the playwright and Whig MP, Richard Sheridan, had this to say:

> Give me but the liberty of the press, and I will give the minister a venal House of Peers, I will give him a corrupt and servile House of Commons, I will give him the full swing of the patronage of office, I will give him the whole host of ministerial influences, I will give him all the power that place can confer upon him to purchase submission and overawe resistance; and yet, armed with the liberty of the press, I will go forth to meet him undismayed; I will attack the mighty fabric he has reared with that mightier engine; I shall shake down from its height corruption, and lay it beneath the ruins of the abuses it was meant to shelter.

The ensuing discussion concentrated largely on the abuse of press freedom and the declining standards to which Mr Jit referred. The first question to be raised was whether it was possible to restore the level of trust between the press and parliament. It was pointed out that the nature of journalism had altered and that its success was measured by the number of members whose reputations could be destroyed. In the British Parliament the press once had access to the House of Commons terrace on the understanding that the confidentiality of any information was respected. Reporters have since been barred because they abused that privilege by indulging in speculative reporting based on lip-reading, the eavesdropping of private conversations and the publication of members' off-the-record comments in order to entrap them.

A number of delegates pointed out that the press looks for sensation and manipulates the news, and that the decline in standards is reflected even in the more serious newspapers, as witnessed by the coverage of the affairs of the British Royal Family. But dissatisfaction with the press coverage of their proceedings seems to be common to all parliaments. One delegate complained that the press never wrote to him directly about issues; journalists preferred to manufacture news rather than undertake the hard work of honest investigation. It was felt that the reason the so-called serious press has also succumbed to this trend is due to drastically falling circulation figures. The respect for and integrity of the press have been sacrificed in the process.

One of the problems, it was suggested, is that journalists are always seeking a story and parliament is often boring. One delegate from Africa referred to what he called the 'blackmail syndrome' whereby the press will either misrepresent or ignore you if you don't say what they want you to say. Sometimes they will support narrow interests, and some MPs compromise with the press on the assumption that if you can't beat it you might as well join it. Another delegate proposed that there should perhaps be legislation to govern parliamentary reporting, but met with little support since any legislation, however mild, would amount to a curb on press freedom.

Another delegate made the point that political reporting covers more than parliamentary proceedings. Television is a force to be reckoned with in the reporting process, and it is important to distinguish between TV and the print media in terms of their impact. What, it was asked, is the point of reporting a speech that has already been televised? Is television perhaps the source of the problem? Since television had, to a great extent, taken over political coverage from the print media, the only way parliament could influence TV coverage was to allow its own proceedings to be televised. Some of the parliaments which have done so control the operation themselves; others have left it to the TV companies. A German delegate explained that, in her parliament, four permanent TV cameras had been installed by TV companies which decide which proceedings to cover, leaving the parliament with no influence at all. She said that the reporting had become very shallow: very short clips are used for broadcasting purposes, and commentators consider themselves properly informed when they do not in fact have the full background to the matters on which they were commenting.

Mr Art Donahoe, who once served as Speaker of the Legislative Assembly of Nova Scotia, informed the Conference of an interesting case which had arisen during his tenure of office. In his capacity as Speaker he was sued by the Canadian Broadcasting Corporation (CBC) after refusing to allow TV cameras unrestricted access into the legislature. The CBC claimed that this refusal violated the rights of the media under the Canadian Charter of Rights and Freedoms; he counterclaimed that the unrestricted right of access demanded conflicted with the parliamentary privilege of the legislature to regulate its own proceedings as it saw fit. The case took four years to resolve and every legislative jurisdiction in Canada was represented at the hearings in support of the Nova Scotia position. The media claim was upheld in the courts of Nova Scotia at two levels, but the judgement was finally reversed by the Supreme Court of Canada by a majority of 8 to 1.

In closing the discussion, Mr Jit acknowledged that the question of how to improve relations between parliament and press was a tough one to resolve. He reiterated that neither one can do without the other, and deplored the damage that the decline in values with respect to factual and honest reporting had done to both institutions. He suggested that holding frank discussions with editors and political correspondents might be a means of improving relations. He supported the idea of a separate parliamentary channel, which exists in some countries, and thought that a daily televised discussion of the events of the parliamentary day would be useful. In Lok Sabha continuous live TV coverage of all parliamentary proceedings has not been instituted; coverage is limited to the President's address at the beginning of the session, important debates, such as the budget debate, and the question period. In many countries it is the question period which attracts most viewer interest. In the UK Prime Minister's Question Time, which takes place for 15 minutes twice a week, is a particularly notable feature of the parliamentary day. However, the question period is not a typical representation of how parliament conducts its business and the viewer would undoubtedly find much of the proceedings extremely tedious.

In Mr Jit's opinion, TV could be used as a corrective towards a better informed public opinion, and it could be made interesting through panel discussions and well presented summaries of the issues before parliament. Currently the media do not represent parliament fairly and, if they do not respond to the overtures he suggested, other solutions would need to be sought. He was opposed to the regulation of the press by legislation but suggested that abuses and excesses might be dealt with by invoking parliamentary privilege. Many parliaments have sought to impose punitive measures against the press by this means, but this, of itself, could be a threat to press freedom.

In my view, parliamentary privilege should be used very sparingly, and never for the purpose of intimidating the press. The line between fair comment and excessive criticism is a very fine one and parliament would be better advised to ignore certain abuses than to place press freedom in jeopardy through an overtechnical interpretation of parliamentary privilege. Nehru's comment, used by Mr Jit in his presentation and quoted on page 36, is of relevance here. In any such confrontation, public opinion is likely to be on the side of the press, and it is the image of parliament that would be most likely to suffer. The laws of defamation are always available to those who may feel they have been libelled or slandered.

One of the many telling comments made during the discussions was to the effect that the press may understand politics but they do not understand parliament. The tendency to seek out scandal as a priority, and to speculate about it even if it cannot be established, gives no incentive to journalists to follow parliamentary proceedings with any seriousness and to educate themselves as to how it works. The quest for the 5-second sound-bite or the mischievous headline is more attractive than the search for truth and knowledge. Although little comfort emerged from the discussions, they were animated and heartfelt, and were greatly enlivened by the incisive wit of the presenter.

6 Ensuring Ethical Standards in Public Life

This session went to the very heart of the overall theme of the Conference, which was fortunate in securing the participation of Dame Anne Warburton as the presenter. Dame Anne is a member of the Nolan Committee, appointed by the British Prime Minister on 25 October 1994:

> ... to examine current concerns about standards of conduct of all holders of public office, including arrangements relating to financial and commercial activities, and make recommendations as to any changes in present arrangements which might be required to ensure the highest standards of propriety in public life.

The Committee was set up against a background of widespread concern about standards of public life in the UK, and will remain in being as a Standing Committee to advise the government of the day. Its first report, *Standards in Public Life*, was published at the end of May 1995 and included in this book as Appendix 1. In the meantime, this chapter will concentrate on Dame Anne's presentation and the resulting discussions, which took place at a time when the contents of the first report could not be definitively anticipated.

The Committee consists of ten members chaired by Lord Nolan, a judge (in fact a Lord of Appeal in Ordinary). The other members are drawn from both the public and private sectors and include representatives of the three main political parties. Lord Nolan himself attended this Conference session and was able to give the benefit of his input.

For the purposes of its mandate the Committee interpreted the term 'public life' to include:

> ... ministers, civil servants and advisers, Members of Parliament, Members of the European Parliament elected in the U.K., members and senior officers of all non-departmental public bodies and of National Health Service bodies, non-

ministerial office-holders, members and other senior officers of other bodies discharging publicly funded functions and elected members and senior officers of local authorities.

The Committee did not enquire into allegations of misconduct against individuals. It is also interesting to note that the appointment of this Committee marks the first occasion on which the British Parliament has submitted to outside investigation.

Dame Anne Warburton began by warning the Conference that she was unable to report on any conclusions reached by the Committee, and that she could only present an unofficial account of the Committee's work. Should any conclusions or opinions intrude, they were to be regarded as hers alone. She elaborated on the background against which the Committee had been set up. In the UK, as in other countries, there had been a perceived decline in the standards of public life, triggered by a series of questionable incidents which had taken place during 1994. These incidents included the case of two MPs who had apparently received payment for putting questions to ministers and, although there was no evidence that this was a widespread practice, the suspicion that these were not isolated cases had taken root in the public mind. There was also public disquiet over the parliamentary activities of lobbying companies and the conflict-of-interest situations in which members risked finding themselves as a result of these activities. Although the House of Commons has adopted rules requiring members to declare their outside interests, there are fears that these are inadequate, largely because they are not statutory and not difficult to ignore. There were also concerns over members receiving gifts or hospitality in return for favours rendered. Criticism had been levelled at ex-ministers and former senior civil servants who had accepted lucrative appointments linked to their previous official duties, thereby profiting from inside knowledge gained while on the public payroll. Further dissatisfaction existed over the extent of government influence over the appointments to quasi-autonomous non-governmental organizations, known as quangos, which are suspected of being comfortable havens of political patronage. There are several thousand such bodies executing government policies, accounting for more than 42 000 appointments, and they are regarded as being insufficiently accountable.

The cumulative effect of these concerns was to create an impression of widespread corruption, conflict of interest and abuse of public office for personal gain. Dame Anne Warburton suggested that such revelations as had been publicized stood out in shocking contrast to the high standards of conduct in public life to which Britons had previously become accustomed, with the result that the suspicions probably outstripped the reality. One of the witnesses who gave evidence before the Committee stated that he would have found it difficult to write a book on corruption in Great Britain between 1930 and 1965 but, in recent years, a different mentality seemed to have taken over. A once-trusting society had become one which questions values and motives. Some witnesses blamed the malaise on the fact that one party had been in power for too long, bringing about a radical change in the political climate. One of the other possible causes to which reference was made was the closer interface between government and business resulting from governmental changes and the spread of privatization. Many, of course, blame the media for their lowered standards and changed attitude towards what is, and is not, acceptable reporting practice. The media, for their part, claim that they report as they find, and no one questioned the indispensable need for a free press in a healthy democracy. Whatever the causes, a Gallup poll taken in the UK in October 1994 revealed an alarming lack of confidence in public institutions, with 64 per cent of respondents believing that MPs were chiefly interested in private gain. Whether or not these fears are exaggerated, something must be rotten when such beliefs take root in the public mind. Although this was not referred to by Dame Anne, one of the Committee's witnesses, Lord Blake, expressed the view that Britain was living in its most corrupt era since Victorian times.

A document entitled *Issues and Questions* was published and circulated by the Committee shortly after its appointment. The public, who were invited to present their views and comments, responded with some 1800 written submissions, and over 100 witnesses gave oral testimony occupying some 55 hours. The hearings took place in public and attracted great interest. The Committee involved the witnesses in wide-ranging discussion of the issues, thereby extending their participation beyond the normal question-and-answer exchanges, and thus taking full advantage of what they had to offer. All expressed serious concerns but, more reassuringly, many of the witnesses, including newspaper editors and academics, felt that the 64 per cent adverse assessment of politicians revealed by the Gallup poll was not accurate. The Committee concluded that it had two problems to deal with – the reality and the public perception – and that it was not only necessary to put in place some reasonable controls but also to reassure the public as to their effectiveness.

Dame Anne Warburton went on to deal with the issues raised in the document referred to above. She pointed out that, before 1911, membership of parliament was an unpaid occupation in the UK and that, even today, parliamentary salaries were comparatively modest. It had long been the practice to allow members to earn additional income, provided any such remuneration did not reward the member for work directly related to his or her parliamentary duties. The parliamentary timetable had been geared to accommodate members with outside interests, although the present century had witnessed the steady development of the member's job as a full-time occupation. Furthermore, many members had made a profession of politics itself and had no other source of income. The combination of constituency work with the demands of parliament itself also added to the pressure, making it increasingly difficult for members to pursue two occupations. MPs giving evidence to the Committee revealed a divergence of view between those who felt that membership of parliament should be regarded as a full-time occupation, and those who expressed horror at the idea of a parliament consisting of professional politicians.

It might be valid to comment at this point that a representative parliament should consist of members drawn from wide-ranging walks of life. On the other hand, once membership of parliament becomes a full-time occupation it almost inevitably becomes a profession in itself. Therefore, if politics becomes a livelihood, then members should be fairly remunerated, particularly if they are to resist the temptation to seek other sources of income.

In the UK it was established as long as 300 years ago that it is a crime to offer or receive money for the purpose of promoting any matter in parliament – a principle endorsed and elaborated in a resolution of the House of Commons of 1947. Consequently, since 1975 members of the House of Commons have been obliged to declare their outside financial interests in a register kept by the Clerk of the House. No details of income are required, but the register specifies nine categories of interests including directorships, remunerated employment, gifts and hospitality, land, property and shareholdings. The requirement to register has been a controversial issue among MPs. Some wish to see it tightened still further; others regard it as an intrusion on their right to privacy. Some MPs feel that they are answerable to their constituents should their extraparliamentary activities be questioned. However, because the requirement to register outside interests has no statutory basis, some MPs have declined to comply with it and the extent to which it acts as a control over unacceptable activities is therefore open to question. This was recognized by a report, presented to the House in 1992 by the Select Committee on Members' Interests, which felt there was a tendency to assume that the act of registration legitimized any interest declared. It warned that MPs holding consultancy positions should ensure that these positions were not used improperly, and concluded: 'A financial inducement to take a particular course of action in Parliament may constitute a bribe and thus be an offence against the law of Parliament.'

When the 'cash for questions' scandal erupted in 1994, the Speaker called for a clarification of parliamentary law in this area. Not only did this appear to violate the rule against receiving money for carrying out parliamentary activities, it raised the whole question of MPs receiving money as consultants, or in any other capacity, from lobbying firms. Lobbying is a legitimate activity, and it is not unusual to consult interest groups whose advice can lead to improvements in legislation. Problems arise when MPs have paid links with lobbying firms. Witnesses before the Committee made various suggestions for regulating lobbying firms and for banning certain activities, such as paying MPs for speaking in debate, putting down questions to ministers, or for lobbying ministers, other MPs or officials. Dame Anne Warburton mentioned that some professional lobbying firms now refuse to employ MPs as consultants on principle.

The association of MPs with lobbying firms raises the question of their relationship to other organizations such as trade unions. Many Labour MPs are sponsored by trade unions – in fact the UK Labour Party has historic ties with the trade unions, without whose financial sponsorship the early party members elected in the days before MPs were paid would not have been able to survive. Union-sponsored MPs giving evidence to the Committee insisted that their independence as parliamentarians was in no way inhibited by trade union ties. It appears that the constituency association, rather than the MP personally, benefits from any financial contribution made by the trade union. The position of MPs who were also company directors was raised by certain witnesses. The prevailing view seemed to be that such MPs could legitimately defend their company's interests in parliament provided they declared their own interest, but opinions differed as to whether a member should be allowed to vote on an issue where an interest has been declared. It is not always easy to determine what constitutes a conflict of interest, and it can be argued that an MP has a fundamental right to vote on any issue which comes before parliament.

Defining the line between acceptable and unacceptable parliamentary activities will not be easy, particularly as past practices which were once deemed acceptable have now come to be seen by some as unacceptable. The bulk of the testimony received regarding MPs having paid relationships with lobbyists leaned towards the view that this was wrong. Some witnesses drew a distinction between advising a lobbying firm and advocating its cause by active promotion in parliament – the former being acceptable and the latter being unacceptable. Indeed, an ex-minister claimed that her activities on behalf of a lobbying firm had been advisory only, and that nothing she did influenced the outcome of the issue in question. Also discussed was the regulation of lobbyists themselves, to the extent of requiring registration and declaration of interest. Undoubtedly the most straightforward solution would be an outright ban on MPs accepting any kind of reward for their outside activities, but such a proposal would probably be strenuously opposed by MPs who have a legitimate need to supplement their incomes.

A key question considered by the Nolan Committee was to decide how to monitor compliance with whatever rules may be adopted and whether they should be statutory, either wholly or in part. There is some doubt as to whether self-regulation by parliament itself can really be effective, and even if it were, whether this could ever satisfy the public demand for openness and transparency. Even the Chairman of the Select Committee on Members' Interests expressed dissatisfaction with the Committee's powers, and the weight of opinion seems to favour some independent form of monitoring. Parliament has always been sensitive to any outside intervention in the regulation of its own affairs but, as pointed out by Dame Anne Warburton, there are precedents for the House delegating certain functions – the review of parliamentary salaries, for example – to outside bodies and a number of possible solutions could be suggested. For example, an independent officer, directly responsible to the Speaker, might be appointed as a monitor, or the responsibilities of the Comptroller and Auditor General or the Parliamentary Commissioner for Administration could be extended for this purpose. An all-party committee of senior parliamentarians was also suggested, although this would still amount to self-regulation by parliament itself. Some witnesses preferred a central independent body with wide responsibilities relating to standards and codes of conduct in public life as a whole, including monitoring compliance and recommending sanctions where necessary. The mechanism recommended by the Committee provides for effective powers, including the right to initiate investigations into complaints.

Dame Anne Warburton went on to deal with the structural changes in the civil service which had led to greater privatization and the growth of so-called 'quangos'. These developments had given rise to morale problems, because of the number of redundancies, the replacement of long-term jobs with short-term contracts, the appointment to senior posts by open competition rather than by progression through internal promotion, and the emphasis on business principles rather than traditional civil service methods. She stated that evidence was also received by the Committee concerning the difficulty of maintaining political impartiality in a political climate which has given one party a hold on power for 16 years. No one questioned the importance of maintaining civil service values, and the Committee was heartened by the positive acceptance of a proposed new government-backed code for civil servants, accompanied by the right to bring complaints to an independent mediator.

Further concerns to which Dame Anne referred were the acceptance by former ministers and former civil servants of appointments in the private sector, and the acceptance of gifts and hospitality while in office. While there is no lack of guidelines in respect of either of these practices, the public perception is that by taking these appointments, politicians and bureaucrats are feathering their own nests by profiting from privileged information they have gained while performing their official functions. Senior civil servants are already required to seek approval from an independent committee for any job they wish to take within two years of leaving the service and, in some cases, delays may be imposed. In the case of former ministers, the decision whether or not to accept further employment is left to their own discretion, although guidelines exist in the form of *Questions of Procedure for Ministers*. This document, while not establishing a code of conduct, states that they will 'naturally avoid any course which would reflect adversely on their or the government's reputation for integrity or the confidentiality of its proceedings'. Some witnesses, including former ministers, told the Committee they would welcome a form of regulation, such as the obligation to refer to an independent committee the offer of any employment which might prove controversial. This was opposed by others, including the government spokesman, who felt that a reasonable degree of flexibility was justifiable in view of the relatively small salaries and severance pay which ministers could command.

Civil service guidelines regarding the acceptance of gifts or hospitality are quite strict, providing that 'civil servants must not make use of their official position to further their private interests, or receive gifts, hospitality or benefits of any kind from a third party which might be seen to compromise their personal judgment or integrity'. Ministers are expected to use their discretion 'to see that no conflict arises or appears to arise between their private interests and their public duties' and, when in doubt, they are called upon to consult the prime minister.

At this point it is interesting to refer to a Canadian practice which is relevant – at least peripherally – to the general question of the acceptance of hospitality by parliamentarians. The standing orders of the Canadian House of Commons provide that members must register any foreign travel which they undertake at the expense of foreign governments or other outside sponsors, together with the name of the sponsoring person or organization. The register is maintained under the authority of the Clerk of the House and, although such travel is not prohibited or regulated in any other way, the information is available to the public.

One of the difficulties faced by the Committee was to get the balance right, but Dame Anne emphasized that it would make every effort to do so. The *Economist*, in its issue of 25 February–3 March 1995, wrote of its approval of the Committee's work and anticipated some of the recommendations it was likely to make. It also suggested that the prime minister might regret having appointed the Committee, as many of his colleagues, some of whose testimony failed to impress the Committee, were furious with him for having done so.

The discussion which followed Dame Anne's presentation revealed that similar concerns existed in all the countries represented at the Conference.

One delegate, speaking in defence of the politicians, said that an investigatory commission had been appointed by his government and, after seven years of operation, no significant corruption had been revealed. One prime minister had actually been driven from office by allegations of corruption, but had subsequently been cleared of corrupt behaviour. This delegate, while acknowledging that MPs lacked sufficient guidance, expressed the view that codified rules could be dangerous and might create unfair situations. Given the rigorous scrutiny which existed in his state (New South Wales), he believed that had there been a high level of corruption it would have been exposed. If a code of conduct is required for MPs, demanded this delegate, why should one not be necessary for all groups and professions? MPs were particularly vulnerable as they could be martyred by the press for no good reason. He pointed out that misconduct could arise from inaction as well as action, and further called for the avoidance of secrecy and insisted that judgements should be based only on facts.

Echoing some of these sentiments, another delegate enquired whether politicians were entitled to the presumption of innocence and asked why different ethical standards should apply to them. He also raised the question of when it is legitimate to accept money. People who contribute to an election campaign expect something in return, and it was difficult to define a precise ethical boundary. In a reference to the countries of the former Soviet bloc, this delegate mentioned that politicians were protected from scrutiny by censorship during the communist era, and the life of a journalist was not easy. Now the situation was reversed, and politicians had become the targets. It was easy to spread rumours, and the public were more likely to believe them than to question them.

The unscrupulous behaviour of the press was referred to in a number of contributions to the discussion. A delegate from a small country suggested that the problem was aggravated in a country where everybody knows everybody else. Politicians in his country were not rewarded while in office and had no choice but to seek further employment. This exposed them to press criticism which was so destructive that, in his words, you couldn't win. A delegate from another small country related a completely different story, saying that the press were so beholden to the government that they hesitated to criticize. He agreed that those in power were much closer to the citizens in a small community, but believed that the public were not necessarily the best judge of what was proper or improper behaviour on the part of politicians. In his country all MPs carried on outside activities and, while he did not oppose the idea of a code of conduct, he felt it would not help to set standards which could not be met. What, after all, is meant by corruption? Suspicion should not be fed by over-reaction – the essential factor was full accountability which was the best protection against rumour and innuendo.

Another delegate felt that a code of conduct should be seen as protective not punitive. The issue to be resolved was whether the code should be statutory or non-statutory. In view of public scepticism concerning the behaviour of politicians, there was an argument for making it statutory, in which case it would be necessary to consider the kind of sanctions which should be provided for. Yet another delegate spoke of the difficulties of monitoring compliance and the dangers of presuming guilt whenever a suspicion is expressed. In his country there was a corruption squad which monitored MPs' activities as well as a leadership code designed to regulate the oversight of government leaders' assets. Neither was very effective – particularly the latter – since assets were not necessarily registered under the leader's name. He also stated that as giving gifts to a leader is regarded as normal in the culture of this African country, it was difficult to define what was legitimate or otherwise with regard to gifts, and questioned whether political patronage is necessarily corrupt.

On the question of the control of assets, one delegate from a small country explained that, in his country, there had been a Public Disclosure Act in operation since 1976 but, since it did not apply to assets registered in the names of children, it was wide open to abuse. A great deal of money was concealed by means of this loophole, and the disclosure requirements revealed only bottom-line income, not wider interests. In one of the Canadian provincial jurisdictions, a Financial Disclosure Act provided for the appointment of a commissioner, and both MPs and their spouses were required to make a declaration, although the spouse's was not made public. The declarations, which must include all gifts of a value in excess of $50, had shown that most parliamentarians were not wealthy people, with the result that attacks on parliamentarians had abated, thus supporting the argument for transparency.

It emerged, during the discussions, that in some countries MPs had only themselves to blame for their negative image, and that the electorate itself sometimes failed to use the remedy at hand by re-electing members who had shown themselves to be at fault. In India the code of conduct laid down by Gandhi and Nehru had largely collapsed, to the point where it was no longer sufficient that an MP should be above suspicion, but should be above proven guilt. Although ministers have to declare their assets to the prime minister this is not enough to satisfy the public as to their integrity. Even so, one minister who was sacked as a result of his activities was re-elected. Similar experiences were reported from other jurisdictions. In Nova Scotia, a minister who was dismissed from cabinet and forced to vacate his seat was also re-elected. A similar experience was reported from Barbados. The public, it seemed, had a double standard: they demanded higher standards from their elected representatives, but failed to act when they had the opportunity. The most effective organ of control in Barbados, it appeared, was the Public Accounts Committee. The Ombudsman had not been very successful because so few complaints are brought to him, and a bill intended to establish a code of conduct died in the Senate.

In Canada, while there have long been specific rules to govern the conduct of ministers, no code of conduct has ever been laid down for MPs. Numerous bills for this purpose had been introduced in the past but all had died on the order paper. Canada has had a Lobbyists Registration Act since 1988, following two decades of attempts by private members to promote legislation requiring the registration of paid lobbyists and the disclosure of their activities. A review of the 1988 Act was undertaken by a House of Commons committee in 1992–93, and an amending bill was introduced, following a general election and a change of government, in June 1994. It was referred for study to the Standing Committee on Industry which presented its report, entitled *Rebuilding Trust*, in March 1995. Extracts from this report can be found in Appendix 2 of this book.

In June 1994 the Canadian Government appointed an Ethics Commissioner who reports to parliament on lobbying activities. His functions include the development of a code of conduct for lobbyists and the investigation of alleged abuses of the code. Also in the same month a revised code of conduct for ministers and other public office holders – which includes guidelines covering the employment of former public office holders – was made public and this, too, is monitored by the Ethics Commissioner. On matters concerning the ethical conduct of ministers the Ethics Commissioner reports directly to the prime minister. In Canada ministers are obliged to make a complete disclosure of their assets and place their investments in a blind trust during their tenure of office. In Canada, as in other countries, the popular image of politicians is very poor, two of the targets of criticism being the generous pension plan provided for parliamentarians and the extent of their overseas travel. As was stated by the participant who described the situation in Canada, rules must be clear in order to be fair, and he suggested that too many rules can have the effect of confirming public suspicion. He echoed a sentiment several times expressed in the course of the discussion that reputations can easily be destroyed by innuendo.

Lord Nolan expressed interest in the Canadian appointment of an Ethics Commissioner with a guiding as well as an investigative function. He felt that, in the UK at least, public scrutiny made it difficult for MPs to cover up any abuses, and wondered whether it was fair to single out parliamentarians for an obligation to reveal their incomes. Public cynicism had led to the appointment of his Committee and, so far, no great evidence of corruption had been revealed. The problem arose from the lack of clear rules to regulate the activities of parliamentarians, and it would probably be reasonable to confine the disclosure obligation to those matters relevant to the parliamentary function. Transparency in government is absolutely necessary if the public is to be persuaded that all is well. MPs themselves know what is acceptable, but a code of conduct similar to those for professions and the civil service would be helpful as a means of clarification. Rules, however, were of no use unless they can be enforced, and it should be possible to enforce them whether or not they are statutory.

So ended a penetrating discussion which highlighted agreement on some key issues, and a revelation of how these matters are viewed in differing political environments. In the opinion of many of those present, the press emerged as the villain of the piece and is perhaps entitled to a forum of its own in order to present its counterarguments.

I myself concluded that matters which might appear straightforward – such as the devising of rules which are both effective and fair, and the distinction as to what is acceptable or unacceptable behaviour – are not so easy to resolve as might be imagined.

7 The Role of Political Parties

The presenter at this session was Professor Philip Norton, Professor of Government at the University of Hull. Political parties are the bedrock of most, if not all, countries which have representative institutions. While the concept of political parties is not new – they may be said to have their origins in the rival factions which fought each other long before there were truly representative assemblies – the growth of modern political parties, formed on the basis of policies and principles by which they could be readily identified, paralleled the evolution of the popular franchise. Some parties are broad coalitions of opinion whose members adhere to certain common ideas and principles; others are formed around narrower and more specific policy themes, admitting fewer shades of difference among its members. Whatever their form, they were shaped by the necessity of appealing to an electorate.

Professor Norton's first comment was that he was concerned with legislatures as representative institutions. Perhaps it was fair to say that the representative function was the common denominator of all legislatures – even those which are not democratically elected. Whatever the political system of the country concerned, and whatever the system of election or appointment, they performed a representative function, whether directly or indirectly. Professor Norton's comments focused on what he termed 'citizen-legislator relations', and were therefore concerned with systems of direct representation through democratic election. To illustrate his thesis he chose three models which he described as the 'mandate model', the 'populist model' and the 'conscience model'.

The mandate model is the one under which the party plays a dominant role. Candidates pledge their loyalty to a particular party and seek election as supporters of their party's platform or manifesto. If elected they are mandated to seek the implementation of their party's programme. The lead is given by the party leadership or the caucus, whose decisions are binding. Party discipline is strong, and if members fail to toe the party line they risk sanctions such as expulsion from the party or withdrawal of the party whip.

Other sanctions used in some jurisdictions might include removal from committees or being barred from participating in a parliamentary delegation travelling overseas.

Professor Norton selected India as the best – or maybe the most extreme – example of the mandate model. The stranglehold which the parties have over their members was embodied in a constitutional amendment of 1985, which provides for the disqualification from membership of the parliament or the state legislatures of any member:

> ... if he has voluntarily given up his membership of such political party; or if he votes or abstains from voting in such House contrary to any direction issued by the political party to which he belongs or by any person or authority authorised by it in this behalf without obtaining in either case, the prior permission of such political party, person or authority and such voting or abstention has not been condoned by such political party, person or authority within fifteen days from the date of such voting or abstention.

Few Westminster-style parliamentary systems go as far as this in limiting the independent action of MPs, although India is not unique in imposing a disqualification upon members who change or resign from their parties.

Under the populist model party control is much looser and the party leadership far less dominant. As explained by Professor Norton, control is exercised from below rather than from the top. Local party supporters and the electorate itself are the influences to which the candidates respond. Consequently, members are less committed to a party programme and more concerned with local interests. In some jurisdictions where the populist model is to be found, the electorate enjoys a measure of control over the activities of its representatives through the power of recall. A member can be unseated should a certain number of electors in a constituency petition for his or her recall, forcing a fresh election in the constituency concerned.

As the best example of the populist model, Professor Norton cited the United States. Parties, he pointed out, have never been dominated by a national leadership, although, at one time, local party bosses wielded tremendous power through local party machines. This power was significantly curbed by the introduction of primary elections which removed the control of the bosses at the state and city level over candidate selection.

The party label is of less significance in American politics than is the case in countries operating a parliamentary system, whereby the executive is responsible to the legislature and can be removed by a vote of no confidence. The separation of powers in the United States enables legislators to enjoy far greater independence, free from party discipline, and they are able to devote themselves to the interests of their state and constituency, wherein lies the key to re-election. Professor Norton pointed out that, in nine states of the USA, all elected office holders are subject to recall, and in six states a similar control exists in respect of all elected officials other than judges.

As an illustration of the conscience model, Professor Norton turned for his example to an earlier British House of Commons, before the party system had become the dominant factor it is today. Under this model, members retained their independence of action whether or not they sought election on a party label. Once elected they were immune from party control or constituency pressure, determining their positions on the nation's interests through the exercise of their own independent judgement. In evoking this conception of the ideal MP, he quoted from Edmund Burke's address to the electors of Bristol, 3 November 1774:

> Your representative owes you, not his industry only, but his judgement; and he betrays, instead of serving you, if he sacrifices it to your opinion. ... You choose a member indeed; but when you have chosen him, he is not the member of Bristol, but he is a member of Parliament.

In other words a member should be a representative, not a delegate, either of a party or a constituency. It must be remembered, however, that Burke was speaking in an age when the electoral system was corrupt, and when many members sat as placemen, or delegates, controlled by the wealthy patrons who owned the boroughs for which they sat. Unlike Burke they exercised no independent judgement. Thus, as Professor Norton indicated, the best example of the conscience model was probably the British House of Commons between the Reform Acts of 1832 and 1867. The Act of 1832 extended the franchise sufficiently to curb the power of the aristocracy who had controlled the rotten boroughs, since voters became too numerous to be bought. The 1867 Act took a further step down the road to universal adult suffrage and enlarged the electorate enough to enable it to hold governments to account. In order to appeal to this greatly extended voting population, political parties had to organize if they were to seek power. The convention whereby governments reflect the will of the people, and depended for their stability on the support of a parliamentary majority, became a recognized element of the British constitution. In 1868 Disraeli became the first prime minister to resign following an election defeat and before the meeting of the new parliament.

During the brief period between 1832 and 1867, MPs were able to bask in the luxury of political independence, although it soon became clear that this was not the way to promote government stability. Many politicians regard this period as the halcyon days of the British Parliament – the time when it really came into its own, before its powers were usurped by the tyranny of the majority. It is ironic that many current MPs feel a sense of nostalgia for this period, and speak of the lost days of glory when there was no party discipline; they do not perhaps always realize that during the many centuries of parliament's existence, there were only 35 years during which their predecessors enjoyed the independence they dream of. Furthermore, to enjoy this independence they had to be already wealthy since MPs were not paid.

In presenting the case for each model, Professor Norton acknowledged that, in most countries, the relationship between legislature and citizenry was a mix of these models, with most Western countries leaning heavily towards the mandate model. Although party control tends to dominate in these countries, this, of itself, does not justify the system. The argument for the mandate model is that if candidates use the benefit of the party label in order to get elected, then the party has a right to expect their loyal support together with their votes in favour of the party's programme. Independents stand little chance of being elected; therefore party-sponsored candidates should not claim the right to act independently having used the party label in order to be elected.

The argument for the populist model is that, while electors may have a preference for a party, they may not necessarily agree with everything the party is proposing. In Professor Norton's words, 'Electors may not want a fixed menu; they may prefer a more *à la carte* menu'. The populist model allows elected representatives to take account of the views of the electors as well as those of the party, and to determine their position on each specific issue rather than be slavishly bound to obey a party whip. It is never possible to anticipate everything in a party programme: unexpected problems can arise, together with issues not covered in a party manifesto. The populist model allows MPs the flexibility to decide where they stand on such issues and be responsive to the views of the electors as well as to the party leadership.

The conscience model may perhaps be described as the idealistic model and, as stated by Professor Norton, 'derives from Burke's perception of a parliament as a deliberative assembly'. In such a parliament, genuine debate would take place – the kind of debate to which all MPs pay attention and whose votes might well be influenced by the arguments. Nowadays, debates in many parliaments are sometimes nothing more than a series of speeches, with everyone knowing what the outcome of the vote is going to be. Under the conscience model MPs are genuinely independent. They consider the principle and detail of each measure proposed and vote according to their own judgement, immune to pressure from either party or electorate. It must be conceded, however, that in a modern parliamentary system the conscience model would be a constant threat to government stability.

Professor Norton suggested that elements of all three models are to be found in many systems, usually with a heavy bias towards the mandate model. Taking the British system as an example, he maintained that, while party is the dominant influence it is not the exclusive influence. MPs take independent positions on certain social issues, sometimes motivated by conscience, sometimes by pressure from constituents. Free votes also take place on private members' bills, although comparatively few reach the statute book and the scope for private members' legislation is limited because the financial initiative is reserved to the government. No private member's bill may contain financial provisions unless the government is prepared to provide the necessary support. Almost all votes in the House of Commons are party votes, although there have always been issues on which some MPs have been prepared to cross party lines, and there have always been MPs who are prepared to defy their whips. Professor Norton stated that this tendency had become more marked since 1970. While it prevents the government taking the House for granted, it does complicate the principle of accountability to the electorate.

A peripheral comment on the Canadian situation might be apposite at this point. It is not unusual during election campaigns for prime ministers to support MPs' calls for more free votes and greater independence, including greater independence for committees. Yet, once elected, there is seldom any enthusiasm evinced by those in power for pursuing these pledges and the slightest deviation from the party line is usually met with sanctions, to the chagrin of the backbenchers concerned. Not that they should be surprised. A prime minister would be very unlikely to be willing to make a difficult job even more difficult for himself or herself. At least dissident Canadian MPs do not face the strictures which would face them in India: they would not be disqualified from membership and are therefore free to act independently – provided they accept the political risks involved.

Professor Norton concluded his presentation by posing the following questions:

> So where does one draw the line, if indeed one should draw a line? Is one of the models to constitute the exclusive model? Or should there be a mix between two or more? If so, where do you draw the line between party, the demands of the electorate, and the dictates of individual conscience? Is it party and nothing else or is it party and something else? If so, what? That is the question I pose for discussion.

It could be concluded from the views of those who spoke in the following discussion that the mandate model was here to stay and could be expected to dominate. A British MP stated that he believed in a strong whipping system, because MPs owed their electoral success to their parties, and it was their job to be party activists at the constituency level. He approved of free votes on conscience issues, and stressed the importance of select committees which offered some scope for independent action. He dismissed the procedure which enabled private members to introduce bills as farcical because they could so easily be talked out or defeated. He also introduced another issue, the selection procedure for candidates, and the steps which might be taken to ensure the adoption of more women candidates. Women-only shortlists in certain constituencies had been proposed, but not everyone was in favour of this solution.

Another British MP felt that an elected executive understands accountability better than one which is not elected. Under the American system of checks and balances the only member of the executive who is elected is the president. Under the populist model there is usually a more widespread use of the referendum – an issue which was dealt with directly at a later session. His comments reminded the Conference that the mandate involved the party as well as the government, and expressed the view that the Labour Party Conference was more effective at policy-forming than its Conservative counterpart. Constitutionally, of course, it is the cabinet that frames government policy, and the extent to which it is influenced by party resolutions is a matter for its own discretion. This participant also emphasized the importance of reconciling the different levels of government – local, national and international – in order to promote harmony and avoid conflict.

Another delegate, while agreeing with Professor Norton's choice of India as the best example of the mandate model, stated that India had started as a quasi-mandate model, but that policy had fallen entirely under the control of government. Today nothing is brought before the party for decision and the party executive has no influence. The anti-defection law had been brought in to deal with political irresponsibility and to prevent any group from hijacking the party. This delegate applauded a German law which regulates the functioning of political parties and felt that India could benefit from a similar law.

Speaking of the German situation, a delegate referred to article 38 of the constitution, which states that MPs vote only according to their consciences. This is a contradiction in practice, because they almost always vote with their parties, although critics never acknowledge that, when voting for the party, one might at the same time be voting according to conscience. Conscience voting is recognized on matters of ethics and on issues such as where the seat of the capital should be, but free votes occur so seldom that the public has become cynical. This participant believed this to be a reason for the public's poor perception of parliament.

It emerged from the discussion that Kenya and Bangladesh were among other countries having an anti-defection law. This had led to difficulties in

Kenya under the recently introduced multi-party system, which had yet to find a stable equilibrium. All parties had to be registered or they were unlawful. In Bangladesh, as in India, MPs are required by the constitution to vote with their parties, but they have discovered a method of defeating a bill by vacating the House so that there is no quorum.

One delegate spoke in favour of coalition governments as a means of removing the mandate from the hands of a single party and making it a shared mandate. He chose South Africa for his example, overlooking perhaps the special circumstances following the democratization of the country which led to the formation, in the first instance, of a government of national reconciliation.

Another delegate enquired as to the means of developing a model to meet what he saw as the Conference objectives, pointing out that the Westminster model pre-dated the party system. How representative are the parties themselves, he wondered. Was there a case for the state funding of parties? His view was that party conferences were not necessarily well informed, but he expressed his confidence in select committees, which were better able to obtain information and work as a team. He proposed that progress could be achieved through participatory democracy, through greater consultation with the people, and cooperation with the various interests affected by policy formation.

Summarizing the discussion, Professor Norton referred to the various points which had been raised. He defended the whips, saying that they were much maligned but could not be effective unless the parties were cohesive. He understood the attraction of free votes, but declared that there were limits as to how far they could be taken if the institution was to remain accountable. Governments are obliged to take responsibility for national policies. He believed that private members' bills were important, but agreed that some modification of the rules would be desirable to make the system more effective. Select committees he described as important adjuncts, which could become the channel for promoting public participation. Their function of hearing witnesses and collecting evidence could be extended, thereby reinforcing their capacity to contribute, while allowing parliament to retain control. If committees are to succeed they must be supported by the House, but they should not be allowed to bypass the chamber as is the case in Italy. Professor Norton could also have cited congressional committees, to which so much power has been delegated by the parent bodies that they have been described as 'little legislatures'.

Professor Norton felt that party membership had been declining because people preferred to work through pressure groups. He believed that candidates should be chosen on merit and was opposed to any kind of quota system. Parties should be free to organize themselves without too much regulation. The right of electors to choose their candidates should not be unduly limited, and they should be able to vote for independent candidates if they wish. With regard to coalitions, broad-based parties are in themselves coalitions, but smaller parties might be the answer in countries where the diversity of beliefs tended to cause larger parties to splinter.

Comparing the congressional and parliamentary systems, he pointed out that, in the USA, there were multiple routes to the political summit, whereas in the UK there is only one route – the parliamentary route to the ministerial level. He said he was opposed to referenda, asking how resources could be channelled in such a way as to be fair to both sides. In his view, parliaments should be held responsible. Referenda enabled governments and parliaments to abdicate responsibility in that they can blame the public should a referendum decision lead to damaging consequences. He raised the question, heard in various countries, of whether there were too many MPs, and suggested there may be an argument for reducing numbers and increasing resources. He also stressed the importance of open voting in parliament, personally favouring roll-call votes as the surest method of forcing MPs to stand up and be counted. As to the future, he said that public attitudes should change before the rules are changed, and the task to be performed was one of public education. This was an area in which parliamentary committees could profitably be involved.

It seems clear that there is no practical alternative to the mandate model except in countries where there is a separation of powers between the legislature and the executive. Governments must be held accountable and, to fulfil this role, they must be assured of a reasonable measure of control over their supporters. On the other hand, the sanctions provided for under the Indian model are too extreme, since MPs should be allowed a certain freedom of action, and at the least the right to face the electorate without first having to suffer expulsion from parliament. When parties impose sanctions on dissident MPs, public sympathy often sides with the latter which is the one consolation that may be available to them. Thus it seems unfair to protect the parties even further by enshrining anti-defection penalties in the law or the constitution.

8 The Evolving Civil Service

The stated theme of this session was 'Ensuring effective interaction between politicians, civil servants and other non-elected officials' and it was introduced by Mr Robin Mountfield, Deputy Secretary of the Treasury of the United Kingdom. He explained that his presentation would deal with the subject largely from the British perspective, adding that he was speaking at a time when major changes were taking place in the British civil service. The modern civil service dates from the reforms implemented as a result of the Northcote–Trevelyan Report on the Civil Service of 1853, which had condemned the incompetence of the system at the time, based as it was on nepotism and patronage. The report called for

> ... an efficient body of permanent officers, occupying a position duly subordinate to the Crown and to Parliament, yet possessing sufficient independence, character, ability and experience to be able to advise, assist and, to some extent, influence those who are from time to time set over them.

The changes currently taking place are probably the most far-reaching since the reforms of the 1850s.

The key characteristic of the British civil service is its political impartiality. It differs in this respect from the civil service in many other countries, and even those which profess to have a non-political civil service may operate rather differently. To many outside observers it seems strange that political programmes are directed by unelected officials, given that, following a change of government, those same officials may find themselves directing a totally different set of programmes. How can the advisers of one government adapt to the responsibilities of advising another government with a totally opposing set of policies? Be that as it may, this is the tradition of the British civil service. Officials are schooled to disregard their own personal views, are probably not even aware of the views of their colleagues, and in the process have become centrists, compromisers or (suggested Mr Mountfield) perhaps cynics.

In addition to political impartiality, Mr Mountfield referred to five key principles for the civil service to which successive governments had subscribed: integrity, objectivity, selection and promotion on merit, and accountability through ministers to parliament. These principles were endorsed in a White Paper mentioned in Chapter 3, *The Civil Service: Continuity and Change* published in July 1994 (Command Paper 2627). It was stressed that, whatever changes might take place, commitment to these principles would remain undiminished. Nevertheless, stresses and strains had developed because of these changes, and Mr Mountfield proceeded to identify four of them.

He saw the first stress as having developed from the fact that one party had been in power for 16 years, and the resultant fear that the official mindset might confuse loyalty to the government with loyalty to the governing party. Mr Mountfield discounted this fear, pointing out that no problems had surfaced in 1964, when a change of government took place after the same party had been in office for 13 years.

The second stress he regarded as more serious, and was due to the political polarization which had taken place in the 1970s and 1980s, when both principal parties adopted radical positions. This gave rise to apprehension in the civil service that the traditional centrist approach would no longer work and that a politically impartial civil service would no longer be able to satisfy either extreme. The presenter believed this fear had abated now that both parties had moved closer to the centre. He quoted a cryptic phrase from a former civil service head, who said that the duty of the non-political civil servant was to withhold the last ounce of commitment – a comment which might not be well received by politicians but which presumably meant that the civil servant should not overstep the barrier between commitment to the government and commitment to a political ideology.

The third stress was the problem of accountability. Politicians and civil servants are both accountable, the former in the area of policy, the latter in the area of administration. Mr Mountfield said that, in the British civil service, personal performance was judged against specific objectives, and great use was made of this in the service delivery areas. When policy goes wrong, and the cry goes up for heads to roll, the suggestion is often heard that the advisers, as well as the politicians, should suffer. The failed policy may have been the adviser's brainchild, or the adviser may have failed to warn against its implementation. Should he or she not pay the penalty? In his argument against this logic, Mr Mountfield postulated a fictitious secretary to the Treasury who failed to meet an inflation target set by the government. Unless that official controlled the levers of economic power it would be wrong to hold him or her responsible, and to do so would make nonsense of ministerial accountability. In any case, officials are accountable to their ministers for what they do, and their careers can suffer if they fail to give sound advice.

The fourth stress arises from the decision to throw open more top positions to open competition in order to create a wider base of recruitment to key positions. Although selections will be supervised by independent civil service commissioners as a safeguard against political bias, the presenter nevertheless saw risks in the process since a well qualified person might be carrying what he termed 'baggage' – deep-rooted convictions which frequently accompany expertise. The even greater risk was probably the blow to civil service morale, since the new system undermines the security of tenure which has always been regarded as a major benefit. While the system would make it easier to get rid of mediocre performers, there was a fear that severance decisions could be politically influenced. For this reason it was decided not to opt for fixed-term contracts for top positions.

Mr Mountfield was optimistic that the civil service would overcome the stresses he described and would continue to provide the same high standards of politically neutral service – a tradition supported by all parties.

He then went on to describe the 'Next Steps' programme, in operation at that time for seven years, which has radically changed the way civil service functions are managed and organized. The report of an Efficiency Unit which undertook an investigation during 1987–88 concluded that: most civil service activity consisted in delivery of services; ministers were overloaded; their closest advisers had no managerial experience and were mainly concerned with their ministers' short-term needs; there was a lack of long-term planning; there was too much focus on inputs rather than outputs; and there was general frustration among managers.

The solution adopted was to establish agencies within departments to deliver services and isolate these executive functions from the area of policy. Ministers are thus freed to concentrate on policy work and the chief executives of the agencies are free to manage within the terms of reference of their delegated authority. The aims and objectives of the agencies are determined by the minister responsible, together with their targets and resources. Taxpayers benefit in terms of better value for money, more efficient management, more reliable delivery of services, and a focus on outputs rather than inputs. Mr Mountfield reported that the programme had been a considerable success, 102 departmental agencies having been set up and 80 per cent of their targets having been achieved during the last complete year [1994]. Nearly two out of three civil servants now work in one of these organizations. However, the establishment of these agencies naturally has implications for the relationships between ministers, civil servants and the public who use the services, which raises the question of accountability.

This will be dealt with below as a broader issue touching other significant developments which have taken place in recent years.

These other more controversial developments are contracting-out, privatization and the turning over of a wide variety of functions to quasi-autonomous non-governmental organizations – the so-called quangos. Between April 1992 and September 1994 over £2 billions' worth of activities were assessed with a view to contracting them out, involving the review of more than 54 000 civil service posts. Of 799 reviews of activities 664 have involved a competitive tender. The current trend on the part of ministers is to press for more contracting-out rather than less. The contracts specify the standards which must be met and the sanctions which may be imposed if they are not, and the minister concerned remains accountable.

In the case of privatization, the government relinquishes all control of the industries concerned, usually public utilities. They are set up under legislation and shares are offered to the public. The telephone service, water, gas and electricity supply are among the utilities privatized; they are mainly monopolies, and the customer deals with them directly. Quangos, sometimes referred to as the 'unelected state', have taken over wide areas of publicly financed activity, and number between 5000 and 7000. They include training and enterprise councils, national health service bodies, housing associations, and schools and colleges no longer directly funded by local authorities and control expenditures in excess of £50 billion. Members of these bodies are appointed by the government but are not directly controlled by ministers or civil servants.

The question of accountability and the rights of consumers is at issue in respect of all these developments – agencies within departments, contracted-out services, privatized utilities and quangos. In the case of agencies set up under the 'Next Steps' programme, the ministers concerned are clearly responsible, since the agencies are incorporated within their departments. They therefore need a means of judging how an agency has been performing, either through advice from within the department itself or through outside advice. Using for his example the prison service, which was recently established as an agency, Mr Mountfield referred to a highly publicized prison escape, and quoted the minister's own words to distinguish between the minister's general responsibility for the prison service and the operational accountability of the director-general of the service. He also quoted from the command paper, *Taking Forward Continuity and Change*, published in January 1995, which made the same distinction, pointing out:

> It is not possible for ministers to handle everything personally, and if ministers were to be held personally responsible for every action of the department, delegation and efficiency would be much inhibited.

In giving evidence before select committees, civil servants account for their actions without exempting ministers from their ultimate responsibility to parliament. In fact, a select committee of the House of Commons recommended in 1994 that the chief executives of agencies 'should be directly and personally accountable to select committees in relation to their annual performance agreements'. Given the increasing tendency of such executives to appear on television to explain and defend their actions, there seems much to justify this recommendation.

When services are contracted out the minister remains accountable, and complaints relating to such services fall under the jurisdiction of the Parliamentary Commissioner for Administration (Ombudsman). This provides the public with a channel of redress, although the Ombudsman's freedom of action is limited by the fact that he can only investigate a complaint if approached through a MP. In the case of privatized industries there is no ministerial responsibility, and the aggrieved customer is obliged to seek a remedy in the same way as with any other private company.

The problem of quangos is one with which the Nolan Committee dealt. Being publicly funded and responsible for vast public expenditures, their activities must be included among those for which government is ultimately responsible. Nevertheless they are not subject to government intervention although, since their members are appointed by the government, they are presumably subject to government dismissal. Government policy seeks to bring decision-making closer to the immediate customer and it is in this direction that the quangos should probably be led in terms of their accountability. They constitute a problem area in the accountability process which will hopefully be successfully resolved.

In concluding his presentation, Mr Mountfield referred to the Citizen's Charter, established by the present British Government, which provides a set of standards for each service to the public, from waiting times in doctors' surgeries to standards of punctuality and cleanliness in trains and buses. The problem for the consumer is how to know what to expect, how to exert pressure to improve standards and how to make complaints. He concluded by suggesting that the issues are the same in all countries and that only the solutions vary.

It seemed, from the subsequent discussion, that in a number of countries the political detachment of the civil service could not be taken for granted. In Canada there are many similarities between their civil service and that of the UK, but heads of departments – styled deputy ministers in Canada – are appointed at the pleasure of the Prime Minister and do not enjoy security of tenure. In some cases Canadian departmental heads develop a close relationship with their political masters and become identified with their policies. A delegate from an African country stated that only the president has direct communication with senior civil servants, a minister may only have direct contact with the principal secretary who holds the purse strings. It is therefore difficult, in these circumstances, to hold ministers responsible for their departments because they are deprived of information. Answers to questions are drafted by civil servants without reference to their ministers, whose only function is to read them out. Speaking of another African country, a delegate said that the government was always nervous of civil servants becoming too independent, and enquired whether any ethical principle was involved with regard to an independent civil service and also whether the formation of policy should be considered a political act. As in the country previously referred to, the answers to questions were drafted for ministers by civil servants, who sometimes conspired in cover-ups.

A delegate from another Third World country stated that, in his country, the civil servants were the real custodians of the public good and that they had only contempt for politicians. On the other hand, they also tended to shelter behind ministerial accountability and seek credit only for successful outcomes. Referring to India, another delegate commented that the prime minister's office had grown too powerful and that some civil servants joined the ruling party on retirement. They are not permitted to seek employment within two years of retirement but are not precluded from pursuing a political career. The speaker felt that the introduction of tenured appointments for certain key officials would improve the situation. A further question was raised as to whether civil servants should be allowed to run for elected office and subsequently return to the civil service. This is permitted in Canada, where they apply for unpaid leave of absence if they wish to seek election, and may return to their employment if they are defeated.

Among other questions raised was the right of civil servants to form or to join trade unions, which is permitted in some countries but not in others. In Canada, for example, collective bargaining in the civil service was introduced some years ago, including the right to strike. Parliamentary staff, except those in managerial positions, may also join unions but are not permitted to strike. The role of political advisers was also raised and, according to one delegate, they were not welcomed by civil servants in the UK. Nevertheless, the speaker believed that they had made a constructive contribution – particularly the policy groups sometimes set up by ministers as think tanks – and secondment of officers to and from industry had also proved valuable. This led to the issue of the extent of university involvement in the civil service, and also how parliamentary staff were affected. In the UK and many other countries, parliamentary staff are independent of the civil service but, in others, the parliamentary staff are civil servants and subject to transfer to and from other departments. The matter of civil servants using their previous experience to obtain high-salaried employment in the private sector was also referred to.

Mr Mountfield dealt with the issues raised when closing the discussion. He stated that security of tenure in the British civil service was increasingly diminishing and that, as in Canada, political support was required in ministers' offices. Some advisers were selected for their expert knowledge; others for their political reliability. A new government might wish to pursue policies which had been advised against, and the historical emphasis on a career civil service was no longer so strong. He added that, in the UK, politicians and civil servants seemed to be two separate breeds of people and that the latter rarely entered politics. With regard to university involvement, senior academics had sometimes been seconded for a specific project but this was rare. However, political appointments to ambassadorial posts were sometimes made from the academic community.

With regard to civil servants accepting subsequent employment, Mr Mountfield agreed that this was a cause for concern but believed it was not a straightforward issue. It was difficult to impose restraints while the civil service was being downsized. In the Treasury alone, staff are being reduced by 25 per cent and it is difficult to prevent these people from offering their skills to other employers. Civil service salaries at the senior levels have always been lower than those of comparable positions in the private sector, and security of tenure has been the historical justification for this. The new policy completely changes the situation. He agreed that if the prime minister's office becomes too powerful, government moves too closely towards a quasi-presidential system. When Edward Heath was prime minister he created a central policy review board within his office, but this was abolished by Margaret Thatcher. Ministers are completely free to consult at any level within their departments, and this can be a means of bringing pressure upon the head of the department to take action. The tradition that the duty of the civil service is to serve the government of the day remains the guiding principle.

This was a particularly interesting discussion to have at a time when the British civil service is undergoing radical change. It is to be hoped that the reforms undertaken, in addition to improving services to the public, will also widen the scope for direct cooperation between ministers and their senior departmental advisers. The role of the latter has always been a crucial one. It was Sir Ivor Jennings who commented that although the politicians, who are supposed to be in touch with public opinion, will tell the bureaucrats what the public will or will not tolerate, there are times when the civil servants find it necessary to deliver the same warning to their political bosses. It is clearly vital to protect the confidential nature of this relationship.

As a postscript to this chapter, it may be of interest to note that, on 11 May 1995, the Auditor-General of Canada published a report which dealt, among other things, with the problem of ethics awareness in the Canadian public service. He found that many public servants are only vaguely aware of what constitutes improper or unethical behaviour and that more than half of those surveyed were totally ignorant of the statutes, rules and policies relating to conflict of interest. The report called on the government to act swiftly to restore public confidence and promote fraud awareness among public servants. It also urged public servants to take advantage of the ethics training courses which are available.

9 Direct Democracy: The Way Forward?

The term 'direct democracy' essentially embraces three processes involving the participation of the electorate: the referendum, by means of which a direct question is put to the people; the recall, which empowers the electorate to unseat a representative and force a new election in the constituency, provided a certain proportion of the electors concerned petition accordingly; and the initiative, a means by which a certain proportion of the electorate may propose a legislative proposition for the consideration of parliament. The Hon. Phil Goff, an MP from New Zealand, and Shadow Minister of Justice, leading the discussion at this session, concentrated on the referendum.

During his presentation Mr Goff described the types of referendum which have been used, the extent to which they have been used, and the arguments for and against the referendum as an instrument of democracy. The background to his remarks was the adoption in 1993 of the Citizens Initiated Referenda Act in his own country. Referenda have long been advocated by those who believe that the only democratic way of reaching decisions on matters of public policy is through the direct participation of the people. This contrasts with the view that the function of the electorate is to elect a parliament and a government and entrust them with the direction of affairs on the basis of stated policies and promises. Mr Goff attributed the growing support for the referendum process in certain countries to the public loss of confidence in the parliamentary process. Parties have failed to fulfil their promises – in fact, in the public perception, parties will promise anything in order to get elected, and not only fail to live up to expectations, but sometimes act contrary to the promises they have made once they gain power. Under the parliamentary system governments have come to be regarded as elective dictatorships, the public having no influence on the conduct of affairs between elections and parliament having become powerless to exert any meaningful restraint as long as the government commands a majority.

Mr Goff proceeded to describe the three most common categories of referenda, which he termed constitutional, government-initiated and citizens-initiated. The constitutional referendum is probably the most familiar, and it is quite widely used when constitutional amendments are contemplated. In some countries, among them Switzerland and Australia, the constitution itself provides that any proposed amendment must be put to a referendum. Government-initiated referenda can take various forms and can also deal with constitutional issues or any other subject on which the government wishes to consult the people. Sometimes they are used to determine the public view on moral issues which cut across party lines. Citizens-initiated referenda require a threshold level of signatures in order to have a proposal put to the popular vote. They are a means of testing public support on a wide range of issues, and a majority vote can either be binding or simply an expression of opinion on which action may not necessarily follow.

Referenda are widely used in some countries, less so in others. They have never, for example, formed a significant part of British political tradition, although in recent decades they have been held on Britain's membership of the European Economic Community and on the devolution of powers to Scotland and Wales. Mr Goff's presentation concentrated on their use in Switzerland and California and the recently adopted legislation in his own country. He pointed out that Switzerland and California have held more referenda than the rest of the world put together.

Switzerland, according to Mr Goff, is the only country in the world where the referendum is central to political life. Between 1848 and 1995 some 414 referenda had been held, more than the total number held in all other countries combined. On average, between six and 12 are held every year. The Swiss system gives a considerable measure of power to the electorate at the expense of the legislators. All constitutional amendments must be submitted to popular vote, and the citizens can themselves initiate constitutional amendments. In addition, they can initiate referenda on virtually every area of national policy. Any law or decree adopted by the Federal Parliament may be challenged by referendum and overturned by a majority vote. All decisions made by the voters are binding. Interestingly, voter turnout in Switzerland is low, averaging less than 50 per cent in the case of referenda, and about 50 per cent at general elections. Switzerland is a stable and democratic country, but Mr Goff questioned whether direct democracy had been a contributing factor. A weakness of such a system, binding as it is in all circumstances, is that referendum majorities frequently reflect popular prejudices. A good illustration of this is that Switzerland was the last country in the Western world to give women the vote – this took place as recently as 1971.

Of the 36 US states which make provision for the popular initiative, California uses it most frequently. Over a 94-year period since 1898, 236 citizens-initiated referenda were launched, of which 78 were approved. The decisions are binding unless struck down by the courts as being unconstitutional. Many of these initiatives have been controversial, and California may well be the best source for those seeking arguments against the use of binding referenda. In 1964 a state law prohibiting discrimination in the sale of residential housing was struck down. In 1978 an increase in property taxes was vetoed, throwing the state budget into chaos and enforcing major spending cuts. In 1990 another proposition imposed term limits of six or eight years on all elected officials, abolished their state pensions and demanded cuts of US$120 million in the state legislature's annual budget. Among the most notorious of California's citizens-initiated propositions were two carried in 1994. One denied schooling and health treatment to illegal immigrants and their children, which was subsequently struck down by the courts. The other imposed a mandatory minimum sentence of 25 years' imprisonment on any person with three or more criminal convictions, no matter how minor the offence.

Another problem inherent in the Californian system is its complexity. The propositions themselves are frequently complicated and they are so numerous that electors can have great difficulty in dealing with them. In 1990, for example, there were 28 state-wide propositions requiring 224 pages of explanation, in addition to a number of county-level propositions. As a result, the process is often incomprehensible to the voters – in fact, a poll conducted in the same year revealed that 78 per cent of voters had difficulty in understanding the propositions.

The Californian experience is far from reassuring. It has not promoted grass-roots democracy, since many propositions are initiated by special interest groups, backed by huge levels of expenditure. In 1988, for example, insurance companies spent US$101 million in promoting their own interests, and the tobacco companies spent US$21 million. As some of the above examples indicate, direct democracy can be used as a tool against powerless and underprivileged minorities. One is forced to the regrettable conclusion that the citizens-initiated referendum provides no guarantee that it will be used in the interests of promoting democracy.

Mr Goff went on to deal with his own country's experiences with regard to referenda. Until recently, referenda in New Zealand had been government-initiated and had dealt mainly with constitutional issues and liquor control. In 1992 and 1993 two major referenda took place. The first resulted in a radical change in the electoral system – a form of proportional representation based on the German model – being introduced with effect from the 1996 election. Although contrary to a Royal Commission recommendation, the National Party included the proposal in its 1990 manifesto, and it eventually secured bipartisan support. The 1993 referendum resulted in the adoption of the Citizens Initiated Referenda Act, empowering voters to initiate non-binding referenda on any subject.

In order to be put to the popular vote, a proposal must be supported by the signatures of at least 10 per cent of registered electors within a 12-month period. Proposals are submitted to the Clerk of the House who, after consultation, determines the precise wording of the question. Within a month of the presentation of the petition the Governor-General must set a date within the following 12-month period when the referendum will take place. In special circumstances parliament may extend this period to 24 months. The process incorporates safeguards which have no place in the Californian system. First, the referendum result is non-binding, the rights of minorities being protected by parliament in the absence of a judicial review process. Second, the Act limits campaign expenditure by groups promoting a referendum to $50 000 at the stage of collecting signatures and to a further $50 000 during the period leading up to voting day. Third, the 10 per cent threshold level acts as a safeguard against frivolous or mischievous initiatives. New Zealand is embarking on an entirely new experience in the hope of showing how the citizens-initiated referendum can be used to enhance democracy with none of the harmful consequences which have occurred in California or elsewhere.

When considering the arguments for and against referenda, there are many aspects to be considered. The general argument in favour is that direct democracy provides for public participation in the decision-making process. It is easy to justify the use of referenda on moral issues, which the public have no difficulty in understanding, or on constitutional issues, since the basic framework of the system of government should not be altered without the consent of a majority of the electorate. Further argument can ensue over the size of majority which should be required to change the constitution. Where government-initiated referenda are concerned, the question arises as to where the major responsibility should lie in deciding questions of public policy. Should the electorate be called upon to decide questions which go to the heart of a country's national interests, when they may be neither properly informed nor possess the necessary expertise to hold a soundly-based opinion on a complex issue? Are governments not elected to take responsibility for such decisions and to take the blame if they go wrong? Much also depends on the framing of the question. A government, in order to obtain the result it wants, may have no scruples about framing the question in such a way as to produce the desired result. Furthermore, complex issues cannot usually be reduced to two simple alternatives and, in the absence of a clear-cut question, a referendum is likely to lead to voter confusion as has been evidenced in California.

In posing the question, 'Are referenda the answer?', Mr Goff examined the reasons for their growing support, together with other possible methods of improving democratic government. Representative government has revealed that it has many weaknesses which have led to the lack of confidence in politicians and their institutions which has grown in recent years. Electoral promises have been ignored; parliamentary debate leaves much to be desired; parliament has shown little effectiveness in supervising the executive. Without direct democracy, electors can only exercise their democratic rights once every few years when they elect a new parliament; even then, their cynicism is such that they feel little enthusiasm in voting for any party. Improvements suggested by Mr Goff included the greater use of select committees as channels of communication with the public as they could at least provide public access to the decision-making process. He also proposed the reorganization of the structure and procedures of parliament to improve its scrutiny and legislative functions, and the revitalization of political parties in order to involve the public in candidate selection and policy-making. In his view, the public should have greater opportunities for participating in the setting of the political agenda, and it was his hope that the referendum process, in conjunction with the other reforms he advocated, would produce the desired results in New Zealand.

An interesting feature of the New Zealand legislation is the responsibility it imposes on the Clerk of the House to frame the referendum question. Although he is required to consult, it is he alone who determines the final wording, which is at once a crucial responsibility and a tribute to the prestige of the office and the confidence in which it is held.

The ensuing discussion revealed both a number of facts concerning practices in other countries and certain differences of opinion. It was generally agreed that popular education was an important factor in promoting the success of direct democracy. In African countries, different communities held different views on many issues. Rural and urban communities saw things differently, and a referendum decision could have an unequal effect depending on the community to which one belonged. Furthermore, the resources available to the various parties or groups varied greatly, and the rich ones would have greater influence. One participant felt that referenda represented a failure of the political process. There was a danger that they could enshrine reactionary attitudes, as in California, which is why judges could be expected to rebel at the results. It was asked whether, in the case of a citizens-initiated referendum, the government should take a position or remain neutral. One delegate declared that he was totally opposed to the use of referenda, claiming that they undermined the system of government. If democracy is the exercise of free will, it becomes a mockery if voters are called upon to register an opinion on matters they do not understand. He cited the example of the Maastricht Treaty, asking how many people understood it, and if they did, how many thought of the consequences when they came to vote on it. While opposed to referenda in principle, he felt that they should be binding if they were used at all. Reference was made to a referendum held in Gibraltar a few years ago on whether Gibraltarians wished to remain a part of the UK. The figures were 13 900 in favour to 44 against. The Spaniards were nevertheless not impressed, claiming that British warships had been sighted off the coast when the referendum was held, which accounted for the result!

Expressing a totally different view, another delegate believed that direct democracy was the way forward. Citing India as his example, he pointed out that, because of its first-past-the-post electoral system, no government had ever achieved power with a majority of the popular vote. By contrast, referenda not only provided a means of obtaining a majority view on an issue, they also threw open issues to public debate and led to a better informed electorate. In his view, rather than give the exclusive power of decision to a government majority, elected with only a minority of the popular vote, the use of referenda would provide a counterbalance – a sharing of power with the electorate – and ensure a genuinely democratic decision on major issues.

Some participants expressed cautious support for referenda, with the qualification that limitations were required to avoid the excesses of the California system, and that they should perhaps be non-binding in the first instance. In Colorado all initiatives must be reviewed by legislative counsel before they can go forward. In Poland any constitutional change must be approved by the people, but a threshold of 500 000 signatures is required if a citizens-initiated referendum is to go forward. The purpose of the high threshold is to deter minor parties, which fail to obtain the minimum 5 per cent of the popular vote required to elect members to parliament, from initiating a referendum on the amendment or rejection of the constitution. If a referendum does take place the result is binding.

Reference was also made to a referendum, held in Canada in 1992, on the amendment of the constitution, which provides a good example of the problems which can arise when a proposal is too complex. An agreement known as the Charlottetown Accord (Charlottetown being the capital of the province of Prince Edward Island where the agreement was finalized) was negotiated between the heads of the federal and all the provincial governments of Canada. It was the kind of agreement known as a 'package deal', each party to it obtaining some of the things it wanted and making the necessary concessions and compromises in order to secure unanimous acceptance. At the political level it was fully supported by all governments and all parties and, backed by such powerful advocacy, it was put to the popular vote. There were many elements contained in the agreement, but the voter had to choose whether to vote for or against the entire scheme. In the event, the Accord was defeated in nearly every province, as most voters agreed with some of the proposals but not others, and the majority therefore preferred to turn it down. The experience of the Charlottetown Accord is probably a good example of how a referendum should not be conducted.

In closing the discussion Mr Goff referred to a number of points which had been raised. Referring to the divergence among communities which is to be found in African countries, he conceded that referenda are a better test of opinion in a unified community. They are not to be recommended in a situation which can only be resolved by compromise. He also conceded that they are only effective in a democratic environment as they can easily be rigged in a totalitarian society. He noted, however, that a referendum held in Chile in 1988 resulted in a vote of 54 per cent to 43 per cent against the continued dictatorship of General Pinochet. This did not bring an immediate end to his rule and, even today, he remains in control of the army. Referring to the Canadian experience with the Charlottetown Accord, he believed that situations in which the thinking of the politicians is not in harmony with the views of the people were not unusual. In New Zealand the politicians were initially opposed to any change in the electoral system, but the people felt otherwise.

He agreed that the choices presented to the people must be clear and simple but rejected the argument that public ignorance was a valid reason for opposing direct democracy, as the same argument could be used against universal suffrage or the basic principles of democracy. He agreed that any system of direct democracy should be tempered with safeguards. For example, campaign expenses should be limited to prevent wealthy parties or interests having too great an advantage. In addition, the Californian experience had shown that there were serious risks of social or financial disaster in the absence of necessary safeguards. The complexity of some of the propositions put to California voters was another defect of the system. One proposition, for example, had run to 15 000 words and, under Californian law, even the initiators are not allowed to change the wording. He suggested that, in order to avoid this kind of confusion, the legislature itself might, subject to the agreement of a specified majority of its members, be given the right to amend the wording of a measure adopted at a referendum.

No consensus emerged from the discussion at this session, and I myself am undecided whether or not the extended use of referenda would greatly change the public perception of politicians. While there are clearly dangers in having a system of binding referenda, on the other hand, a system which permits a government to ignore a clear expression of the will of the majority would only increase public cynicism. It is also true that the majority are not always necessarily right, and that government by referendum is unlikely to be viewed by the defeated minority as particularly democratic. At least in a representative assembly minorities have a stronger voice and are better placed to exert an influence.

10 Who do Politicians Really Represent?

Mr Charles Miller, Secretary to the Association of Professional Political Consultants of London, spoke on the theme 'Interest groups, lobbyists or constituents: who do politicians really represent?' There is no doubt as to the 'right' answer to this question: politicians represent their constituents – those who voted against them no less than those who voted for them. The framing of the question, however, reflects the distrust in which politicians are generally held, the suspicion that they are more concerned with furthering their own interests than those of the people they are supposed to represent. Mr Miller quoted the results of certain opinion surveys which bear out the low esteem in which politicians are held. A MORI poll taken in 1983 revealed the degree of public confidence in the integrity of certain occupational categories according to the following scale: doctors 82 per cent; teachers 79 per cent; TV newsreaders 63 per cent; the police 61 per cent; politicians in general 18 per cent; government ministers 16 per cent. A similar poll taken ten years later revealed that all the above categories except the two last-mentioned had gained in public confidence. Politicians in general had fallen to 14 per cent and ministers to 11 per cent. Only journalists fared worse. This was the public perception which led to the appointment of the Nolan Committee and to committee investigations by both Houses of the British Parliament into matters affecting the standards of public life.

Mr Miller began his presentation by reminding the Conference of certain basic principles which risk being overlooked. The institutions of government are the servants of the public: they do not govern us; they govern on our behalf. Politicians, he pointed out, should never forget who pays their salaries. The public have a right to demand they be accountable and to know what their agents – those who govern on their behalf – are doing. The right to petition the sources of power is basic to parliamentary democracy – in fact it pre-dates it – but some petitioners are in an influential position that is not enjoyed by all.

MPs should never forget that the least of their constituents – the weak, the uneducated, those who are not aware of their rights – are entitled to the help of their elected representatives no less than the strong and influential.

The corridors of power are more accessible to those with close contacts with ministers and government institutions than to the ordinary citizen. One might say, to plagiarize George Orwell, that some petitioners are more equal than others, the others being the non-privileged majority. Major corporations and powerful interest groups do not have to push very hard to open the doors: they have money to spend; they can subscribe large sums to the coffers of political parties; they can hire high-priced lawyers to challenge administrative decisions in court; and they are able to use political insiders, including MPs, to speak in their favour and arrange meetings with decision-makers. In some countries, where corruption is endemic, ministers can be bribed directly to award contracts or grant favours. The UK has happily never fallen into this abyss, and ministers rarely behave other than with rectitude. They would not allow outside influences to shape policy decisions which are unbalanced or contrary to the national interest.

The fact remains that, in Mr Miller's words, 'there is still a healthy market in paying legislators'. The question as to what kind of payments are legitimate and what are not surfaced earlier in this Conference, and has become a matter for public enquiry. Generally speaking they are paid for giving advice, for arranging meetings, for advocating a cause and for using such influence as they possess in opening doors and making representations. Some receive payments from trade unions, which usually go towards covering election expenses. This has led to the public perception that they represent those who pay them rather than those who elected them. According to Mr Miller, lobbying firms do not normally hire politicians – it is the exception rather than the rule. His own firm never does so and, in his words, 'Regulated lobbyists do not pay politicians. Full stop.'

Mr Miller did not believe that abuses were widespread. He referred to the steps taken in both UK Houses of Parliament to monitor the interests of parliamentarians. In the House of Commons members are required to register their interests although there is little guidance as to what kind of interests are proper or improper. In the House of Lords there are no specific rules, although it has been made clear that, while it is legitimate to lobby a minister it is improper to accept money for speaking for or against a bill in debate. Ministers are required to place all their major interests in trust during their tenure of office. The lobbying profession has proposed six further safeguards to regulate the behaviour of politicians:

1   An independent element should be introduced into Parliament's current system of self-regulation.

2   The system should be more transparent. At present, parliamentary committees considering cases of impropriety sit behind closed doors, which does not encourage effective accountability.
3   MPs should be barred from booking entertainment and other facilities other than for their constituency party association. The question as to whether this ban should also apply to peers, who have no constituencies, is left open.
4   Members of both Houses should not be permitted to ask questions or introduce motions on subjects relating to their retained interests.
5   Members should not be permitted to arrange meetings with ministers on behalf of organizations who pay them.
6   Paid advocacy should be banned.

The presenter conceded that such rules, if implemented, would pose problems of their own. There are ways of concealing that a question to a minister is motivated by a payment. A ban on ministerial meetings may have the effect of blocking a case which has merit. Open enquiries would be subject to media distortion and could lead to unjust charges against innocent members. There was no infallible system of control. His conclusion was that supervision needed to be tightened up, and that fear of severe reprisals in the event of abuse taking place may be an essential ingredient of any solution which is eventually adopted.

The discussion which followed the presentation indicated that lobbyists were not viewed in the same light in every country. Contrasting the perception of lobbyists in Canada and the UK, one participant said that, in the UK, MPs were regarded as the villains of the piece; in Canada the villains were the lobbyists. In India, it appears that 'lobbyist' is a dirty word, because lobbying activities involve a great deal of bribery and corruption. In Barbados there is no statutory regulation of lobbyists, but parliamentarians had formed their own voluntary regulatory body and a code of conduct had been drawn up as a guide to MPs in their relations with interest groups. One delegate enquired whether lobbying was an integral part of a democratic system or a shelter for corruption. Another responded that a lobbyist was like a lawyer, hired to advance an issue and undertake the necessary research and advocacy. He maintained that most lobbying was not carried out by professional lobbying firms but by lawyers and accountants. There is no shame in lobbying provided representations are accurate, honest and in the public interest. The idea that lobbying is a shelter for corruption reveals the cultural differences which exist between countries. There is nothing wrong with helping people promote legitimate interests; problems arise only when an MP is supported by a large organization and, because he or she is expected to serve its interests, might accept all it says as the truth.

The view was expressed that members should not accept money for promoting issues which were in the national interest. Another delegate enquired whether it was possible to lessen the impact of lobbies, suggesting that the government was the strongest lobby when it came to persuading parliament to change the law. In Poland, lobbies, as they are recognized in other countries, do not exist: members are lobbied by their constituents who often expect more than their representatives can deliver. An MP has a duty to represent his constituents, and to lobby on their behalf, in return for their support. This, it was suggested, involved no impropriety. It was pointed out that MPs represent their countries as well as their constituencies, and that their interests should not be limited to their constituencies. The question of relations between lobbyists and ministers was also raised. In Canada this was a matter of particular concern, and since the executive usually initiated contacts with interest groups, transparency was not the complete answer. The Lobbyists Registration Act, to which an amending bill was under consideration at that time, requires lobbyists to name their clients. An association of business groups which maintain contacts with government has been formed, and it is anticipated that they will develop their own code of conduct.

One delegate declared that the only answer to the problems raised was to elect honest people, without elaborating on how to ensure that this was always the case. A delegate from New South Wales suggested that most elected representatives were honest, at least in his own parliament, pointing out that investigative activities had led to an increasing level of transparency and very little corruption had been exposed. Exposure of corruption can ruin a political career, and this in itself was a deterrent.

This session offered a useful insight into the central theme of the Conference from the perspective of the lobbying industry, contradicting the popular view that many MPs were hand-in-glove with lobbying firms. The presenter made it clear that his industry shared the public's concerns and was in favour of tighter regulation of MPs activities. It was also evident from what he said that he recognized the perception in the public mind that politicians were tending to forget who they were supposed to represent. His view, nevertheless, was that abuses were not as widespread as many feared. Some politicians were venal but their colleagues usually knew who they were. This view was expressed more than once during the Conference, not only by those involved in political life, and perhaps provides some basis for reassurance – at least so far as the UK is concerned.

11 Conclusion

This chapter is being written a few days after the publication of the first report of the Nolan Committee, which is included in Appendix 1 to this book. There is little in the recommendations to surprise anyone who has been following the progress of the investigation, although proposals for the appointment of two new public officials are of particular interest. The appointment of a Parliamentary Commissioner for Standards to monitor MPs' paid activities and to investigate complaints is recommended. A second recommended innovation is the appointment of a Commissioner for Public Appointments to oversee appointments to quangos and draw up a code of practice to govern such appointments. The report was agreed to unanimously.

The report was issued at a time when John Major's beleaguered government was facing ever increasing adversity. Recently held municipal elections had proved disastrous for the Conservative Party and, in the House of Commons, an already depleted government majority anticipated further inroads into its fragile margin in the face of forthcoming by-elections. If this was not enough, yet another scandal involving a government member was exposed, the member concerned having put down an amendment in the name of another member to a bill in which the former had a financial interest. Given the prevailing political climate there was press speculation as to how far the government would go in implementing the Nolan Committee recommendations. Government members, it was argued, might be reluctant to accept the rigid restrictions on their paid activities proposed by the Committee at a time when they could be facing imminent defeat in an enforced general election. Nevertheless, the prime minister's immediate response was to embrace the recommendations in principle and provide time for the House of Commons to debate them. The debate showed that the press speculation was not unfounded. A bid by the Nolan Committee to direct its next enquiry into the financing of political parties was not favourably received by the government. One hopes that the Committee's important recommendations will not be stultified by partisan debate and that the maintenance of standards in public life will remain a priority of all parties.

Also included in the appendices are summaries of the discussions of two committees which met during the Wiston House Conference taken from a concise survey of the Conference entitled 'The Democratic Deficit' which appeared in *The Parliamentarian* (vol. LXXVI, April 1995, pp. 129–38) and was written by the CPA's Editor and Assistant Editor of Publications, Andrew Imlach and Diana Reynolds. The themes dealt with by these committees were 'Making Laws Make Sense' and 'Committees and Committee Systems' and the summaries are included as Appendix 3 and Appendix 4 respectively. The discussion leader in the former committee was Senator the Hon. Margaret Reynolds of the Senate of Australia. In the latter committee the discussion was led by Senator the Hon. Gerald Ottenheimer, Deputy Speaker of the Senate of Canada.

In terms of the quality of the discussions, the Conference was a great success. Nevertheless it offered few solutions to the questions it raised. There were divergences of view on specific issues, such as the use of referenda, and varying perspectives on ethical issues which reflected the different political environments represented. One delegate suggested that there were areas where the activities of parliamentarians were better regulated by cultural dynamics than by codified rules. He also expressed the view that politics was not a shameful, but a noble, profession, and that one of the problems was that the community did not always get to know their MPs. It takes years of experience before an MP can gain recognition and respect, and he felt there was a need to examine the training process. As had been pointed out during the Conference, no special qualifications are required to be a politician, and no formal training was available other than what the parliament or the political parties could provide. Parliamentarians of long experience should perhaps be enlisted to organize training courses for their less experienced colleagues, either on a non-party basis or within party caucuses. The CPA and the IPU are already making commendable efforts to assist the parliaments of developing nations in the area of training.

Great concern was expressed throughout the Conference at the poor public perception of parliaments and parliamentarians in general. There was general agreement that the public has a right to be outraged whenever corruption is exposed, but that the extent of corruption is nowhere near as widespread as the public seem to believe. Unfortunately cynicism has become so ingrained in the public psyche that, even without evidence of corruption, people are persuaded that politicians are more concerned with serving their own interests rather than those of the people. Much of the responsibility for the malaise was placed on the media, which were cast as the villains of the piece by a number of delegates. They were not strongly represented at the Conference and were therefore unable to make the case for the defence. Not all the organs of the media, nor all journalists, are irresponsible, but toleration of certain excesses is the price of a free press. It is true that the press can destroy reputations, but politicians are aware of this, which should provide them with an incentive to take every precaution to ensure that their probity cannot be impeached. Since the press is a significant force in moulding public opinion, it is important that there should be competition among the media, and it is always a matter of concern to hear of a press closure. It is right that the media should be vigilant. It is right that they should comment frankly and critically. They also have a right to take a partisan position, provided no organ of opinion has a monopoly. The most total monopoly is to be found in countries where the government controls the media and it is idle to talk about standards when they cannot operate in a democratic environment.

The Conference agreed on certain things which could be done to counter the negative attitudes of the public and inspire greater confidence in the political process. The people need to know and understand what is happening. They need to be informed and consulted. While no radical changes were proposed to any particular system of government, there seemed to be agreement on the need to simplify parliamentary procedures and get rid of archaic practices. Parliamentarians should accept that they have an educative role to play in encouraging their constituents to take an interest in how they are governed and helping them to understand the process. Delegates seemed to agree that a more productive use of parliamentary committees would be an ideal way of involving the public since too many decisions are taken without any public consultation at all. Committees could provide a forum for public participation. Outside input could be invited into the framing of legislation and the formulation of policy. Committees could provide a non-partisan environment in which members of all parties could work in concert instead of against each other. The right of final decision would remain with parliament but committees backed by public participation could be an influential force.

There was a feeling that the adversarial system was too dominant among political parties. People were tired of hearing promises which were never kept, the trading of insults and accusations, oppositions which were ineffective, the myth of parliamentary control in the face of a government majority. Cooperation, as well as confrontation, should be seen as an essential feature of the party system, since the national interest should take precedence over narrow party interests. There was therefore a need for political parties to examine their own methods of operation and think about reforming themselves. They share responsibility for the malaise and should seek a more constructive role in the political pattern.

Some delegates felt there was much to be said for power-sharing in preference to a system whereby one party arrogated to itself all the spoils of office. This can be construed as an argument for coalition government or else for separation of powers. Under a congressional system the executive and the legislature are not necessarily controlled by the same party. This can lead to conflict but it also makes cooperation obligatory if breakdown in government is to be avoided. Coalition government normally arises from an electoral system based on some form of proportional representation. This also makes for cooperation and compromise since no one party dominates the government and the legislature. It was agreed that an electoral system must be fair and be seen to be so in every aspect of its operation, although no consensus emerged in favour of one electoral system over another. What was agreed was that public participation should not be limited to general elections but that consultation should take place continually throughout the mandate of a Parliament and a government. Ordinary people should be brought into the consultation process, which should not be limited to those close to the centre of power.

If the public are to be more closely involved, then, clearly, they have to respond to such opportunities as are created. There was general agreement among the delegates that there was widespread ignorance in all the countries represented as to how the system of government worked. Educative programmes had to be designed in such a way as to induce public participation. There had to be a willingness to listen and to learn. There are limits as to how far parliamentary procedure, for example, can be simplified, since much of its complexity is due to the need to protect the rights of all members. An effort is required on the part of the public if they are to be better informed, and it is up to all the institutions of government – the legislature, the executive, the public service and all institutions supported by the taxpayer – together with the political parties, to share the responsibility for stimulating public interest and encouraging participation. Secrecy in government should be kept to the essential minimum. Access-to-information legislation and directives to politicians and public servants to be forthcoming in providing information have been effective in jurisdictions which have adopted these measures and represent an important step in assuaging public suspicion and reassuring a public which has come to believe that government neither pays attention to, nor cares about, it.

The public, for its part, should recognize that its elected representatives and public servants are entitled to fair and reasonable pay and benefits. This is not the case in all countries, and inadequate remuneration can lead to corruption. Indeed, in some developing countries, public officials would find it difficult to sustain a livelihood without supplementing their incomes by bribes. At the Conference the discussion of this issue concentrated on the pay and benefits of parliamentarians. There were countries where membership of parliament was a full-time job and therefore became a livelihood; the provision of adequate salaries and pension benefits is therefore not unreasonable. It was said that the salary should be generous enough to attract candidates of calibre but not so generous as to attract unscrupulous candidates attracted by monetary reward. The problem with this somewhat trite statement is that it offers no guidance as to where the line might be drawn. In most countries MPs have opportunities to supplement their incomes from other sources and, in the UK, the Nolan Committee has recommended that this should not be prohibited provided that such paid employment is unrelated to their parliamentary role. In parliaments which do not sit for the greater part of the year, it is the norm for MPs to have other employment – in fact, it is undoubtedly essential in the majority of cases. In parliaments such as the British, MPs incur considerable expenses and sometimes need to supplement their incomes, which is not improper provided no conflict of real or potential interest is involved. It is reasonable to argue that there is a case for increasing parliamentary salaries in exchange for tightening the restrictions on outside interests. Hours of work as well as pay and benefits figure among the conditions of service of any job. Members of the British and other parliaments which sit long hours endure severe stresses on their private lives. When the reform of parliamentary procedure is being considered, the hours of sitting should not be overlooked.

Democracy works best when parliament and government are not remote from the people. In this respect, the extent to which people and nations are governed by supranational organizations raises problems. For instance, the European Union, although it has a democratically elected Parliament, cannot be regarded as close to the many peoples whose lives it governs to such a great extent. The European Parliament itself is not a sovereign parliament as its powers are severely limited, and it is perceived more as an instrument of the European Union than as a representative body protective of the rights of the people who elect it. To what extent do the members of the European Parliament deal with their constituents? What kind of problems do their constituents bring to them? What are they able to do for constituents alleging grievances against the mighty faceless authorities of the European Union? The answers to such questions would provide a test of the democratic reality of this supranational association.

It was suggested during the Conference that the evolution of more cohesive political parties which could fight Euro-elections with a recognized identity would do much to improve the credibility of the European Parliament. This would mean that electors would vote for European parties just as they now vote for their own national parties. It seems, however, that only by equipping the European Parliament with the powers enjoyed by national parliaments could it really pass the democratic test. It was argued, not without justification, that a certain sacrifice of national sovereignty is worthwhile in the interests of the greater good. But, as one delegate from a developing country pointed out, what is national sovereignty worth when a country's economy is controlled by the dictates of the World Bank and the International Monetary Fund? The undemocratic nature of supranational organizations and their remoteness from ordinary people are issues which should have a place in any discussion of promoting democracy and accountability. Few people know how they operate. Few people know the extent of their powers, or understand how their decisions can affect the lives of people at the grass-roots level.

The Nolan Committee's first report deals with standards in public life in respect of one country only, the UK. The seven principles of public life which it propounds – selflessness, integrity, objectivity, accountability, openness, honesty, and leadership – would hold good, however, on a global basis. Elaboration of these principles may be found on the first page of Appendix 1 (page 91) and there is no need to repeat the details here. Although concern about a decline in standards and the public's highly negative perception of politicians led to the appointment of the Nolan Committee, it is important to emphasize that a country which has the courage to investigate its own public life cannot be completely degenerate. The same can be said for the USA during the investigation of the Watergate scandal. The country's image at the time, both nationally and internationally, was at an all-time low, but the investigation which took place and its outcome was a vindication of the country's system of checks and balances. Sadly, there is no shortage of countries in the world where corruption in public life is normal and unlikely to be subject to such investigation. We should therefore take heart whenever action is taken to root out corruption.

Ultimately, the truth that every individual is responsible for his or her own behaviour is inescapable. Integrity in public life finally rests on the shoulders of the individual, and that individual must be governed by mechanisms which ensure accountability and the exposure of improper conduct. If democratic institutions are to become more responsible to, and representative of, those they serve, and more relevant to their needs, this is unavoidable. Cosmetic changes to the electoral process, parliamentary procedure, administrative structures, party organization, or any other effort to reform the institutions of a political system will prove meaningless unless all those in positions of trust recognize their collective and individual responsibility to uphold those principles so effectively enunciated by the Nolan Committee. This realization emerged very clearly from the Conference discussions, unclouded by any divergences of opinion, digressions or ambiguities which inevitably arise at a dynamic conference and which are no doubt reflected in this account. The Wiston House Conference was, in itself, an expression of concern regarding standards of public life and attracted delegates from a number of countries where these concerns are shared. The fact that no cast-iron solutions were discovered to the problems which were aired need not be a source of disappointment. Major problems do not respond to easy solutions. What is needed is the will to solve them, and the realization that it is essential to do so.

APPENDICES

Appendix 1   Standards in Public Life

First Report of the Committee on Standards in Public Life

Summary

1. At the request of the Prime Minister, this Committee has spent six months inquiring into standards in British public life. We have concentrated on Members of Parliament, Ministers and Civil Servants, executive Quangos and NHS bodies.

2. We cannot say conclusively that standards of behaviour in public life have declined. We can say that conduct in public life is more rigorously scrutinised than it was in the past, that the standards which the public demands remain high, and that the great majority of people in public life meet those high standards. But there are weaknesses in the procedures for maintaining and enforcing those standards. As a result people in public life are not always as clear as they should be about where the boundaries of acceptable conduct lie. This we regard as the principal reason for public disquiet. It calls for urgent remedial action.

3. Our conclusions are summarized below. They are followed by a full list of recommendations, together with an indication of the timescale in which each should be implemented.

General recommendations

4. Some of our conclusions have general application across the entire public service:

Principles of public life

5. The general principles of conduct which underpin public life need to be restated. We have done this. The seven principles of selflessness, integrity, objectivity, accountability, openness, honesty and leadership are set out in full on page 14. (*see page 105.*)

Codes of Conduct

6. All public bodies should draw up Codes of Conduct incorporating these principles.

Independent Scrutiny

7. Internal systems for maintaining standards should be supported by independent scrutiny.

Education

8. More needs to be done to promote and reinforce standards of conduct in public bodies, in particular through guidance and training, including induction training.

Members of Parliament

9. A fall in public confidence in the financial probity of MPs has coincided with an increase in the number of MPs holding paid consultancies which relate to their Parliamentary role. Some 30% of backbench MPs now hold such consultancies.

10. The House of Commons would be less effective if all MPs were full-time professional politicians, and MPs should not be prevented from having outside employment.

11. It reduces the authority of Parliament if MPs sell their services to firms engaged in lobbying on behalf of clients. This should be banned.

Appendix 1 93

12. Other Parliamentary consultancies and the fact that some MPs have more than one are also a cause for concern. It is impossible to be certain that MPs with such consultancies never allow their financial interests to affect their actions in Parliament, yet this would clearly be improper.

13. Guidance associated with the Register of Members' Interests has led to some confusion among MPs as to what conduct is acceptable. The long-established law of Parliament in this area should be reaffirmed.

14. Full disclosure of consultancy agreements and payments, and of trade union sponsorship agreements and payments, should be introduced immediately. Over the next year Parliament should review the merits of allowing MPs to hold consultancies, taking into account the wider implications of greater restrictions.

15. The Register of Interests should be more informative. The rules on declaring interests, and on avoiding conflicts of interest, should be set out in more detail. A Code of Conduct for MPs should be drawn up. We have set out a draft. The Code should be restated at the start of each new Parliament. More guidance for MPs, including induction sessions, should be available.

16. The public needs to know that the rules of conduct governing MPs' financial interests are being firmly and fairly enforced. There have been calls for these rules to be put into statute law and enforced by the courts. We believe that the House of Commons should continue to be responsible for enforcing its own rules, but that better arrangements are needed.

17. By analogy with the Comptroller and Auditor General, the House should appoint as Parliamentary Commissioner for Standards, a person of independent standing who will take over responsibility for maintaining the Register of Members' Interests; for advice and guidance to MPs on matters of conduct; for advising on the Code of Conduct; and for investigating allegations of misconduct. The Commissioner's conclusions on such matters would be published.

18. When the Commissioner recommends further action, there should be a hearing by a sub-committee of the Committee of Privileges, comprising up to seven senior MPs, normally sitting in public, and able to recommend penalties when appropriate. MPs who are being heard should be entitled to be accompanied by advisers.

Ministers and Civil Servants

19. Very high standards of conduct are rightly expected from Ministers and civil servants. While there is public disquiet, this focuses on fairly narrow issues.

20. A Code of Conduct for civil servants has recently been announced. The existing guidance for Ministers is sound but needs to be drawn together into a clear set of principles.

21. The public interest requires that allegations of Ministerial misconduct should be promptly investigated. Normally this is a matter for the Prime Minister. Who should investigate, and whether to publish a report, will vary from case to case, but in such cases civil servants should not be drawn into the party debate and their advice should remain confidential.

22. There has been much concern over Ministers who, on leaving office, take positions in companies with which they have had official dealings. For two years after leaving office senior civil servants have to seek clearance from an independent advisory committee before joining private companies. The same need to protect the public interest arises with Ministers and special advisers, who should be subject to a similar clearance system.

23. For both Ministers and civil servants the system should be made more open to public scrutiny than at present.

24. There is insufficient monitoring of the effectiveness of similar arrangements for more junior civil servants, and these should be reviewed.

25. Very large changes in the management and structure of the civil service have taken place. Greater delegation and diversity mean that more positive action has to be taken to reduce the risk of impropriety. In particular, political interference in the pay and promotion of individuals must be avoided.

26. While the new independent appeal system for civil servants is welcome, better arrangements within departments for the confidential investigation of staff concerns on propriety are needed.

27. More needs to be done to ensure that all civil servants remain aware of the standards of conduct required in the public sector.

28. The rules on acceptance of gifts and hospitality for both Ministers and civil servants are sufficiently strict, and need not be changed.

Quangos (Executive NDPBs and NHS bodies)

29. Executive Non-Departmental Public Bodies (NDPBs) and National Health Service bodies are public bodies with executive powers whose Boards are appointed by Ministers. They have almost 9000 Board Members and spend some £40bn a year.

30. There is much public concern about appointments to Quango Boards, and a widespread belief that these are not always made on merit. The Government has committed itself publicly to making all appointments on merit.

31. While individual posts should always be filled purely on merit, it is important that the overall composition of boards should represent an appropriate mix of relevant skills and background. This range should be clearly and publicly set out in job specifications.

32. Ministers should continue to make board appointments, but an independent Public Appointments Commissioner should be appointed to regulate, monitor and report on the public appointments process.

33. The government is already taking steps to develop best practice and to ensure that the widest range of candidates is secured. In future the Commissioner should recommend best practice and departments should have to justify any departures from it.

34. Formal and impartial assessment of candidates is essential. The advisory panels being introduced in the NHS should become universal, and they should all include an independent element. All candidates whom Ministers consider for all appointments should have been approved as suitable by an advisory panel.

35. Following recent scandals, much has been done to improve and standardise arrangements to secure high standards of conduct in NDPBs. This process needs to continue. All NDPBs and NHS bodies should have codes of conduct, in line with the principles which apply to all public bodies, for board members and staff.

36. There remain differences in the legal framework governing standards of conduct in NDPBs, NHS bodies and local authorities. The government needs to review this area and consider whether greater consistency can be achieved.

37. Further steps are needed to safeguard propriety both internally and externally. Internally, the Accounting Officer's responsibility for propriety as well as financial matters needs to be emphasised, and better confidential avenues are needed for investigation of staff concerns about propriety.

38. Externally, the role of auditors in propriety matters needs to be emphasised. Audit arrangements should be reviewed to ensure that best practice applies to all bodies.

List of Recommendations

We set out below our specific recommendations under each of the main headings of our report (followed in brackets by the paragraph number within the chapter).

We believe it would be helpful to those to whom we have addressed the Report if we gave some broad indication of the timescale within which we consider that recommendations could be implemented. We therefore place our recommendations into one of three broad categories.

- A   those recommendations which we believe could be implemented with the minimum of delay;

- B   those recommendations which could in our view be implemented—or on which we would expect to see significant progress towards implementation—by the end of this year;

- C   recommendations which we recognise will take longer to implement, but on which we would wish to re-examine progress in the latter part of next year.

Members of Parliament

1. Members of Parliament should remain free to have paid employment unrelated to their role as MPs. (para 2.21) A

2. The House of Commons should restate the 1947 resolution which places an absolute bar on Members entering into contracts or agreements which in any way restrict their freedom to act and speak as they wish, or which require them to act in Parliament as representatives of outside bodies.
(para 2.59) A

3. The House should prohibit Members from entering into any agreements in connection with their role as Parliamentarians to undertake services for or on behalf of organisations which provide paid Parliamentary services to multiple clients or from maintaining any direct or active connections with firms, or parts of larger firms, which provide such Parliamentary services.
(para 2.59) B

4. The House should set in hand without delay a broader consideration of the merits of Parliamentary consultancies generally, taking account of the financial and political funding implications of change. (para 2.59) A

5. The House should:

- require agreements and remuneration relating to Parliamentary services to be disclosed;

- expand the guidance on avoiding conflicts of interest;

- introduce a new Code of Conduct for Members;

- appoint a Parliamentary Commissioner for Standards;

- establish a new procedure for investigating and adjudicating on complaints in this area about Members. (para 2.59) B

6. On disclosure of interests we recommend:

- the Register should continue broadly in its present form, and should be published annually. However the detailed entry requirements should be improved to give a clearer description of the nature and scope of the interests declared;

- updating of the Register should be immediate. The current updated version should be made more widely available electronically;

- from the beginning of the 1995/96 session (expected in November) Members should be required to deposit in full with the Register any contracts relating to the provision of services in their capacity as Members, and such contracts should be available for public inspection;

- from the same time, Members should be required to declare in the Register their annual remuneration, or estimated annual remuneration, in respect of such agreements. It would be acceptable if this were done in bands: eg under £1,000; £1,000–5,000; £5,000–10,000; then in £5,000 bands. An estimate of the monetary value of benefits in kind, including support services, should also be made;

- Members should be reminded more frequently of their obligations to Register and disclose interests, and that Registration does not remove the need for declaration and better guidance should be given, especially on first arrival in the House. (para 2.70) B

7. Members should be advised in their own interests that all employment agreements which do not have to be deposited should contain terms, or be supported by an exchange of letters, which make it clear that no activities relating to Parliament are involved. (para 2.71) B

8. The rules and guidance on avoiding conflicts of interest should be expanded to cover the whole range of business pertaining to Parliament, and particular attention should be paid to Standing Committees. (para 2.85) B

9. The House should draw up a Code of Conduct setting out the broad principles which should guide the conduct of Members; this should be restated in every new Parliament. (para 2.89) B

10. The Government should now take steps to clarify the law relating to the bribery of or the receipt of a bribe by a Member of Parliament.
(para 2.104) C

11. On procedure we recommend:

- the House should appoint a person of independent standing, who should have a degree of tenure and not be a career member of the

House of Commons staff, as Parliamentary Commissioner for Standards;

- the Commissioner should have the same ability to make findings and conclusions public as is enjoyed by the Comptroller and Auditor General and the Parliamentary Commissioner for Administration;

- the Commissioner should have independent discretion to decide whether or not a complaint merits investigation or to initiate an investigation;

- the Commissioner should be able to send for persons, papers and records, and will therefore need to be supported by the authority of a Select Committee with the necessary powers;

- we consider that a sub-committee of the Committee of Privileges, consisting of up to seven very senior Members, would be the best body to take forward individual cases recommended by the Commissioner for further consideration; we recommend that such a sub-committee should be established;

- in view of the fact that there would be a prima facie case to investigate, we recommend that hearings of the proposed sub-committee should normally be in public. We also recommend that the sub-committee should be able to call on the assistance of specialist advisers and that a Member who so wishes should be able to be accompanied by advisers before the sub-committee;

- the sub-committee should be given discretion to enable an adviser to act as the Member's representative at hearings;

- as the sub-committee would report to the full Privileges Committee this would have the practical effect of giving the Member a right of appeal to that Committee. Only the most serious cases should need to be considered by the whole House. (2.104) B

The Executive: Ministers and Civil Servants

12. The first paragraph of Questions of Procedure for Ministers (QPM) should be amended to say: 'It will be for individual Ministers to judge how best to act in order to uphold the highest standards. It will be for the Prime

Minister to determine whether or not they have done so in any particular circumstance.' (para 3.13) A

13. The Prime Minister should put in hand the production of a document drawing out from QPM the ethical principles and rules which it contains to form a free-standing code of conduct or a separate section within a new QPM. If QPM is to remain the home for this guidance, we recommend that it is retitled 'Conduct and Procedure for Ministers' to reflect its scope.
(para 3.15) A/B

14. Careful consideration should be given to ensuring that the most appropriate means is used for the investigation of cases of alleged impropriety affecting Ministers. Other than in exceptional circumstances, the general rule that advice from civil servants to Ministers should not be made public should apply in these cases. (para 3.22) A

15. A system similar to the civil service business appointment rules should apply to Ministers. The system should operate on an advisory basis, and it should be administered by the existing Advisory Committee on Business Appointments. (para 3.31) A

16. In parallel with the civil service arrangements for permanent secretaries, an automatic waiting period of three months should apply to former Cabinet Ministers, but not to other Ministers or Whips. In cases where a further waiting period is recommended, the maximum waiting period should be set at two years from the date of leaving office. (para 3.33) A

17. The advisory committee should be able to advise an applicant, whether a civil servant or a former Minister, that they feel that the application is not appropriate, and to make public that advice if it is not taken. (para 3.34) A

18. Former Ministers, having received the advice of the advisory committee, should have the right of appeal to the Prime Minister of the day, who would be able to reduce any waiting period or relax any conditions if the appeal were well-founded. (para 3.36) A

19. The system should be as open as possible, while protecting the personal privacy of Ministers. (para 3.38) A

20. The Government should monitor the workload of the advisory committee under the new arrangements and put in place contingency arrange-

ments for its staffing to be augmented to deal with the aftermath of any change of administration. (para 3.39) B

21. Departments, as well as maintaining records of gifts, should maintain records of hospitality accepted by Ministers in their official capacity and should make these records available if asked to do so. (para 3.41) A

22. The new performance pay arrangements for the senior civil service should be structured so as not to undermine political impartiality.
(para 3.48) A

23. The draft civil service code should be revised to cover circumstances in which a civil servant, while not personally involved, is aware of wrongdoing or maladministration taking place. (para 3.51) A

24. The operation of the appeals system under the Code should be disseminated as openly as possible, and the Commissioners should report all successful appeals to Parliament. (para 3.52) B

25. Departments and agencies should nominate one or more officials entrusted with the duty of investigating staff concerns raised confidentially.
(para 3.53) A

26. The new civil service code should be introduced with immediate effect, without waiting for legislation. (para 3.55) A

27. The Cabinet Office should continue to survey and disseminate best practice on maintaining standards of conduct to ensure that basic principles of conduct are being properly observed. (para 3.59) A

28. There should be regular surveys in departments and agencies of the knowledge and understanding staff have of ethical standards which apply to them; where such surveys indicate problem areas, guidance should be reinforced and disseminated appropriately, particularly by way of additional training. (para 3.61) A

29. The Advisory Committee on Business Appointments should, when an appointment has been taken up, give the reasons for its decision in that particular case. (para 3.66) A

30. The operation, observance and objectives of the civil service business appointment rules should be reviewed. (para 3.68) B

31. Special advisers should be subject to the business appointment rules.
(para 3.70) A

32. A central or local record of invitations and offers of hospitality accepted should be kept in all departments and agencies. There should be clear rules specifying the circumstances in which staff should seek management advice about the advisability of accepting invitations and offers of hospitality. (para 3.72) A

Quangos

(Executive Non-Departmental Public bodies and National Health Service Bodies)

Appointments

33. The ultimate responsibility for appointments should remain with Ministers. (para 4.29) A

34. All public appointments should be governed by the overriding principle of appointment on merit. (para 4.35) A

35. Selection on merit should take account of the need to appoint boards which include a balance of skills and backgrounds. The basis on which members are appointed and how they are expected to fulfil their role should be explicit. The range of skills and background which are sought should be clearly specified. (para 4.46) A

36. All appointments to executive NDPBs or NHS bodies should be made after advice from a panel or committee which includes an independent element. (para 4.48) C

37. Each panel or committee should have at least one independent member and independent members should normally account for at least a third of membership. (para 4.49) C

38. A new independent Commissioner for Public Appointments should be appointed, who may be one of the Civil Service Commissioners.
(para 4.53) B

39. The Public Appointments Commissioner should monitor, regulate and approve departmental appointments procedures. (para 4.55) C

40. The Public Appointments Commissioner should publish an annual report on the operation of the public appointments system. (para 4.56) C

41. The Public Appointments Unit should be taken out of the Cabinet Office and placed under the control of the Public Appointments Commissioner. (para 4.57) B

42. All Secretaries of State should report annually on the public appointments made by their departments. (para 4.62) B

43. Candidates for appointment should be required to declare any significant political activity (including office-holding, public speaking and candidature for election) which they have undertaken in the last five years. (para 4.68) B

44. The Public Appointments Commissioner should draw up a code of practice for public appointments procedures. Reasons for departures from the code on grounds of "proportionality" should be documented and capable of review. (para 4.72) C

Propriety

45. A review should be undertaken by the Government with a view to producing a more consistent legal framework governing propriety and accountability in public bodies, including executive NDPBs, NHS bodies and local government. This should involve all relevant departments and be co-ordinated by the Cabinet Office and the Treasury. (para 4.81) C

46. The adoption of a code of conduct for board members should be made mandatory for each executive NDPB and NHS body. (para 4.91) B

47. It should be mandatory for the board of each executive NDPB and NHS body to adopt a code of conduct for their staff. (para 4.91) B

48. Board members and staff of all executive NDPBs and NHS bodies should be required on appointment to undertake to uphold and abide by the relevant code, and compliance should be a condition of appointment. (para 4.95) B

49. Sponsor departments should develop clear disciplinary procedures for board members of executive NDPBs and NHS bodies with appropriate penalties for failing to observe codes of conduct. (para 4.96) C

50. The role of executive NDPB and NHS accounting officers should be redefined to emphasise their formal responsibility for all aspects of propriety. (para 4.102) B

51. The Audit Commission should be authorised to publish public interest reports on NHS bodies at its own discretion. (para 4.105) B

52. The Treasury should review the arrangements for external audit of public bodies, with a view to applying the best practices to all.
(para 4.109) C

53. Each Executive NDPB and NHS body that has not already done so should nominate an official or Board Member entrusted with the duty of investigating staff concerns about propriety raised confidentially. Staff should be able to make complaints without going through the normal management structure, and should be guaranteed anonymity. If they remain unsatisfied, staff should also have a clear route for raising concerns about issues of propriety with the sponsor department. (para 4.116) B

54. Executive NDPBs, supported by their sponsor departments, should:

- develop their own codes of openness, building on the government code and developing good practice on the lines recommended in this report;

- ensure that the public are aware of the provisions of their codes;

sponsor departments should:

- encourage executive bodies to follow best practice and improve consistency between similar bodies by working to bring the standards of all up to those of the best;

the Cabinet Office should:

- produce and periodically update guidance on good practice for openness in executive NDPBs and NHS bodies. (para 4.123) B

The Seven Principles of Public Life

Selflessness
Holders of public office should take decisions solely in terms of the public interest. They should not do so in order to gain financial or other material benefits for themselves, their family, or their friends.

Integrity
Holders of public office should not place themselves under any financial or other obligation to outside individuals or organisations that might influence them in the performance of their official duties.

Objectivity
In carrying out public business, including making public appointments, awarding contracts, or recommending individuals for rewards and benefits, holders of public office should make choices on merit.

Accountability
Holders of public office are accountable for their decisions and actions to the public and must submit themselves to whatever scrutiny is appropriate to their office.

Openness
Holders of public office should be as open as possible about all the decisions and actions that they take. They should give reasons for their decisions and restrict information only when the wider public interest clearly demands.

Honesty
Holders of public office have a duty to declare any private interests relating to their public duties and to take steps to resolve any conflicts arising in a way that protects the public interest.

Leadership
Holders of public office should promote and support these principles by leadership and example.

• •

These principles apply to all aspects of public life.
The Committee has set them out here for the benefit of
all who serve the public in any way.

55. New board members should on appointment make a commitment to undertake induction training which should include awareness of public sector values, and standards of probity and accountability. (para 4.125) B

Chapter 1

Introduction

1. In October 1994 the Prime Minister asked this Committee to enquire into the growing public concern about standards in public life. Evidence of such concern was reflected in the correspondence which we received, nearly 2,000 letters of all kinds from people in every walk of life. It was also voiced by many of the 100 witnesses who gave evidence to us in public over a period of six weeks. Further indications of widespread public concern over the trustworthiness of politicians were contained in recent opinion surveys, details of which are set out in Appendix 1 to this report.

2. It was equally clear from a considerable body of this evidence that much of the public anxiety about standards of conduct in public life is based upon perceptions and beliefs which are not supported by the facts. Taking the evidence as a whole, we believe that the great majority of men and women in British public life are honest and hard working, and observe high ethical standards.

3. There is, and always will be, a minority who fall short. Deliberate corruption is, however, notoriously difficult to measure. As our predecessors on the Salmon Commission wrote, 'there is no objective way of making a true assessment of the amount of public sector corruption that exists now or whether the amount has changed over recent decades.'*

4. It is equally difficult to say whether there has been any decline in overall standards in public life. The public's concerns about the conduct of people in public life certainly seem to have increased in recent years, but part of the explanation may be that the public's expectations of the behaviour of those in office are now higher†. The amount of media interest in the subject of misconduct in public life, particularly sexual misconduct has certainly intensified. Politicians of previous generations, and their families, were largely free from the invasions of privacy by the press which are now common. In recent years there have been periods when instances of real or alleged malpractice seemed to be reported in the newspapers every few weeks. There is no precedent in this century for so many allegations of

---

* Report of the Royal Commission on Standards of Conduct in Public Life, Cmnd 6524, 1976, paragraph 34.
† A brief look at the historical background to our work is contained in appendix 1.

wrongdoing, on so many different subjects, in so short a period of time. It is not therefore surprising that opinion polls suggest that people believe that there is more actual misconduct than in the past.

5. It would be comforting to think that the public believe that standards have declined only because of the growth in media activity and intrusion into the private lives of public figures. Yet we do not believe that this is the whole answer. The newspapers may have run with or encouraged the 'sleaze' issue, but they generally print what they believe to be the facts and can be challenged in court if what they say is defamatory or untrue. A free press using fair techniques of investigative journalism is an indispensable asset to our democracy. We would prefer more acknowledgement from the media that the overwhelming majority of public servants work hard and have high standards. We would prefer more recognition of the value of our democratic mechanisms and the dangers of undermining them. We would prefer less concentration on private sexual behaviour. But we do not hold the media in any way to blame for exposing genuine wrongdoing. They have a duty to enquire—coupled with a duty to do so responsibly—and in that way can contribute to the preservation of standards in public life.

> "... We are in a period which I think is nothing like as bad as the Edwardian and early Georgian period but is, nonetheless, one that does give rise to a good deal of unease." **Lord Blake (witness)**
>
> "The principles of honesty, truth and integrity have become debased at the highest levels of society, by people who should be in their personal and private lives examples to ordinary people." **Mavis Evans (correspondent)**
>
> "The standard of public behaviour of politicians in this country does compare well with many comparable countries." **Ivor Crewe (witness)**
>
> "Most people who join the House of Commons as Members are as animated with the idea of public service as they were 50 years ago." **Lord Callaghan (witness)**
>
> "As a parent of two teenagers and a schoolteacher of pupils aged 11–16 years, I am deeply disappointed that public figures appear to escape retribution for actions and attitudes which set such a poor example to our youth." **David Powell (correspondent)**

6. Frequently in our work we heard the expression 'grey area' used as a rationalisation of morally dubious behaviour. The ubiquity of the phrase, and the implication that some no longer seem to be certain of the difference between what is right and what is wrong in public life, concern us. When people in public life are in doubt about whether a particular action is consistent with the standards expected of them, the only proper course is not to do it.

7. The erosion of public confidence in the holders of public office is a serious matter. One of our aims in this report is to rebuild this public confidence. The other is to try to restore some clarity and direction wherever moral uncertainty has crept in. In so far as a culture of moral vagueness, a 'culture of sleaze', has developed, we seek to put an end to it. A degree of austerity, of respect for the traditions of upright behaviour in British public life, is not only desirable, but essential.

8. We recommend procedures and institutions that will deter and detect wrong-doing. We seek to restore respect for the ethical values inherent in the idea of public service. Formal procedures have a role to play, but in the end it is individuals' consciences that matter.

9. There are two reasons why this is important. First, we in Britain have, with reason, always prided ourselves on the standards of conduct of the vast majority of our public servants; that pride must be restored. Second, experience elsewhere warns that, unless the strictest standards are maintained and where necessary restored, corruption and malpractice can become part of the way of life. The threat at the moment is not great. Action needs to be taken before it becomes so.

10. Changes in the public sector have increased the need to take action. Decentralisation and contracting out have varied the format for organizations giving public service. There is greater interchange between sectors. There are more short term contracts. There is scepticism about traditional institutions. Against that background, it cannot be assumed that everyone in the public service will assimilate a public service culture unless they are told what is expected of them and the message is systematically reinforced. The principles inherent in the ethic of public service need to be set out afresh. We have done so on page 14. (*see page 105*.)

11. To consider what lessons might be learned from experience overseas, we have obtained information (both written and in talks with knowledgeable visitors) about arrangements existing or under consideration in a number of

110 *Parliament and the People*

other European Union and Commonwealth countries and the United States. We found closer analogies where the constitutional framework was based on the Westminster model. While we noted a tendency in recent years to underpin rules of conduct with statute law, we also noted a current of opinion in Canada and elsewhere that there are advantages in having a more flexible non-statutory basis for Codes of Conduct. We concluded that it was appropriate to United Kingdom circumstances to tailor our recommendations closely to our largely non-statutory mechanisms.

12.   Our remit covers the whole of public life. In order to make our task more manageable, we decided to concentrate in this first report on three of the areas which seemed to cause most immediate public concern: the House of Commons, central Government (Ministers and civil servants) and executive quangos, including NHS bodies. These represent a broad swathe of public life, and they are covered in the next three chapters of our report. We believe that the seven principles set out on page 14 (*see page 105*) are applicable to them all, and to those parts of public life we will cover later.

Common threads

13.   We have also given thought to the mechanisms which need to be put in place to ensure that our principles are understood.

Codes of Conduct

14.   We believe that the principles set out above should form the basis of codes of conduct throughout the public sector. Ministers have recently accepted a new code for the civil service. Most of the quangos mentioned in this report already have codes. Later in this report we comment on these and also recommend codes for Ministers and Members of Parliament.

15.   Such codes should be drawn up within each organisation concerned, so that they will be appropriate to their circumstances and will form part of the culture of the organisation. But they should all be based on the principles set out above. In addition to the principles and the codes two other common elements will be found throughout this report.

Independent Scrutiny

16.   First, wherever there is scope for behaviour falling below the highest standards, then internal systems must be supported by independent scrutiny

and monitoring. Part of this will be routinely performed by auditors, but in certain circumstances an independent body to oversee the framework within which actions are taken and to monitor compliance can be an important additional safeguard in maintaining public confidence.

Guidance and Education

17.   Second, because of the pace of change, it is essential that more is done to inculcate high ethical standards through guidance, education, and training, particularly induction training, than has been thought necessary in the past. In this context guidance means the planned promotion and reinforcement throughout every public body of ethical standards. It involves the active participation of people in public life in formulating key ethical standards; it requires those in senior positions to set a good example; and it requires organisations to monitor the awareness of those standards and take remedial action when necessary.

Conclusion

18.   We have inherited a legacy of immense value from those who laid the foundations of a public service in the last century and in this that people could trust and in which they could take pride. As Robert Sheldon MP, the Chairman of the Public Accounts Committee, told us:

> 'We are extraordinarily fortunate—there are, what, 184 countries in the United Nations. The number of them which have standards somewhere approaching ours are just a handful. We are a rare exception and it is up to us to make sure that we retain those standards... Once you lose them I am afraid it is extraordinarily difficult to return to them'.

19.   The recommendations we make in this report are designed to ensure that public life in Britain retains the highest standards.

Chapter 2

Members of Parliament

Principal Conclusions

Members of Parliament should remain free to have paid outside interests unrelated to the work of Parliament. Paid work as general multi-client Parliamentary consultants should be banned. The House of Commons should review the law of Parliament with regard to the other Parliamentary consultancies. We will review the situation further in a year's time.

Agreements and remuneration in respect of permitted Parliamentary consultancies and sponsorships should be declared in full. Other entries in the Register of Members' Interests should more clearly identify the nature of the interest.

The 1947 Resolution of the House on paid outside interests should be reaffirmed. Clearer and more detailed guidance should be issued on declarations of interest, and on action to avoid conflicts of interest.

A code of Conduct for Members of Parliament should be drawn up.

The House should appoint a person of independent standing as Parliamentary Commissioner for Standards, who would maintain the Register of Interests, advise on the Code of Conduct, provide guidance and advice on matters of conduct and interests, and investigate and report on complaints about Members' conduct.

When the Commissioner has found in a matter of conduct that a Member has a case to answer, this should be heard by a sub-committee of the Committee of Privileges under arrangements which would combine the rules of natural justice more effectively with the established procedures of the House.

The Public Perception

1. The House of Commons is at the heart of our democracy. The standards of conduct observed by its Members are crucially important to the political well-being of the nation. Those standards have always been self-imposed and self-regulated because Parliament is our supreme institution.

2. It is vital for the quality of Government, for the effective scrutiny of Government, and for the democratic process, that Members of Parliament should maintain the highest standards of propriety in discharging their obligations to the public which elects them. It is also essential for public confidence that they should be seen to do so.

3. In recent years the confidence of the public in politicians has declined sharply. Our first witness, Professor Ivor Crewe, told us that:

> *'Whenever surveys have asked people to compare various occupations for honesty or trustworthiness or a moral example, Members of Parliament have been at or near the bottom of the league, competing with estate agents and journalists to avoid the wooden spoon.'*

4. He went on to mention a recent Gallup survey result that 64% of the public agreed that 'most MPs make a lot of money by using public office improperly', a figure which has risen from 46% nine years ago. The same survey found that 77% of people believed that 'MPs care more about special interests than about people like themselves', while only 28% agreed that 'most MPs have a high personal moral code'.

5. Such figures must be treated with caution. On the suggestion that most Members of Parliament make a lot of money from using public office improperly, Professor Crewe told us 'I myself do not believe that for one moment'. Professor Crewe also told us that constituents would normally take a different view of their own Member. Iain Duncan-Smith MP, among others, agreed. He said:

> *'As politicians generally we are rated fairly low in people's regard [but] often you find that regard for an individual MP puts them high in the list of public perception within [the constituency]'.*

6. There is no evidence either of a growth in actual corruption. When asked whether it was the considered judgement of the Metropolitan Police that, whatever the problems with Members of Parliament accepting payment

for lobbying services, these did not extend to corruption in the legal sense, Assistant Commissioner David Veness replied 'As of now that is correct.'

7. John Witherow, Editor of 'The Sunday Times', and Peter Preston, Editor in Chief of 'The Guardian', both told us that they would not agree with the view that most Members were 'in it for the money', but nevertheless felt that public cynicism created a real problem. Not surprisingly, they took the view that this was Parliament's own fault, rather than the media's. A comment by Lord Callaghan is relevant. Asked whether the House of Commons had turned its back on the strict approach of earlier years, he said:

> *'I think we have slipped into an easing of these sorts of arrangements rather than taken a deliberate decision about it, and our own standards, I think, have fallen into disuse in some ways.'*

8. Members of Parliament themselves are aware of this loss of confidence, which to some extent reflects trends affecting democratic institutions elsewhere. Emma Nicholson MP told us:

> *'I think the sadness is that MPs feel that these great efforts that they make to help other people are no longer recognised and respected as such.'*

while Dale Campbell-Savours MP set out the issue succinctly:

> *'At the end of the day what do the public want? The public want to be assured that standards of propriety are being maintained—that is all.'*

Members' Financial Interests

9. The reasons for the public's reduced confidence in the financial probity of Members of Parliament are not hard to identify. The public reads extensive press reporting of cases in which Members have accepted money for asking Parliamentary Questions, are said to have stayed at expensive hotels at others' expense without declaring an interest and are employed by multi-client lobbying firms, an attitude which has become known as 'MPs for hire.' Public confidence in MPs' overall standards of conduct has been further eroded by a regular flow of sexual revelations involving politicians.

10. It is harder to pin down precisely whether there has been an actual decline in the financial probity of Members. It would be surprising in a body

of some 650 men and women if all had standards which were uniformly impeccable. There have been financial scandals in the past. The political historian, Lord Blake compared the present era with the Edwardian age when a 'get rich quick' mentality prevailed, and suggested that while the problems were worse at that time the present situation nonetheless gave rise to 'a good deal of unease'.

11. This unease undoubtedly has much to do with the growth of professional Parliamentary lobbying and the very substantial increase in the number of Members of Parliament employed as consultants and advisers to companies, trade associations and the like. Those with long experience of Parliament referred to the growth of lobbying and the problems it posed. For example, Chris Moncrieff, veteran lobby journalist, told us:

'Over the past four or five years there has been a massively increased influx of commercial lobbyist activity in the House of Commons and I think Members are far more vulnerable now than they have been ever before to outside and commercial pressures.'

12. A number of witnesses pointed to another possible reason for increased commercial pressure on Members of Parliament. This is the relative decline in the pay of MPs and Ministers over recent years, and the greatly increased workload making MPs more likely to accept outside help. Alex Carlile MP said:

'... it is a great honour and privilege to be an MP, but that does not feed, educate or clothe one's wife or husband and children'.

Sir Terence Higgins MP spoke of the workload, and also told us that in real terms average incomes in Britain were now 80% higher than when he entered the House in 1964, while the pay of MPs was the same and that of Ministers had declined by between 50% and 60%. Peter Thurnham MP, making a similar point, wrote of the extent to which he personally subsidised his constituency office:

'I found politics to be more demanding than I realised, with a commitment of over 100 working hours per week needed to defend a highly marginal seat through three general elections. ... I determined from the outset to establish a well staffed and equipped constituency office. ... Over the years this office has cost me a very substantial sum above the official allowances.'

13. Whatever the reason, there has been a significant growth in the number of Members of Parliament who have entered into consultancies or other forms of agreement which might reasonably be thought to influence their Parliamentary conduct. Analysis of the 1995 Register of Members' Interests suggests that 26 Members have consultancy agreements with public relations or lobbying firms and a further 142 have consultancies with other types of company or with trade associations. These 168 Members hold between them 356 consultancies. If Ministers and the Speaker are excluded there are 566 MPs. Thus almost 30% of eligible Members of Parliament hold consultancy agreements of these types.

14. A similar, though by no means identical, relationship which has of course existed for many years is that of sponsorship arrangements between Members and trade unions. The roots of trade union sponsorship go much further back into Parliamentary history than do those of modern consultancy. In the past, when Members were not paid, election to the House without such sponsorship would have been financially impossible for many Members. The importance of the financial link for the Member concerned may be less than it was. The financial support is generally limited to payment of a proportion of the Member's constituency office and election expenses. There is no remuneration for the Member personally. Yet it is only natural that it should give rise to feelings of obligation which have the potential to influence the Member's conduct in the House. According to the 1995 Register a total of 184 Members (over 30% of MPs excluding Ministers) have sponsorship arrangements with Trade Unions. In addition, 27 Members have paid consultancies with Trade Unions. A further 10 receive other financial help from Trades Unions.

15. While the lack of detail in the Register makes precise analysis difficult, it appears in their different ways that some 389 of the 566 eligible MPs—almost 70%—have financial relationships with outside bodies which directly relate to their membership of the House. It is not surprising, therefore, that the financial question which gives rise to most public concern is the paid outside employment of Members.

16. The specific issues are these. Should any new restraints be placed on Members' freedom to take up outside jobs? If any outside employment is to be permitted how far can transparency protect the public interest? Are there circumstances in which a conflict of interest needs to be resolved by requiring a Member to withdraw from Parliamentary business? Do Members need further guidance? Can the public be confident that the rules on Members'

interests are being firmly and fairly applied? We consider each of these in turn below.

Paid outside employment

17. A significant section of opinion holds that, as in certain other countries, Members of Parliament should have no outside paid interests, and that their only earned income should be their Parliamentary salaries. The majority of people who wrote to us took this view, as did Harry Barnes MP who gave oral evidence.

18. However most Members, journalists and business people from whom we heard took a different view, Ivor Crewe again told us that:

> '... a recent poll suggests that the public accept that MPs should be able to earn additional income from outside interests, so long as those interests are declared.'

while Tony Newton MP, the leader of the House of Commons, said:

> 'None of us would gain from a House of Commons made up of 651 people who were completely cut off from the rest of life, except on the basis of representations they received, rather than of experience of contacts they continued to have in various walks of life.'

19. We believe that those Members who wish to be full-time MPs should be free to do so, and that no pressure should be put on them to acquire outside interests. But we also consider it desirable for the House of Commons to contain Members with a wide variety of continuing interests. If that were not so, Parliament would be less well-informed and effective than it is now, and might well be more dependent on lobbyists. A Parliament composed entirely of full-time professional politicians would not serve the best interests of democracy. The House needs if possible to contain people with a wide range of current experience which can contribute to its expertise.

20. As well as having Members with continuing outside interests, it is important that the House of Commons should continue to contain Members from a wide variety of backgrounds. We should be worried about the possibility of a narrowing in the range of able men and women who would be attracted to stand for Parliament if Members were barred from having any outside paid interests. We believe that many able people would not wish to

enter Parliament if they not only had to take a substantial drop in income to do so but also ran the risk of seeing their source of livelihood disappear altogether if they were to lose their seats. Several of our witnesses regretted the tendency for Members of Parliament to be drawn increasingly from those who have had no employment experience outside the political field.

21. The onward march of the professional politician may be an irresistible feature of modern life, but we believe that nothing should be done by way of institutional arrangements which would hasten it.

We recommend that Members of Parliament should remain free to have paid employment unrelated to their role as MPs.

Parliamentary Consultancies

22. A more specific issue then arises as to whether some paid outside interests are less acceptable than others. As we have noted above, the greatest current concern about the independence of the House arises when organisations seek the services of a Member of Parliament specifically as a Parliamentary adviser or consultant.

23. The need to protect the House against improper influences on Members has long been recognised. There is a statutory ban on Members holding various offices of profit under the Crown, including positions in the civil service and on the boards of publicly owned industries. The statutory position reflects the history of conflict between the monarchy and Parliament, and the fear that patronage could be used by the Crown to buy votes. It does not have much relevance to modern conditions.

Historical background

24. Although the same statutory prohibition as applies to public employment has not been extended to financial interests, concern about the influence of external financial pressures on Members, and the need to preserve their independence, is not new. In 1695, following the expulsion of Speaker Sir John Trevor for accepting a bribe of 1000 guineas from the City of London in connection with the Orphans Bill, the House resolved that 'the offer of money, or other advantage, to any Member of Parliament for the promoting of any matter whatsoever, depending or to be transacted in Parliament is a high crime and misdemeanour and tends to be subversion of the English constitution.'

25. In 1858 the House resolved that 'it is contrary to the usage and derogatory to the dignity of this House that any of its Members should bring forward, promote or advocate in this House any proceeding or measure in which he may have acted or been concerned for or in consideration of any pecuniary fee or reward.' This rule was specifically aimed at barristers.

26. By 1947 the position had not changed greatly. In that year the House declared that:

'... it is inconsistent with the dignity of the House, with the duty of a Member to his constituency, and with the maintenance of the privilege of freedom of speech, for any Member of the House to enter into any contractual agreement with an outside body, controlling or limiting the Member's complete independence and freedom of action in Parliament or stipulating that he shall act in any way as the representative of such outside body in regard to any matters to be transacted in Parliament; the duty of a Member being to his constituency and to the country as a whole, rather than to any particular section thereof.'

27. In 1969 the Select Committee on Members' Interests (Declaration), known as the Strauss Committee, reviewed the rules on declaration of Members' Interests. While rejecting at that stage the concept of a Register of Interests, it proposed a new code of conduct for MPs. One arm of that code was a much stricter rule on declaration of interests. The other arm would have placed considerable restrictions on Members' freedom of action in the House in situations where they had financial interests. The Committee proposed that the House should adopt this resolution:

'That it is contrary to the usage and dignity of the House that a Member should bring forward by any speech or question, or advocate in this House or among his fellow Members any Bill, Motion, matter or cause for a fee, payment, retainer or reward, direct or indirect, which he has received, is receiving or expects to receive.'

28. The Strauss Committee's report was never debated by the House, and their resolution was not adopted. In 1971 the then Leader of the House (Rt Hon William Whitelaw MP), clearly speaking following consultations via 'the usual channels', said:

'... following the Report there was very careful consideration of whether the Resolutions proposed would be suitable or would, in certain circumstances, be very much more restrictive than would be wise. It was felt that

they would be so restrictive. ... there is widespread support in the House for the view that it is right to rely on the general good sense of Members rather than on formalised rules. That is certainly the view of the official Opposition.'

The 1947 resolution and the rules of the House

29. The Strauss report did not therefore change the formal position. In principle this has remained unchanged for 50 years, and perhaps even for 300 years. The resolution of 1947 remains binding on Members of Parliament, and is the most detailed statement of the Law of Parliament on this subject. However, this resolution, which appears at first sight clear and unequivocal, contains within itself the seeds of the current problem.

30. The 1947 resolution was drawn up in response to concern about an outside body—a trade union, as it happens—attempting to instruct a Member. It clearly prohibits any contracts which in any way limit a Member's freedom of action in the House. Thus it prohibits a Member from entering into a consultancy agreement which imposes, in return for payment, a binding obligation to speak, lobby or vote in accordance with the client's instructions, or to act as the client's representative in Parliament.

31. Although the resolution therefore prohibits a Member of Parliament from entering into any agreement requiring action on behalf of an outside body 'in regard to any matters to be transacted in Parliament', it does not prohibit a binding obligation to advise the client on Parliamentary matters. The Member remains free to enter an agreement to act as an adviser or consultant about Parliamentary matters. On the face of it therefore, this resolution might appear to draw the clear line between paid advice and paid advocacy which very many people, in Parliament and outside, have told us would be appropriate.

32. However the resolution does not prohibit Members from voluntarily speaking, lobbying or voting in support of their clients' interests if the Members think it right to do so, and if to do so is consistent with Members' duties to their constituents and to the public.

33. The voluntary nature of any action by the Member is important. No outside body would be able to use any financial arrangement with an MP to seek to secure any particular action in Parliament without committing a punishable contempt of Parliament. The Privileges Committee in 1946/47,

in a passage which has been the basis of subsequent Privileges Committee reports, said:

> '... *if an outside body may properly enter into contractual relationships with, and make payments to a Member as such, it must in general be entitled to terminate that relationship if it lawfully can where it considers it necessary for its own interests to do so. What, on the other hand, an outside body is certainly not entitled to do is to use the agreement or the payment as an instrument by which it controls or seeks to control the conduct of a Member or to punish him for what he has done as a Member.'*

34. The rules of the House, therefore, as established over many years, focus very much on maintaining the privileges and freedom of action of Members, so that they cannot be compelled by outside bodies to act in a particular way in Parliament.

35. However the rules are much less explicit as regards restricting the freedom of Members to place themselves in situations where they are liable to be improperly influenced.

36. It is clearly established that it is an offence against the law of Parliament for a Member to accept a bribe. For lesser misdemeanours, however, the rules are much less clear. In the recent 'cash for questions' case, the Privileges Committee recommended action against the Members concerned on the basis that their conduct 'fell below the standards which the House is entitled to expect of its Members.' In his memorandum published in Volume II of the Privileges Committee Report, the then Clerk of the House (now a member of this Committee) stated:

> *'The House has never attempted to deal comprehensively with the potential conflicts of interest that can arise when the business and professional interests of Members touch upon their duties and responsibilities as Members. ... the House has preferred instead to deal with particular instances of conflict pragmatically when difficulties arise.'*

37. This position is entirely consistent with the 1971 statement of the then Leader of the House, referred to in paragraph 28 above, that 'it is right to rely on the general good sense of Members.'

Recent developments

38. Two major changes over the last fifty years have combined to concentrate attention on this latter area of Members' behaviour, and to bring into sharp focus the ambiguities left by the existing law of Parliament.

39. First, there has been a radical change in the nature of MPs' outside employment. Until recently, Members with paid outside employment typically pursued careers and occupations which, with the possible exception of journalism or the law, were largely unconnected with Parliament. Usually these were the same occupations that they had pursued before entering parliament. Only a few Members were paid in connection with their Parliamentary duties. That position has now, however, been radically transformed. The proportion of Members pursuing careers largely unconnected with Parliament, such as farming, has fallen, while—as the figures in paragraph 13 above show—the proportion whose outside employment arises directly out of their Membership of the House of Commons has risen to a very significant level.

40. Second, the introduction of the Register of Members' Interests, designed to further the wholly admirable concept of disclosure of interests, has tended to create a false impression that any interest is acceptable once it has been registered, and so to add to the confusion which has developed.

41. Some of this confusion may stem from the 'defining purpose' of the Register as set out in the First Report of the Select Committee on Members' Interests 1991/92. This purpose is 'to provide information of any pecuniary interest or other material benefit which a Member receives which might reasonably be thought by others to influence his or her actions, speeches or votes in Parliament, or actions taken in his or her capacity as a Member of Parliament.'

42. In the 1995 edition of the Register of Members' Interests consultancy agreements come under the third of the listed categories of registrable interests. Under the heading 'clients' it provides that Members must disclose the names of clients 'for whom they provide services which depend essentially upon, or arise out of, Membership of the House; for example, sponsoring functions in the Parliamentary buildings, making representations to Government Departments or providing advice on Parliamentary or public affairs.'

43. The position is, therefore, that the 1947 resolution prevents a Member from agreeing to act for a client in Parliament, but the rules governing the

Register of Members' Interests expressly contemplate that the Member may have received material benefits 'which might reasonably be thought by others to influence his or her actions, speeches or votes in Parliament' and which, in the case of consultancy agreements, may involve Members being paid for making representations to government departments on issues which inevitably will normally be concerned with matters to be transacted in Parliament.

44. The contrast between the 1947 Resolution and the rules governing the Register is in our view totally unsatisfactory. It is small wonder that it has given rise to confusion in the minds of Members of Parliament themselves. We agree with the comment made by Madam Speaker on 12 July 1994 (Official Report col 829) that there is an urgent need to clarify the law of Parliament in this area.

45. Although it is not comprehensive, the 1947 resolution is a clear statement of entirely sound principles. As a first step, therefore, we believe that it would clarify the position, and reinforce the impact of this resolution, if the House were to restate it at an early date.

The issues surrounding paid consultancies

46. The principal argument advanced in favour of allowing Members to put forward the views of their consultancy clients in Parliament is that many entirely respectable, and in some cases highly deserving, organisations can thereby gain a voice in the nation's affairs which would not be open to them by way of the normal constituency machinery. As a result, it is argued, the House as a whole is more fully informed and better able to debate the issues in question. Moreover, it is said, an imbalance is thus avoided between firms, professions and occupations whose members happen also to be Members of Parliament, and so can speak with authority on relevant subjects, and organisations such as trade associations, or charities, or the Police Federation which may be unable to command any such direct representation.

47. On the other hand, the consequence of the enormous growth in paid consultancy has been to create a real issue out of the distinction between paid advice and paid advocacy. Where once it might have mattered less that the occasional Member of Parliament who was a paid adviser spoke in the client's interest in Parliament, this has become a matter of significant public concern.

48. If a Member is engaged to advise a client on Parliamentary matters affecting the client, and is at the same time free to speak, lobby and vote on those same matters in the House, it is not merely possible but highly likely

that the Member will use Parliamentary opportunities in a way consistent with that advice.

> *'If your Committee were to conclude that certain activities—for example paid advocacy on behalf of outside bodies—are incompatible with a membership of the House I would regard this as thoroughly helpful both to Members and to those, such as the Registrar, who have to advise them.'* **Sir Geoffrey Johnson Smith MP**
>
> *'I think for a Member to be a paid-up lobbyist is outrageous and I am amazed, if I may say so, that your confreres ever tolerated it...'*
> **Simon Jenkins**
>
> *'... we had no problem in deciding recently, when we first set up, that one of the first rules should be that we would not pay Members in any way whatsoever.'*
> **Andrew Gifford, President and founder of the Association of Professional Political Consultants**
>
> *'... we cannot have a situation where somebody only says something because they are paid, but nor can we have a situation where somebody does not say something even though they know more about it than anyone else.'* **Ann Taylor MP**
>
> *'I think there is a distinction between the advocates and the general advisers. But I think of the advocates, the lobbyist is by far the strongest and clearest example.'* **Sir Norman Fowler MP**
>
> *'The very word "lobby" implies promoting a cause in the lobby. It seems to me it is a very difficult relationship to regard with enthusiasm.'* **Lord Howe**
>
> *'There are some people who say they don't want a House of Commons full of professional politicians. Well I don't want a House of Commons full of part-time London lawyers, London journalists, London heart surgeons, City financiers or West End shop managers.'*
> **Jeff Rooker MP**

49. It is more likely than not that Members who enter into consultancy agreements will do so with clients to whose viewpoints they are sym-

pathetic, although Members who have such agreements have been at pains to tell us that they would not hesitate both to make clear to their clients where their views differed, and to express views in the House which their clients did not share. Nevertheless the impression can easily be gained, however unfair this may be in individual cases, that not only advice but also advocacy have been bought by the client. The evidence which we have received leaves us in little doubt that this is the impression which many people have. It is one of the most potent sources of public suspicion about the true motivation of Members of Parliament. In recent years Members have acquired paid consultancies on a large scale. Over the same period public scepticism about MPs' financial motives has increased sharply. It must be more likely than not that these two developments are related, but in any case their combination can only tend to undermine the dignity of Parliament as a whole.

50. We would consider it thoroughly unsatisfactory, possibly to the extent of being a contempt of Parliament, if a Member of Parliament, even if not strictly bound by an agreement with a client to pursue a particular interest in Parliament, was to pursue that interest solely or principally because payment, in cash or kind, was being made. A Member who believes in a cause should be prepared to promote it without payment; equally a Member ought not to pursue a cause more forcefully than might otherwise have been the case as a result of a financial interest. We believe that such action would breach the spirit if not the letter of the 1947 resolution, and we cannot be confident that all Members are as scrupulous in this respect as some have claimed to be.

51. With these factors in mind we have carefully considered whether we should recommend an immediate and total ban on all forms of advocacy in the House by Members pursuing the interests of those with whom they hold consultancy or sponsorship agreements. The effect of this would be to prevent members with such interests from speaking, and perhaps from voting, when a relevant subject was under consideration. We have little doubt that such a ban would receive not only widespread public support but also support from many Members. A number of MPs who gave evidence to us endorsed the principle that paid advice is acceptable but paid advocacy is not. There is also a substantial body of opinion which holds that it is wrong in principle for Members to accept money for any services, even purely advisory services rendered in their capacities as Members.

52. We have concluded, however, that an immediate ban in that particular form, would be impracticable. It would involve asking three-fifths of the

Members of the House and their clients or sponsors to amend with immediate effect arrangements which have been made perfectly lawfully and are often of very long standing. Because so many Members have such interests, and so would be excluded from particular pieces of business, there would be a short term disruption of the business of the House. The impact on the income of many Members would have implications which could not be ignored. And the issues it would raise for the equilibrium of party political funding could only be addressed by a fundamental re-examination of that issue.

53. We have also concluded that further thought is needed before a firm decision can be taken on whether such a ban would be appropriate and on what the consequences would be of a decision to introduce such a ban. Parliament itself needs to debate further what it considers the Law of Parliament should be in this area. Parliament also needs to consider the implications for matters such as loss of income and party funding which are outside our terms of reference. Above all it needs to establish the facts. In this context, our recommendations below that agreement and remuneration in relation to Parliamentary consultancies should be disclosed in full are crucial. There is not sufficient information at present to enable a sound judgement to be made on whether the undoubted benefits of having well-informed and remunerated Members are outweighed by the risk of wealthy clients buying undue influence in Parliament.

54. While the further consideration suggested will need to be undertaken in some depth, and changes could take time to implement, the need to set the action in hand is urgent. The House may therefore think it right to hold an early debate with a view to commissioning the further work we propose. We ourselves will return to the subject in a year's time to review the position. In the meantime, individual Members may wish to consider whether in undertaking Parliamentary consultancies they may not have unwittingly put themselves under an obligation to advocate specific causes in Parliament in a manner contrary to the spirit, if not necessarily the letter, of the 1947 Resolution.

General consultancies

55. There is one area where we have no doubt that immediate action can and should be taken. Whatever arguments there may be in favour of Members who are retained as consultants by outside organisations acting as principles in their own right, we can see no justification for consultancy

agreements between Members and public relations or lobbying firms, which are themselves acting as advisers and advocates for a constantly changing range of miscellaneous and often undisclosed interests. Similarly, it seems to us inappropriate for Members who are connected with legal and other professional firms which offer clients Parliamentary services of any type to retain that connection unless arrangements can be made to separate completely the Member's interest in the firm from that part of its work. We consider that this is precisely the situation which the Prime Minister has described as 'a hiring fair'. We believe that the House should act immediately to stop this practice by outlawing agreements which commit Members to giving Parliamentary advice for payment to multi-client lobbying organisations or to the clients of such organisations. We also believe that the House should prohibit Members from maintaining direct or active connections with firms, or those parts of firms, which provide paid Parliamentary services to multiple clients.

Immediate practical measures

56. We also believe that, whatever the longer term decision on consultancies, a package of practical measures should be introduced as soon as possible. These will clarify how Members with outside interests should behave in order to avoid conflicts of interest. We believe that they will remove the area of doubt about the law of Parliament, and so be helpful to Members. We also believe that they will restore public confidence that Members of Parliament are not being improperly influenced by outside financial interests. The measures we set out below combine strong re-affirmation of the existing rules of the House; more effective disclosure of relevant interests; better arrangements for preventing conflicts of interest, including a Code of Conduct for Members; better guidance on and more equitable enforcement of the rules, involving the creation of a new officer of the House.

57. We are well aware that some will consider that we are over-reacting to a few isolated cases, and that the individual judgement of Members of Parliament can be relied on. Others will feel we should have gone further, and moved immediately to recommend statutory controls.

58. It is clear that, while some cases have been so bad as to require direct action even under the existing rules, there are problems of principle and practice over the separation of public and private interests, which damage the standing of Parliament. Neither we nor the media have invented the

problems. The House itself has recognised them and has made efforts to respond to them over the last quarter century. But the 1969 Strauss report was shelved without debate; the introduction of a Register of Interests was resisted until the Poulson scandal forced the hand of a new government in 1974; it has taken Members 20 years to accept the Register fully, with senior Members even in recent years feeling free to defy a Resolution of the House in respect of entries in the Register; and doubt has been expressed about whether justice has always been done to Members whose conduct has been judged by the House in recent years. While we accept that in the recent 'cash for questions' case the Privileges Committee has acted firmly, and that this should be fully recognised, the long-drawn out preliminaries to the committee's hearings were not such as to promote public confidence. The overall picture is not one of an institution whose Members have been quick to recognise or respond to public concern.

59. On the other hand we do not believe that the position is so grave that it has to be addressed outside the framework of the House's own rules. The question is whether the House is prepared to clarify and to implement those rules fully and objectively. An elected representative has a unique position, but it cannot be assumed that this inevitably makes that person's judgement of the balance of public and private interest infallible. The House collectively has a responsibility to safeguard the public interest against the possible misjudgement of individual Members, and it has the ability to do so. It also needs to reassert forcefully to the public that Members of Parliament, collectively and individually, have a sense of both the responsibilities and the dignity of the role with which they are entrusted. We believe that the House can do this itself, and that the package which we set out below will help it do so. It is a powerful and flexible mixture of disclosure and enforcement which will serve the public interest better than the inflexibility of statutory procedures.

We recommend that the House should restate the 1947 resolution which places an absolute bar on Members entering into contracts or agreements which in any way restrict their freedom to act and speak as they wish, or which require them to act in Parliament as representatives of outside bodies.

We recommend that the House should prohibit Members from entering into any agreements in connection with their role as Parliamentarians to undertake services for or on behalf of organisations which provide paid Parliamentary services to multiple clients or from maintaining any direct or active connections with firms, or parts of larger firms, which provide such Parliamentary services.

Appendix 1 129

We recommend that the House should set in hand without delay a broader consideration of the merits of Parliamentary consultancies generally, taking account of the financial and political funding implications of change.

We recommend that the House should:

- require agreements and renumeration relating to Parliamentary services to be disclosed;

- expand the guidance on avoiding conflicts of interest;

- introduce a new Code of Conduct for Members;

- appoint a Parliamentary Commissioner for Standards;

- establish a new procedure for investigating and adjudicating on complaints in this area about Members.

The detailed proposals for immediate action are set out in the following paragraphs.

Disclosure of interests

60. The House has for long operated on the principle that transparency is in most cases the best safeguard against conflicts of interest. Sir Terence Higgins MP said in evidence to us:

> *'Transparency is all important; wherever one draws the line on the issues you are considering, it is vital that there should be proper registration and it should be apparent both to the public, the House and Members themselves whether a person has an interest or not.'*

61. When the Register of Interests itself was established in 1974, it did not supersede the practice of declaring an interest at appropriate times. In fact the House in setting up the Register took the opportunity to enshrine in a formal resolution the long-standing convention of declaring an interest:

> *'In any debate or proceeding of the House or its Committees or transactions or communications which a Member may have with other Members or with Ministers or servants of the Crown, he shall disclose any relevant*

pecuniary interest or benefit of whatever nature, whether direct or indirect, that he may have had, may have, or may be expecting to have.'

This requirement casts its net wider than the Register, and it is not clear that its extent is always fully appreciated.

62. The House already goes to some lengths to ensure that Members of Select Committees know when to declare an interest. Declarations are required when putting a question to a witness and at deliberative meetings of the Committee. In addition, the Chairman is expected to seek declarations of interest immediately after the Committee is established, and to remind Members of their obligations from time to time.

63. There is much to be said for more systematic action to remind Members of their obligations to declare interests at other times. It is particularly important to emphasise that this obligation exists on each and every occasion when a Member approaches other Members or Ministers on a subject where a financial interest exists. Such contacts are often informal and private, and are therefore where the greatest risk of impropriety arises. It is clear that declaration at present is not always made in accordance with the rules, often through forgetfulness or misunderstanding. We have been told that Ministers always know when a Member who approaches them has a financial interest. But that is unlikely, especially given the number and extent of Members' financial interests. In any event the onus is on the Member to declare, not on the Minister to know. A Minister who discovers that an interest exists which has not been declared ought normally to consider whether the omission is sufficiently serious to report to the Select Committee on Members' Interests.

64. It has been suggested by some of our witnesses that the Register of Members' Interests is not particularly effective because it gives the appearance of declaration while permitting a form of declaration which may yield little information as to the true nature of the interest.

65. We agree. While the new 1995 register is an improvement on earlier editions, it lacks a standardised form of description and the nature of the interest is often difficult to discern. It is important that the Register should give a clear picture of the nature of the interest in question, and in particular of the nature of any activity that a Member is undertaking for payment, in order that a possible conflict of interest can be readily discerned. This is needed in respect of all declarable interests. At the same time, registration of

minor interests, which obscure the real purpose of the register, should be discouraged.

66. Full declaration is especially important in respect of paid activities related to Parliament. We consider that in those cases, because the risk of impropriety is greater, it is essential that the full terms of all consultancy and sponsorship agreements, if not already in writing, should be reduced to writing and deposited along with the Register, so as to make them open for public inspection in full.

67. The need to deposit the contract in full is illustrated by the recent 'cash for questions' case. At several places in the evidence there is discussion of the form of entry which would have been put in the Register, and it is clear that whether or not payment was being made for a single question, or for a consultancy, the entries would have been wholly uninformative. One example will suffice. The Cash for Questions Report* contains the following exchange. Mr John Morris says:

> '... Mr Calvert asks "How much information will you have to give when..." You reply: "What I shall say is something like this. I would put 'July 1994, consultancy project carried out for Mr Jonathan Calvert."'

Mr Riddick responds:

> 'May I point out that this is how the Registrar had suggested to me that I register this.'

68. The Registrar is not blamed for suggesting an uninformative description, because the Member did not go into detail with him. But it is clearly unsatisfactory that such opaque descriptions are routinely being entered so that there is disclosure in appearance but not in practice.

69. Depositing the agreement will inevitably involve disclosure of the remuneration. We believe that the public, and in particular Members' constituents, have a right to know what financial benefits Members receive as a consequence of being elected to serve their constituencies. We consider it right, therefore, that remuneration should be disclosed in these cases. We also believe that information about the remuneration or other financial consideration received by a Member for Parliamentary services, or by way of sponsorship, should be entered in the register itself, possibly in banded

---

* Committee of Privileges Report, Volume II, page 25, Q233.

form. It has been argued that actual remuneration is irrelevant, and that the mere existence of a financial relationship is what matters. That argument is not at all convincing. A Member who gets £1000 a year as a Parliamentary adviser is less likely to be influenced by the prospect of losing that money than one who receives £20,000 a year. The scale of the remuneration is in practice relevant to a full understanding of the nature of the service expected. We have notes that several MPs with whom we raised this issue did not object to disclosure of remuneration so long as this related strictly to Parliamentary services.

70. We are aware that in a number of other countries the practice is to require full disclosure of assets and income. But it is by no means clear that full disclosure of financial matters unrelated to Parliamentary business is relevant to the public interest. No-one has put a convincing case to us as to why that might be necessary.

On disclosure we recommend:

- the Register should continue broadly in its present form, and should be published annually. However the detailed entry requirements should be improved to give a clearer description of the nature and scope of the interests declared;

- updating of the Register should be immediate. The current updated version should be made more widely available electronically;

- from the beginning of the 1995/96 session (expected in November) Members should be required to deposit in full with the Register any contracts relating to the provision of services in their capacity as Members, and such contracts should be available for public inspection;

- from the same time, Members should be required to declare in the Register their annual remuneration, or estimated annual remuneration, in respect of such agreements. It would be acceptable if this were done in bands: eg under £1,000; £1,000–5,000; £5,000–10,000; then in £5,000 bands. An estimate of the monetary value of benefits in kind, including support services, should also be made;

- Members should be reminded more frequently of their obligations to Register and disclose interests, and that Registration does not remove the need for declaration, and better guidance should be given, especially on first arrival in the House.

71. In addition, Members with employment agreements (including Directorships and Partnerships) which are unrelated to their role as Members, and which under our proposals would not therefore have to be deposited, should be advised to ensure that those agreements do not imply that they will perform any activities related to their Parliamentary role. Such action is necessary to reduce the risk of misunderstandings.

We recommend that Members should be advised in their own interests that all employment agreements which do not have to be deposited should contain terms, or be supported by an exchange of letters, which make it clear that no activities relating to Parliament are involved.

Lobbyists

72. Mention has been made in evidence to us of a proposal for a Register of Lobbyists. We are not attracted by this idea. It is the right of everyone to lobby Parliament and Ministers, and it is for public institutions to develop ways of controlling the reaction to approaches from professional lobbyists in such a way as to give due weight to their case while always taking care to consider the public interest and the interests of the constituents whom Members of Parliament represent. Our approach to the problem of lobbying is therefore based on better regulation of what happens in Parliament.

73. To establish a public register of lobbyists would create the danger of giving the impression, which would no doubt be fostered by lobbyists themselves, that the only way to approach successfully Members or Ministers was by making use of a registered lobbyist. This would set up an undesirable hurdle, real or imagined, in the way of access.

74. We commend the efforts of lobbyists to develop their own codes of practice, but we reject the concept of giving them formal status through a statutory register.

Conflicts of interest

75. Disclosure of interests clearly goes a long way to reducing the risk of impropriety. But even when an interest has been disclosed, it may still be necessary in the public interest for the person with the interest to withdraw from the business in question.

76. Such a procedure is now universal in government, local government and other public bodies, and common in the private sector. People with an interest must declare it, often withdraw from meetings, and take no further part in the business. In local government, following Poulson, failure to do this may be an offence.

77. The Select Committee on Members' Interests has considered this issue on more than one occasion. In a report published in 1992*, it responded to suggestions that Members should be subjected to similar rules by saying:

> 'Comparisons are often drawn between the position of Members of Parliament and that of local authority councillors. These should be treated with caution. There are significant differences of function between the two.'

78. The Committee went on to quote with approval a witness who stated that all Members had an interest in all areas of public policy and must be allowed to participate in their deliberation, adding that the local government solution, if strictly enforced, would bring the work of the House to a halt. It then said:

> 'we heard ingenious arguments suggesting that there was little real distinction between the duties of Ministers of the Crown and the duties of other Members and proposing that both should comply with variants of the same rules. We did not find these arguments convincing. There is a world of difference between the position of Ministers, who have the responsibility for initiating policy and for taking executive decisions, and backbench Members, the powers of whom (as individuals) are confined to the exercise of influence.'

79. On this basis the Committee went on to conclude that full and public disclosure of relevant pecuniary interests was sufficient, and suggested that

---

* Select Committee on Members' Interests, Session 1991/92 First Report. Registration and Declaration of Members' Financial Interests.

the only occasion on which a Member should withdraw from business was when the possibility arose of making private gain as a result of access to information:

> 'As we have pointed out in an earlier report, if some Members, such as Chairmen and Members of Select Committees, acquire privileged insight into the development of policy they must expect that public opinion will eventually require that they should abide by rules which prevent them from holding particular interests or which require their withdrawal from certain proceedings.'

80. In fact, the Committee had understated the strength of the position adopted in its previous report*. That report, which was adopted on 13 July 1992 in a Resolution of the House, said:

> 'We feel that it is right that when a Member of a Committee, particularly the Chairman, has a pecuniary interest which is directly affected by a particular inquiry, or when he or she considers that a personal interest may reflect upon the work of the Committee or its subsequent report, the Member should stand aside from the Committee proceedings relating to it. This convention is so fundamental to the proper conduct of select committee business that we recommend that it should be reinforced by an appropriate resolution of the House.'

81. It has long been accepted that Members should not take part in Private Business in which they have a pecuniary interest, and there is one recorded case of Members being prevented from voting in Public Business in such circumstances. The 1992 Resolution extends the principle of requiring Members to withdraw from Public Business to cases where the pecuniary interest 'is directly affected' by a particular inquiry or where 'a personal interest may reflect upon the work of the Committee or its subsequent report.'

82. This was an important and welcome development, in that the House recognised that the public interest could be a factor in determining whether a Member should withdraw. However we agree with the Select Committee's 1992 comment that the position of Members is not entirely analogous with Ministers or local councillors, and that there are many areas of Parliamentary business where following a declaration of interest a Member can still make a valuable, and quite proper, contribution to public business. What is

---

* Select Committee on Members' Interests, Session 1990/91 First Report.

still needed is further guidance to Members on the appropriate action in differing situations.

83. There can be few cases where any damage to the public interest can result from a Member who has declared an interest speaking in the House, even in a Second Reading Debate of a relevant Bill or in a Committee of the whole House. And there is little risk of damage to the public interest at large, as opposed to the risk of damage to the credibility of Members of Parliament, when a Member who has a financial interest signs an early day motion, votes at a Division of the whole House, or puts down a Parliamentary Question, so long as the interest is declared on every occasion in the appropriate way. We believe that arrangements should be devised, possibly through the use of symbols on the Order Paper, to achieve this: it is already done for the proposers, though not other signatories, of Early Day Motions.

84. But there are other circumstances when the public interest may well demand that a Member with a financial interest should stand aside. In addition to the Select Committee position which the House has already addressed (see paragraph 80 above), the question of Standing Committees needs to be considered. A Member who takes part in Standing Committee on a Bill is one of a small group which shapes the legislation in detail, some of whose amendments may well be accepted by government.

85. There will be circumstances where a Bill is sufficiently relevant to a sectional interest to make it against the public interest for Members with a financial interest to serve on such a Committee. In at least one recent case it has been suggested to us that the House failed to appreciate the risks of such a conflict of interest, to the possible detriment of the final legislation. This was the Cable Bill Standing Committee, when several Members of the Committee had financial interests, which they declared, in the industry in question. At present the House's own practice increases the risk, because it is customary for the Committee of Selection to make appointments to a Standing Committee from among those Members who have expressed a willingness to take part, and to reflect the balance of contributions in the Second Reading debate. This practice needs to be amended to incorporate a presumption against appointing Members with a financial interest.

We recommend that the rules and guidance on avoiding conflict of interest should be expanded on the lines we have suggested to cover the whole range of business pertaining to Parliament, and that particular attention should be paid to Standing Committees.

A Code of Conduct

86. Two recurring themes throughout our oral evidence were, first that any line drawn in order to ban particular Parliamentary activities by Members would give rise to anomalies, and second that the elected representatives of the people need to be trusted to exercise their own judgement. A comment by Lord Callaghan illustrates the point:

> '*I regard the sense of propriety of a Member of Parliament himself as to what he should do as being the ultimate test. ... I hope you will be able to draw up a set of principles of conduct that will govern Members' financial interests. I would suggest that the Code, when drawn up and accepted by the House, should be adopted afresh by the House of Commons at the beginning of every Parliament after a general election ... so that every new Member would understand what was expected of him and what was the normal code of behaviour.*'

87. We have suggested above a number of firm rules, and have also indicated a number of areas where difficulties arise. We share the view of those who warn against unduly detailed and prescriptive rules, but we also consider that it is unreasonable to expect that the view of every Member of Parliament of what is and is not acceptable will produce without guidance a universally acceptable standard.

88. While "Erskine May's Parliamentary Practice" is a thorough guide to the procedures and rules of Parliament it is a very weighty document, and we doubt that it is closely read by all Members. We believe therefore that more needs to be done in future to ensure that new Members are fully aware of all the rules on conflict and disclosure of interest, through induction sessions, a code of conduct and the preparation of guidance.

89. The Code of Conduct should provide a framework against which acceptable conduct should be judged, but should not contain excessive detail. It should avoid the type of detailed rules which can give rise to anomalies, but should set out principles clear enough to enable appropriate decisions to be made. It ought to be supplemented by detailed guidance from time to time. We believe too that the proposal that such a Code should be restated and debated early in the life of every new Parliament has much to commend it. We have set out our suggestion for a Code on page 39 (*see page 138*), and we commend this to the House, but we believe, in line with best practice in the private sector, that such a Code is more effective if the institution to which it is to apply draws it up and is committed to it.

A Draft Code of Conduct for Members of Parliament

General Principles

It is the personal responsibility of every Member of Parliament to maintain those standards of conduct which the House and the electorate are entitled to expect, to protect the good name of Parliament and to advance the public interest.

Members should observe those general principles of conduct which apply to all people in public life. [These are set out on page 14 of this report, and should be incorporated into the final code]

The primary duty of Members is to their country and their constituents. They should undertake no actions in Parliament which conflict with that duty.

Because Members of Parliament enjoy certain privileges in law, which exist to enable them to fulfil their responsibilities to the citizens they represent, each Member has a particular personal responsibility to comply fully with all resolutions and conventions of the House relating to matters of conduct, and when in doubt to seek advice.

Financial Interests

A Member must not promote any matter in Parliament in return for payment.

A Member who has a financial interest, direct or indirect, must declare that interest in the currently approved manner when speaking in the House or in Committee, or otherwise taking part in Parliamentary proceedings, or approaching Ministers, civil servants or public bodies on a matter connected with that interest.

Where, in the pursuit of a Member's Parliamentary duties, the existence of a personal financial interest is likely to give rise to a conflict with the public interest, the Member has a personal responsibility to resolve that conflict either by disposing of the interest or by standing aside from the public business in question.

In any dealings with or on behalf of an organisation with whom a financial relationship exists, a Member must always bear in mind the overriding responsibility which exists to constituents and to the national interest. This is particularly important in respect of activities which may not be a matter of public record, such as informal meetings and functions.

In fulfilling the requirements on declaration and registration of interests and remuneration, and depositing of contracts, a Member must have regard to the purpose of those requirements and must comply with them, both in letter and spirit.

We recommend that the House should draw up a Code of Conduct setting out the broad principles which should guide the conduct of Members, and that this should be restated in every new Parliament.

Enforcement of obligations

90. Because the House of Commons is responsible for enforcing its own rules, we regard it as a matter of concern that over recent years the procedures for their enforcement have appeared to be less than satisfactory. Proceedings related to conduct of Members in general have been carried forward on an ad hoc basis. Given the inevitable tendency for party politics to influence decisions on matters of conduct it is even more important for Parliament, the highest court in the land, to have established procedures which operate as a matter of course rather than chance. The public needs to see that breaches of the rules by its elected legislators are investigated as fairly, and dealt with as firmly, by Parliament in such cases as would be the case with others through the legal process. The recent arguments over how to conduct proceedings in the 'cash for questions' case point clearly to the need for fixed and fair arrangements which provide for proper investigation and demonstrably fair hearings.

91. Parliamentary Privilege is designed to ensure the proper working of Parliament, and is an essential constitutional safeguard. In the recent report on the 'cash for questions' case, the Committee of Privileges helpfully defined both its role and the concept of privilege:

'It may be helpful to the wider public to describe briefly the role of this Committee. Having been directed to examine a matter by the House, our essential function is to take evidence on its behalf in order to advise Members generally on whether and to what extent there appears to have been a breach of the privileges of the House or any action amounting to a contempt and to make recommendations to the House. It is for the House in all cases to take the final decision. Partly through precedent and partly by statute the House has over the years obtained certain rights known as "privileges". Their purpose is not to protect individual Members of Parliament but to provide the necessary framework in which the House in its corporate capacity and its Members as individuals can fulfil their responsibilities to the citizens whom they represent. Parliament defends its privileges by the law of contempt'.

92. One of the consequences of privilege is therefore that the House of Commons regulates the activities of its Members itself. Where Parliamentary business is concerned, they are answerable to the House and not to the Courts. Because Parliamentary privilege is important for reasons entirely unconnected with the standards of conduct of individual Members of Parliament, we believe that it would be highly desirable for self-regulation to continue.

93. For self-regulation to continue successfully, however, it is essential that Resolutions of the House—in effect the legal framework which the House imposes on its own operations—should be regarded as binding by all Members, and should be firmly, promptly and fairly enforced. Comments in evidence by Sir Geoffrey Johnson Smith MP, Chairman of the Select Committee on Members' Interests, illustrate the problem:

> *'I feel sure that the rules [on registration of interests] are now better understood by Members and more widely accepted by them than was the case some five or ten years ago. ... Some Members, when [the register] was introduced, did not quite understand the force of it. ... I used to spend some part of my time going round and reminding Members that they had not yet signed the register.'*

94. Sir Geoffrey added that on occasion in the past he had to threaten to report a Member to the House, but that the Register was now accepted and this was no longer necessary.

95. In more recent years a number of senior Members did not accept a resolution of the House in respect of the Register, and refused to comply with it. In due course it was changed to meet their concerns. Yet when Parliament passes a law with which some people disagree, the expectation is that the law will be enforced until its opponents succeed in getting it changed.

96. We give this as an example. But there are other instances too which lead us to believe that Resolutions of the House in matters of conduct are not perceived by all Members as having the same impact as laws or regulations, even though they are the law of Parliament. In part this is because the House as a whole, and in consequence its staff, is clearly reluctant to sit in judgement on fellow Members unless a matter is very serious.

97. Such an attitude is entirely understandable, but wrong. Unless obligations are routinely and firmly enforced a culture of slackness can develop

with the danger that in due course this could lead on to tolerance of corruption.

98. While we share with Chris Moncrieff the view that:

> *'Members of Parliament, generally speaking, are not corrupt and are well intentioned ... ',*

we firmly believe that the House of Commons needs to develop and implement a culture in which Resolutions of the House are automatically regarded as binding on Members, where there is a certainty of action when there is a breach of the rules, and where the procedures are fair and well understood. We believe that if the rules are clear, and enforcement is certain, the overwhelming majority of Members of Parliament will readily embrace and adhere to the standards which the House requires.

99. We consider that this can best be taken forward by combining a significant independent element with a system which remains essentially self-regulating. We believe that this should be done by appointing an officer of the House, called the Parliamentary Commissioner for Standards, to take responsibility for advising Members on, and playing an independent role in the enforcement of, the House's rules in respect of Members' conduct. If the House accepts our recommendation that a Code of Conduct should be drawn up, the Commissioner would take on the task of advising on that and producing guidance. We believe this would be helpful to Members themselves. Ann Taylor MP told us:

> *'It really is remarkable how, when Members of Parliament are first elected, they don't actually get a guide to the House of Commons which tells them the rules: just as there is no job description of a Member of Parliament, there is no set of rules which you are given once you arrive and by which you must abide.'*

100. Mrs Taylor accepted the need for an element of independence in enforcement, as did a number of other witnesses, including Lord Howe and Roy Hattersley MP. Professor Sir William Wade, the leading constitutional lawyer, wrote to us as follows:

> *'The question is how breaches ... should be adjudicated. Traditionally the House has been jealous of its privilege of self-regulation, but some Members have now proposed that there should be an independent element so as to eliminate political bias. In my opinion that would be a very desir-*

able step. It would add to the reputation of the House and be well worth the surrender of privilege. Comparison might be made with election petitions, which until 1868 were decided by the House itself, but after that date were transferred to election courts manned by High Court judges, much to the benefit of justice.'

101. We do not believe it is necessary to rehearse in detail the weaknesses of the present arrangements, but Lord Callaghan, John MacGregor MP (a former Leader of the House) and Sir Geoffrey Johnson Smith MP (Chairman of the Committee on Members' Interests) all commented on this. John MacGregor said:

'I have become concerned about the extent to which the Select Committee on Members' Interests is asked to be judge and jury, working out the evidence and so on. The procedures of the Select Committee may not be appropriate where there are serious issues affecting a Member's total career. ... For example, a Member is not entitled to question witnesses who are putting the case against him. I therefore feel that there is a case for having outside involvement in a Select Committee when it is dealing with such matters.'

102. We consider that our proposals to appoint an independent Commissioner and to overhaul the entire disciplinary procedure for Members should be sufficient to achieve the necessary detachment without recourse to the courts or indeed any surrender of privilege. The recommendations set out below should enable Members to secure a fair, thorough and expeditious hearing without removing the jurisdiction of the House of Commons. We should say, however, that among others John Biffen MP (a former Leader of the House), Lord Blake and Professor Dawn Oliver have told us in effect that such procedures should be put on to a statutory basis. If adopted, the test of whether our recommendations are sufficient, or further change is needed, will be their operation in practice.

103. There is one area of conduct where a need already exists to clarify, and perhaps alter, the boundary between the courts and Parliament. Bribery of a Member, or the acceptance of a bribe by a Member, is contempt of Parliament and can be punished by the House. The test which the House would apply for bribery would no doubt be similar to that which would apply under Common Law. However it is quite likely that Members of Parliament who accepted bribes in connection with their Parliamentary duties would be committing Common Law offences which could be tried by the courts. Doubt exists as to whether the courts or Parliament have jurisdiction in such cases.

104. The Salmon Commission in 1976 recommended that such doubt should be resolved by legislation, but this has not been acted upon. We believe that it would be unsatisfactory to leave this issue outstanding when other aspects of the law of Parliament relating to conduct are being clarified. **We recommend that the Government should now take steps to clarify the law relating to the bribery of or the receipt of a bribe by a Member of Parliament.** This could usefully be combined with the consolidation of the statute law on bribery which Salmon also recommended, which the government accepted, but which has not been done. This might be a task which the Law Commission could take forward.

On procedure we recommend:

- **the House should appoint a person of independent standing, who should have a degree of tenure and not be a career member of the House of Commons staff, as Parliamentary Commissioner for Standards.** The Commissioner would take over responsibility for maintaining the Register of Members' Interests; advising on the code of conduct and questions of propriety; have responsibility for preparing guidance and providing induction sessions for new Members on matters of conduct, propriety and ethics; and have responsibility for receiving complaints about and investigating the conduct of Members in this area. **The Commissioner should have the same ability to make findings and conclusions public as is enjoyed by the Comptroller and Auditor General and the Parliamentary Commissioner for Administration.**

- **the Commissioner should have independent discretion to decide whether or not a complaint merits investigation or to initiate an investigation.** An investigation by the Commissioner would be conducted in private. Following an investigation the Commissioner would again have discretion either to dismiss a complaint, to find it proved and agreed a remedy with the Member concerned, or to find a case to answer and refer the complaint to a Committee of the House. The Commissioner would be expected to publish the reasons for dismissing a case after investigation, the finding and remedy agreed when it was being taken no further, and the report to the Committee when a case was being taken further;

- **the Commissioner should be able to send for persons, papers and records, and will therefore need to be supported by the authority of a Select Committee with the necessary powers.** To give the powers personally to the Commissioner would require primary legislation, and we do not believe that to be necessary at this stage;

- there has been hitherto considerable uncertainty about the respective roles of the Select Committee on Members' Interests and the Committee of Privileges in enforcing the rules in this area. **We consider that a sub-committee of the Committee of Privileges, consisting of up to seven very senior Members, would be the best body to take forward individual cases recommended by the Commissioner for further consideration. We recommend that such a sub-committee should be established.** The enlarged responsibilities envisaged for the Commissioner might make it possible for the Select Committee on Members' Interests to be dispensed with altogether, with any residual functions being transferred to the Committee of Privileges with its sub-committee. But this is a matter for the House to determine;

- **in view of the fact that there would be a prima facie case to investigate, we recommend that hearings of the proposed sub-committee should normally be in public. We also recommend that the sub-committee should be able to call on the assistance of specialist advisers and that a Member who so wishes should be able to be accompanied by advisers before the sub-committee.** The arrangements should be such as to enable all concerned to see that the rules of natural justice are being applied. **We recommend that the sub-committee should be given discretion to enable an adviser to act as the Member's representative at hearings.** In exercising this discretion, it would be appropriate for the sub-committee to follow these principles set out in Halsbury*.

'Factors which ought to be taken into account in exercising the discretion include the seriousness of any allegations made or any potential penalty, whether any points of law are likely to arise, the capacity of the particular individual to present his or her own case, whether it will be necessary to cross-examine witnesses whose evidence has not been disclosed in advance, any potential delay, and the need for fairness as between all persons who may appear.'

- Where a formal penalty is thought to be appropriate, we commend the practice adopted in the recent Privileges Committee report on 'cash

---

* Halsbury's Laws of England, Fourth Edition.

for questions' for a specific recommendation to that effect to be included in the sub-committee's report;

- an advantage of establishing a Commissioner and a sub-committee to deal with conduct cases would be that minor cases could be handled with maximum despatch and minimum fuss. **As the sub-committee would report to the full Privileges Committee this would have the practical effect of giving the Member a right of appeal to that Committee. Only the most serious cases should need to be considered by the whole House.** We believe that it should not be necessary for the House formally to endorse every adverse finding by the Privileges Committee, although it might be appropriate in certain cases for a Member to make a personal statement of regret. More severe penalties, involving suspension and possible loss of salary (in practice the equivalent of a fine) would continue to require the authority of the whole House.

Chapter 3

The Executive: Ministers and Civil Servants

Principal conclusions

There is a need for greater clarity about the standards of conduct expected of Ministers. The Prime Minister should draw up specific guidance on this subject, based on the principles set out in this report

Careful consideration should be given to ensuring that the most appropriate means are used for the investigation of cases of alleged impropriety affecting Ministers. Other than in exceptional circumstances, the general rule that advice from civil servants to Ministers should not be made public should apply in these cases

There should be a new advisory system regulating the employment taken up by ex-Ministers. The system should be based on the existing civil service rules and should be flexible and as transparent as possible, while protecting personal privacy

The new system of appeal for civil servants to the civil service commissioners proposed by the Government should be extended by introducing systems for handling confidential appeals within civil service departments and agencies. The civil service commissioners should report the details of all appeals which have been upheld to Parliament

The civil service business appointments system should be more open. It should be actively monitored to ensure that the rules are being observed and complied with. It should cover special advisers.

Introduction

1. While the backbench Member of Parliament has a good deal of influence, it is the executive—Ministers and civil servants—which plays the major role in the making and execution of policy. Ministers are accountable

to Parliament and the public for the work of their departments and agencies; less publicly, senior civil servants may substantially influence the policy process. Both are likely to be the target of lobbying.

2. Despite the great difference in their formal responsibilities and their public profile, standards of conduct of both Ministers and civil servants must be of the highest. Combined, they exercise power directly over the lives of their fellow-citizens. Whether that power belongs to a Secretary of State approving a contract worth many millions, or a benefits clerk handling a claim for a few pounds, the maintenance of public trust is essential.

3. During the course of our work we have been made aware of circumstances in which public trust has been weakened. For example, many of our correspondents and witnesses have commented on the ease with which Ministers can obtain employment with commercial firms with which they have had connexions while in office; disquiet has been expressed about the private lives of some Ministers; serving and retired civil servants have suggested that initiatives designed to improve efficiency in the provision of public services, such as the next steps programme and the contracting-out of public sector functions, have put at risk established standards of conduct.

The Conduct of Ministers

4. The public is entitled to expect very high standards of behaviour from Ministers, as they have profound influence over the daily lives of us all. The example they set is closely scrutinised by the public and the media. As Vernon Bogdanor told us, 'it is from Ministers that standards in public life must flow'.

5. We believe that a response is needed to the increased media and public interest in standards of ministerial conduct. In principle this interest is welcome. Yet the media does not confine itself to the public life of Ministers. It reports their sexual behaviour, their private conversations and in some cases the activities of their children and relatives. It can be oppressive and intrusive: to the extent to which it involves those who are not in public life through choice, it is seldom justified by legitimate public interest.

6. In our view, there is a significant difference between media coverage of sexual behaviour, and accounts of financial impropriety, unacceptable conflicts of interest, or other forms of misconduct in office. Financial misbehaviour in particular matters to us all, because it strikes at the very heart of

that confidence which people must have in Ministers and the motives behind their decisions. The same cannot normally be said of sexual misconduct. It is true that the private lives of Ministers may occasionally be relevant to the performance of their public duties, for example when their private conduct runs directly counter to some public policy, gives rise to embarrassing publicity, or involves a security risk. We do not, however, feel that there are rules which can usefully be made about the sexual conduct of Ministers in the same way as those which apply to their financial interests.

7. The evidence we have heard and received does not indicate that the public believes that Ministers are implicated in widespread wrong-doing. It does, however, suggest that people would welcome greater clarity about the standards of conduct to be expected of Ministers and how these are enforced.

Questions of Procedure for Ministers (QPM)

8. What guidance there is for Ministers on standards of conduct, as well as on procedural matters, is contained in Questions of Procedure for Ministers. In the context of the British constitution, QPM is a youthful document, dating from 1945 (although elements within it are older). For many years, Questions of Procedure was a confidential document. It was only in 1992 that the present Prime Minister took the decision to publish it.

9. QPM has no particular constitutional status, but because it is issued by each Prime Minister to ministerial colleagues at the start of an administration or on their appointment to office, and any changes can only be authorised by the Prime Minister, it is in practice binding on all members of a Government. The records show that QPM has grown organically over the years, beginning as a document that was not much more than what Lord Trend described as 'tips on etiquette for beginners' but with fresh sections being added to deal with new circumstances. Over the years, the growth in QPM has largely been in the area of conduct and not procedure.

10. We do not believe that the explanation for this is a decline in ministerial standards of conduct. We think that the addition of ethical material to QPM has resulted from a combination of responses to specific incidents and a general trend, not confined to Government, towards codification of what might once have been assumed to be common ground.

Ministers and the Prime Minister

11. QPM begins by setting out some fundamental principles:

> '*It will be for individual Ministers to judge how best to act in order to uphold the highest standards. Ministers will want to see that no conflict arises or appears to arise between their private interests and their public duties. They will wish to be as open as possible with Parliament and the public. These notes should be read against the background of these general obligations*'*.

12. Ministers themselves are individually and separately responsible for upholding the standards of conduct applicable to their office. Everyone in public life has a personal responsibility for judging a course of action—the acceptance of hospitality, for example—weighing up its ethical implications using their own judgement. In the case of Ministers, their need to account to Parliament for their actions reinforces that responsibility.

13. Yet Ministers do not make their ethical judgements in isolation. To remain in office they must retain the confidence of the Prime Minister and, in a question of conduct, that will involve the Prime Minister's own judgement of the ethics of the case. This is axiomatic and should be reflected in QPM.

We recommend that the first paragraph of Questions of Procedure for Ministers should be amended to say: 'It will be for individual Ministers to judge how best to act in order to uphold the highest standards. It will be for the Prime Minister to determine whether or not they have done so in any particular circumstance.'

Guidance to Ministers on Conduct

14. We believe that there are general principles of conduct which are applicable to Ministers; that it is possible to set these out in a clear and comprehensible form that will be of assistance to the Prime Minister, to Ministers themselves and to members of the public; and that this can indicate unacceptable aspects of ministerial behaviour. This approach will not, of course, stop misconduct. But it will do much to counter present public uncertainty about what is and is not acceptable.

---

* Questions of Procedure for Ministers (Cabinet Office 1992), paragraph 1.

15. QPM does not offer a coherent series of principles which can be applied by Ministers who are in doubt about possible courses of action. The document is a miscellany: 'a mix of immutable principles with housekeeping practicalities', as Professor Peter Hennessey described it to us.

We recommend that the Prime Minister puts in hand the production of a document drawing out from QPM the ethical principles and rules which it contains to form a free-standing code of conduct or a separate section within a new QPM. If QPM is to remain the home for this guidance, we recommend that it is retitled 'Conduct and Procedure for Ministers' to reflect its scope.

16. The precise wording of the new guidance will be a matter for the Prime Minister. We believe, however, that the following essential principles should be spelt out, supported where necessary by detailed rules, some of which already exist in QPM:

Ministers of the Crown are expected to behave according to the highest standards of constitutional and personal conduct. In particular they must observe the following principles of ministerial conduct:

i) *Ministers must ensure that no conflict arises, or appears to arise, between their public duties and their private interests;*

ii) *Ministers must not mislead Parliament. They must be as open as possible with Parliament and the public;*

iii) *Ministers are accountable to Parliament for the policies and operations of their departments and agencies;*

iv) *Ministers should avoid accepting any gift or hospitality which might, or might appear to, compromise their judgement or place them under an improper obligation;*

v) *Ministers in the House of Commons must keep separate their roles as Minister and constituency Member;*

vi) *Ministers must keep their party and ministerial roles separate. They must not ask civil servants to carry out party political duties or to act in any other way that would conflict with the Civil Service Code.*

17. Setting out these principles for Ministers might seem unnecessary or obvious. We do not share that view. The Government has accepted the proposition that there should be a code of conduct for civil servants. It is difficult to see why the same approach should not apply to Ministers. The advantages of a code can be seen by considering the number of Ministers who have had to resign since the war because of avoidable errors of judgement. We do not, though, believe that express sanctions need to be set out to prevent Ministers from doing wrong. Public and media scrutiny of ministerial conduct in the light of the principles we have listed above is likely to be far more effective. Ministers themselves will be able to judge possible courses of action against these principles, supported by the useful rules-of-thumb recommended to us by Lord Howe: 'Would you ... feel happy to see all the relevant facts of any transaction or relationship fully and fairly reported on the front page of your favourite newspaper', and 'If in doubt, cut it out'.

Scrutinising Ministerial Conduct

18. The way in which allegations of ministerial misconduct are dealt with will depend very much on the circumstances of each case. In the nature of things, such allegations may well be made publicly or become public. It is important for the public interest, the reputation of the Minister concerned, and that of the Government that allegations are investigated promptly and effectively.

19. The handling of allegations of criminal misbehaviour is relatively straightforward. The police will investigate the alleged offence. It may be necessary for a Minister to stand down in these circumstances, but there is no ambiguity about the process of investigation. Fortunately, such cases are extremely rare. It is more common for allegations of misconduct to fall well short of criminal behaviour and to be concerned with sexual behaviour, conflicts of interest, or financial impropriety.

20. Recent cases have shown that there may be circumstances in which the Prime Minister needs further advice or information. There are various people to whom the Prime Minister may turn for this. There is no reason why the advice of the Cabinet Secretary should not be sought on how best to proceed. Indeed it would be usual to do so, particularly if it is alleged that a Minister breached the principles of ministerial conduct in QPM. In some circumstances the preparation of advice may require investigation into the facts: this will depend on the nature of the case. However, if the allegations relate to past behaviour before entering office, or personal misbehaviour

unconnected in any way with ministerial duties, they are not matters for the Cabinet Secretary, who should advise the Prime Minister to that effect.

21. It is impossible to foresee all the circumstances which then arise. In some cases, it may be a matter for the police, in others, for the Chief Whip or other ministerial colleagues, the security services or the Law Officers. In some cases, where Parliamentary rules are involved, the Prime Minister might refer the case to the proposed Parliamentary Commissioner for Standards. A very serious and complex case might merit a Tribunal of Inquiry. Occasionally a suitably qualified individual might be engaged to carry out an investigation. In a good many cases, an internal administrative investigation may suffice.

22. During or after any investigation, by whomever it is carried out, into a Minister's conduct, the Cabinet Secretary may well have to advise the Prime Minister, or (acting on the Prime Minister's behalf) to advise the Minister concerned on the best course of action to take in respect of his or her ministerial office. We believe that a clear distinction must be drawn between the report of an investigation, which it might be appropriate to publish, and the Cabinet Secretary's advice, which should never, or very rarely, be made public. The political impartiality of the civil service has to be protected, and it is wrong for such advice to become part of the debate over a Minister's behaviour.

We recommend that careful consideration should be given to ensuring that the most appropriate means is used for the investigation of cases of alleged impropriety affecting Ministers. We recommend that, other than in exceptional circumstances, the general rule that advice from civil servants to Ministers should not be made public should apply in these cases.

Employment After Leaving the Government

23. One aspect of the conduct of Ministers has been repeatedly raised in evidence to us: the absence of rules on employment after leaving public office. We have considered whether this is a justified area of concern. We have concluded that it is.

24. Ministers have the opportunity while in Government to take decisions which may favour or disadvantage outside bodies, including individual firms. For civil servants (and members of the armed forces) in a similar position, regulations have existed for many years to reassure the public that decisions

made while in office have not been influenced by the prospect of employment after leaving the civil service. These rules, administered by an independent committee, are known as the business appointment rules. Although they are non-statutory, they are flexible, understood, and seldom disobeyed. Cabinet Ministers have much greater responsibility for decisions about Government policy than even the most senior civil servants. Yet Ministers can take any post they wish—subject to the dictates of their own consciences—whereas senior civil servants must have their plans approved for a full two years after the date of their departure from government service. That is difficult to justify.

25. We have heard arguments both in favour of and against the introduction of a business appointment system for Ministers. The Government's view was given by the Chancellor of the Duchy of Lancaster, David Hunt MP, who argued that 'it is still right to leave decisions about these matters to the judgement of the individuals concerned'. We recognise the force of some of the points which he made. We have also, however, to take into consideration other evidence which we received, not least from former Conservative Ministers, people of considerable experience in public life. Sir Norman Fowler MP said that 'the aims of the civil service code seem to me ... equally applicable to Ministers'. His view was shared by Lord Callaghan, Lord Younger, and many of our other witnesses. Sir Norman Fowler also pointed out that 'both the public and former Ministers would benefit from a clearly stated set of rules'. We agree. The risk of abuse, or of unfounded and malicious criticism, would be much reduced by a vetting system.

26. It has been argued that in most cases, senior civil servants will leave public service at a retirement age which is known in advance, and that on departure most will receive a full pension. In the case of Ministers, their departure from government may be abrupt and their severance pay is likely to be very much less. Nevertheless, the same principles of public interest apply. The reassurance of the public that standards of conduct are being maintained is an overriding necessity. As Lord Younger said, 'Ministers have to take the rough with the smooth on this'. We have also taken note of the argument that a restrictive system will discourage talented people from becoming Ministers. In the commercial world, restrictions on freedom of future employment are normally compensated in the renumeration package, but we accept that this is unlikely to happen with Ministers. We consider, however, that the risk of discouraging candidates for ministerial office will be minimal if, just as with the civil service rules, any rules for Ministers are drawn so as to affect only the limited number of possible moves which give

genuine reason for concern. Lord Carlisle, the Chairman of the Advisory Committee on Business Appointments, which advises on the application of the present rules, told us that approximately 70% of the cases put before his Committee attract neither waiting period nor other restriction. We have no reason to suppose that the pattern for ministerial applications would be very different.

27. We share the view that there should be as much interchange as possible between the public and private sectors. The civil service rules restrict interchange between the sectors, but on a narrow and defensible basis. Ministers should be able to contribute their expertise and their knowledge of government to companies that wish to employ them, because the benefits to the country and economy may be substantial. A flexible system, which curtails employment plans only when they might threaten public confidence in standards of conduct, would not prevent those benefits from being realised.

The Civil Service Business Appointment Rules

28. The salient points of the existing civil service business appointment system are as follows:

i) all civil servants at grades 1 and 1A (permanent secretary) and 2 (deputy secretary) must submit their future job plans to the Advisory Committee on Business Appointments for approval, unless the job is unpaid and in a non-commercial organisation, or is a public appointment;

ii) they must seek approval both for their first job and for any others within two years of leaving the civil service. Approval is given by the Prime Minister on the advice of the Advisory Committee;

iii) there is an automatic waiting period of three months imposed on all grade 1 and 1A (permanent secretary) civil servants, except fixed-term appointees;

iv) the advisory committee may recommend a waiting period of up to two years (from the date of leaving the civil service) before the ex-civil servant can take up the job, and may also impose what are called 'behavioural conditions'. These govern what the ex-civil servant may not do for his or her new employer: they may, for example, prevent ex-civil servants from contacting their former departments or working on tenders for Government projects. These conditions may also last for up to two years from the date of leaving Government service.

v) the rules are not designed to detect corruption, which would be a criminal matter. 'The aim of the application of the rules is to maintain public trust in [the civil and military] services and in the people who work in them'*;

vi) The advisory committee recommends whether a waiting period or behavioural condition should be applied under two headings. It considers whether a proposed move creates 'any suspicion, no matter how unjustified, that the advice and decisions of a serving officer might be influenced by the hope or expectation of future employment with a particular firm or organisation'. It also takes into account 'the risk that a particular firm might gain an improper advantage over its competitors by employing someone, who, in the course of their official duties, has had access to technical or other information which those competitors might legitimately regard as their own trade secrets or to information relating to proposed developments in Government policy which may affect that firm or its competitors.'*;

vii) the rules apply equally to civil servants below grade 2, although these cases are not normally dealt with by the advisory committee. Final decisions rest with departmental Ministers. Applications at Grade 3, and the more sensitive cases below Grade 3, must be referred to the Cabinet Office for advice.

A Ministerial Business Appointments System

29. The civil service system is tried and tested; our view is that it appears to be accepted by civil servants and it provides a strong reassurance to the public. Public concern now demands a similar reassurance in the case of Ministers. We believe that the evidence we have heard indicates that the civil service system, with some slight modifications, could be applied to Ministers.

30. We have considered whether a Ministerial system should be enforceable by statute, or purely advisory. We believe that a transparent advisory

* Civil Service Management Code 4.3 Annex A.

system will achieve the necessary liberty of movement for individuals but nevertheless secure public confidence and ministerial compliance, without the complication of a statutory power. In other words, if ex-Ministers knew that a failure to seek the views of an advisory body or to abide by its advice would be reported in public, the fact that there were no legal sanctions would not matter. The threat of hostile public reaction and media comment would be a powerful disincentive. However, we would not rule out returning to this subject in the future, should practical experience convince us that a voluntary system was insufficient to sustain public confidence.

31. A purely advisory system places great weight on those advising. We have considered whether some form of new advisory machinery needs to be created which would be of sufficient standing and expertise to offer advice to Ministers. We do not feel that fresh arrangements are necessary. The existing Advisory Committee on Business Appointments draws its membership from senior retired politicians, civil servants, the diplomatic service and the armed forces. Its members have long experience in applying the rules sensibly and flexibly to senior civil servants and they are supported by a secretariat in the Cabinet Office. In principle, we see no reason why the advisory committee should not take on the task of advising Ministers on their future employment plans. We are confirmed in this view by the evidence given to us by Lord Carlisle, who said 'if you ask me whether [the advisory committee] could take on the task of advising Ministers, I think my answer must be yes'. The former Cabinet Secretary, Lord Armstrong, agreed. Among our own members are two members of the advisory committee who endorse that proposition.

We recommend that a system similar to the civil service business appointment rules should apply to Ministers. The system should operate on an advisory basis, and it should be administered by the existing Advisory Committee on Business Appointments.

32. Under the civil service system, permanent secretary grades (1 and 1A) are required to undergo an automatic three-month waiting period before taking up outside employment. We have heard no evidence in favour of abolishing that basic safeguard and have therefore considered whether this should also apply to Ministers. The automatic three months waiting period recognises the special position of permanent secretaries within the civil service and the breadth of their responsibilities. Similar considerations apply to Cabinet Ministers.

33. Under the civil service arrangements, two years from the date of leaving office is the maximum delay that can be applied and, except for

permanent secretaries, there is no automatic waiting period. Is a similar maximum waiting period for former Ministers sufficient to allay public criticism? On the face of it, it seems that it may not be. Ministers have been criticised for joining companies which they have privatised, or which have advised them on privatisations, after intervals well in excess of two years. We feel that this criticism, while understandable given the many other firms which former Ministers might have joined, is nevertheless based on a misunderstanding of the function of the rules. Any waiting period would be insufficient in a case of genuine corruption. Waiting periods are not punishments, but a means of maintaining public confidence. Neither do we feel that Ministers outside the Cabinet should be subject to automatic waiting periods. The circumstances of each case should determine the decisions of the advisory committee. That will help the new system attract the co-operation of those whose freedom of action it may impair.

We recommend that, in parallel with the civil service arrangements for permanent secretaries, an automatic waiting period of three months should apply to former Cabinet Ministers, but not to other Ministers or Whips. In cases where a further waiting period is recommended, the maximum waiting period should be set at two years from the date of leaving office.

34. We accept, however, that there may be rare situations which create such suspicion of impropriety that it would simply be better for the applicant not to proceed. In these circumstances, the advisory committee should be able to advise an applicant, whether a civil servant or a former Minister, that they feel that the application is not appropriate. If the applicant persisted, then a two-year waiting period would be imposed, and if the applicant then took the employment, the committee's comments on the wisdom of the application would become public in the normal way. In reality, we believe that the publication of the committee's advice, and the subsequent public scrutiny, would stop an unwise application in its tracks.

We recommend that the advisory committee should be able to advise an applicant, whether a civil servant or a former Minister, that they feel that the application is not appropriate, and to make public that advice if it is not taken.

35. No waiting period, of course, is free from anomaly. Under the civil service rules, civil servants can wait for two years and a day and take whatever employment they wish without the advisory committee being involved, although we have heard no evidence that this is done from im-

proper motives. We have had to strike a balance between the rights of individuals and the need to reassure the public. We believe that requiring Ministers to seek the advice of the Committee for two years after leaving office, and a maximum waiting period of the same length, achieves those aims. We expect that Ministers who are in doubt about the propriety of an appointment after the two years has expired will continue to bear in mind the injunction in QPM 'that they should naturally avoid any course which would reflect on their or the Government's reputation for integrity or the confidentiality of its proceedings'*. If they remain in doubt about a particular offer of employment, we believe that they should be able to seek the advice of the advisory committee, even after the expiry of the two year period.

36. Under the present system, the advisory committee, as its name suggests, merely puts recommendations to the Prime Minister of the day who may vary the conditions or waiting periods which the committee applies, although this happens rarely. We do not feel, for reasons which have been pointed out by a number of witnesses, that the ministerial system could work in precisely the same way. It might seem invidious, for example, for Ministers who have just been dismissed by the Prime Minister to have to submit their future employment plans to the same Prime Minister for consideration. On the other hand, to exclude the Prime Minister would deny Ministers any form of appeal.

We recommend that former Ministers, having received the advice of the advisory committee, should have the right of appeal to the Prime Minister of the day, who would be able to reduce any waiting period or relax any conditions if the appeal were well-founded.

37. If there were no appeal, then the Prime Minister would not be involved. We have considered whether a change of administration would make that appeal system unworkable, but we have confidence in the traditions of courteous relations between political opponents and see no reason to doubt that a Prime Minister of one party would deal fairly with appeals from the former Ministers of another.

38. As soon as a former Minister has taken up a job which the advisory committee has scrutinised, the committee should make public the advice it had given and its reasons. A summary of all cases dealt with that year should be subsequently published in an annual report. There would be no

---

* Questions of Procedure for Ministers, paragraph 105.

announcement if a Minister decided not to go ahead with an appointment after hearing the views of the advisory committee: that would be an unjustified intrusion into personal privacy.

We recommend that the system should be as open as possible, while protecting the personal privacy of Ministers.

39. Some concern has been expressed to us about the capacity of the present advisory committee and its secretariat to cope with the additional workload that would be generated by having to advise Ministers. In recent years the advisory committee has been asked to advise on between 34 and 48 cases per year, covering applications from Grade 1, 1A and 2 staff in the Home Civil Service and their equivalents in the diplomatic service and armed forces. The committee's secretariat has an internal target to put cases to the advisory committee within 5 days of receiving application forms from departments. If the applicant asks for a personal hearing in front of the committee, which happens in only a small number of cases, the secretary of the advisory committee told us that they are dealt with in three weeks. It is impossible to predict precisely what will happen if a ministerial system is introduced, but research carried out on our behalf* indicates that under normal circumstances the present advisory committee would be able to administer the new arrangements, although there might be consequences for the staffing of its secretariat. Maintaining the present rapid processing of cases will be important however, and in the special case of a general election leading to a change of government, there might well be a rush of applications.

We recommend that the Government should monitor the workload of the advisory committee under the new arrangements and put in place contingency arrangements for its staffing to be augmented to deal with the aftermath of any change of administration.

The Acceptance of Gifts and Hospitality

40. We have considered the rules on acceptance of gifts by Ministers set out in QPM (paragraphs 80–81) and are satisfied that they are sufficiently detailed. The rules on the acceptance of hospitality are necessarily less rigid, because of the difficulty of defining all possible circumstances. The principle set out in paragraph 126 of QPM is an important one:

---

* 'Ex-Ministers' Business Interests 1979–94', research carried out by the Labour Research Department.

> *'It is a well-established and recognised rule that no Minister or public servant should accept gifts, hospitality or services from anyone which would, or might appear to, place him or her under an obligation.'*

41. We have considered whether recent cases, in which Ministers have accepted hospitality or had their travel costs paid, indicate that this principle needs to be strengthened or clarified. We have concluded that additional detail is unnecessary. The rules are 'pretty clear' though Lord Younger, and Lord Armstrong felt that more detail would encourage a legalistic approach. We believe, however, that it is important that the public should be reassured that standards of propriety are being maintained.

We recommend that departments, as well as maintaining records of gifts, should maintain records of hospitality accepted by Ministers in their official capacity and should make these records available if asked to do so.

Ministers who accept hospitality on the basis of personal friendship, involving accommodation or holidays, or other significant cost, should be advised to record that they have done so if they think there is any possibility that the failure to do so might otherwise be misunderstood or misrepresented.

42. Such a record would supplement the declarations made by Ministers who are Members of the House of Commons in the Register of Members' Interests, which requires the declaration of gifts above £125 in value, and hospitality if above £160 in value.

The Civil Service

43. As Giles Radice MP said to us, 'it is a priceless gift that we have an impartial, non-corrupt civil service'. The civil service is well provided with codes of behaviour, with detailed rules on conduct and with generally accepted principles which have been in place since the mid-nineteenth century. From 1854 until the late 1960s the civil service developed greater uniformity and tighter central control. In the 1980s, that process was deliberately reversed, with the establishment of executive agencies and the delegation from the centre of many management responsibilities. The question of standards of conduct was not much considered when those changes were made: the need for efficiency and effectiveness in the delivery of services was given pre-eminent place.

44. The remit of this Committee does not extend to reviewing the merits of particular ways of managing the civil service. Our concern is strictly with any developments which might imperil long-standing rules of conduct and with how such threats might be averted without weakening the entirely proper drive towards better public sector management.

45. We believe that standards of behaviour in the civil service as a whole remain very high, and that cases of outright corruption and fraud are rare, although individual cases can be very serious. Nor have we received evidence that other important standards—political impartiality or the ideal of public service—are under systematic threat. We will, however, study with interest the conclusions reached by Sir Richard Scott in his inquiry into the export of defence equipment. If it appears that misconduct by civil servants was widespread or if the report raises general issues of propriety or impartiality, we may need to return to this subject in our future work.

46. Our task has been made much easier by two recent reports on the civil service. The Treasury and Civil Service Select Committee produced a perceptive and thorough analysis of many of the most pressing issues facing the civil service. The Government responded with a positive White Paper, 'Taking Forward Continuity and Change', reflecting the welcome degree of common ground that exists between the political parties about the future of the civil service*.

Core Values

47. In the White Paper, the Government restated and endorsed the core values of the civil service: 'integrity, political impartiality, objectivity, selection and promotion on merit and accountability through Ministers to Parliament'. We agree with the Government's view that 'with greater delegation and more movement in and out of the civil service, there is a need for even greater vigilance about standards throughout the civil service'. The Government lists four policies intended to help:

i) the establishment of a new senior civil service;

ii) a new handbook for agency chief executives;

iii) a new civil service code;

---

* Treasury and Civil Service Committee, Fifth Report, House of Commons 27, 1993–94, 'Taking Forward Continuity and Change', Cmnd 2748, 1995.

iv) an independent line of appeal for civil servants to the Civil Service Commissioners.

48. We welcome the establishment of a new senior civil service as a symbol of the importance of shared values throughout the whole civil service. We agree, however, with the view of some of our witnesses that caution should be exercised in the introduction of performance pay and appraisal arrangements for this group. Many, though not all, of the senior civil service will be in contact with Ministers and will handle sensitive policy matters. A perception that reward and promotion may depend in any way on commitment to Ministerial ideology inconsistent with the impartiality required of a civil servant would of course be wholly unacceptable.

We recommend that the new performance pay arrangements for the senior civil service should be structured so as not to undermine political impartiality.

49. A guide for Agency Chief Executives on core values and standards properly responds, in our view, to the pressures which may occur when traditional public sector values are applied in an organisation with a sharper commercial focus, such as some executive agencies. However, we note here that the issuing of guidance and codes is not the end of the matter. We return to this in paragraph 61 below.

The Code and Appeal System

50. Devising a clear and brief code for civil servants setting out the constitutional framework within which they work is entirely in keeping with the principles which we have recommended in this report and we welcome it. We hope that it will be a helpful element in sustaining civil service morale. Well-motivated and self-confident organisations find it much easier to maintain good standards of conduct among their staff.

51. In order for the appeal to the Civil Service Commissioners to work effectively, two changes to the proposed code would be helpful. The present draft paragraph 11 envisages an appeal being made by a civil servant who has been asked 'to act in a way which is illegal, improper, unethical, or in breach of constitutional convention, which may involve possible maladministration, or which is otherwise inconsistent with this code or raises a fundamental issue of conscience'.

We recommend that the draft civil service code should be revised to cover circumstances in which a civil servant, while not personally involved, is aware of wrongdoing or maladministration taking place.

Similarly, paragraph 7 of the draft should be made more general by deleting the words underlined:

> 'civil servants should endeavour to ensure the proper, effective and efficient use of public money <u>within their control</u>'.

52. We are disappointed by the Government's proposal that the Civil Service Commissioners should report to Parliament only those cases in which the Government has failed to heed their recommendation. There seems to be no pressing constitutional reason for this limitation on openness. If the Commissioners were to report to Parliament in all cases when an appeal has been upheld, it would then be open for the Government to respond in public. This system has the great advantage that there will be no barrier to the dissemination of best practice arising out of the Commissioners' recommendations. The Government has already accepted this principle in the case of the Parliamentary Commissioner for Administration and the Public Accounts Committee.

We recommend that the operation of the appeals system should be disseminated as openly as possible, and the Commissioners should report all successful appeals to Parliament.

53. The institution of an independent appeals system is a step forward. We remain concerned, however, that the minimal use made of the previous appeal mechanism to the Head of the Home Civil Service (only one appeal in eight years) may be replicated under the new system because of the requirement that all internal avenues of appeal must be exhausted before the Civil Service Commissioners become involved. As Lord Armstrong observed, 'I don't know that an appeal to the First Civil Service Commissioner is any less intimidating than an appeal to the Head of the Home Civil Service'. What we believe is needed is a parallel system allowing staff to raise concerns in confidence without necessarily having to take them through the management structure in the first instance. We believe that departments and agencies should nominate one or more officials entrusted with the duty of investigating staff concerns raised confidentially. Such a person must stand outside the line management structure of the complainant but should expect and receive the support of senior management when investigating alleged abuses. The limits of the person's powers of investigation should be

set out on the lines of those laid down for the Commissioners in the new civil service code (amended, as we propose, in paragraph 51 above).

We recommend that departments and agencies should nominate one or more officials entrusted with the duty of investigating staff concerns raised confidentially.

54. We recognise that this represents something of a novelty, although the use of confidential appeal systems and hotlines is not uncommon in the private sector. Structured in the way we suggest, however, such a system could be introduced within the framework of the constitutional conventions governing the work of civil servants and their relations with Ministers. We accept the Government's view that most issues can safely be resolved by the normal mechanisms within departments and agencies. We think, however, that the prevention of corruption and maladministration is hampered if an individual civil servant has to identify him or herself as a complainant before superiors who may have direct influence over his or her career. That has been found to be a powerful disincentive to 'whistleblowers' in other organisations. The independent charity, Public Concern at Work, has set out Good Practice Guidelines which recommend that employees are offered confidential routes to raise concerns*. Indeed, the result of failing to provide a confidential system for matters of conscience is, ironically, to encourage leaks, which are damaging to the cohesiveness of civil service bodies and weaken the relationship between Ministers and civil servants.

A Civil Service Act

55. The Government has begun a process of consultation on whether the civil service should no longer be regulated under the Prerogative but should be the subject of a narrowly drafted statute. We see merit in the idea of a statutorily based civil service, provided that a consensus can be reached between the parties as to the scope of the legislation.

We recommend that the new civil service code should be introduced with immediate effect, without waiting for legislation.

The code should not itself appear in primary legislation, which would make it difficult to amend in the light of changing circumstances. Instead, it should be contained in secondary legislation subject to the affirmative resolution of both Houses, ensuring that flexibility is joined with scrutiny.

* Public Concern at Work, First Annual Report (1994), page 12.

56. We acknowledge the force of the government's argument that any such legislation should not alter the constitutional basis for the civil service or confer on civil servants special rights over and above those of other employees.

Political Misconduct

57. From time to time there have been allegations, repeated by witnesses at our inquiry, that civil servants were being asked by Ministers to undertake duties which were not appropriate to their non-political status, such as writing constituency speeches or supplying MPs with pro-Government parliamentary questions. It has also been suggested that some civil servants have allowed themselves to become so publicly partisan and enthusiastic about Government policies that it would be difficult for them to retain the confidence of any incoming administration of a different political colour. No evidence was offered to us that these are other than isolated cases. The existing guidance offered both to Ministers and civil servants has always been clear on the point that there is a boundary beyond which a civil servant should not be asked, or volunteer, to go. We have recommended as an additional safeguard (paragraph 16 (vi) above) that guidance for Ministers should spell this out more clearly.

Conduct in the Civil Service

58. We turn now to the detailed arrangements governing conduct in the civil service. Under the Civil Service Management Code (CSMC), departments and agencies are given delegated powers to introduce regulations on conduct, so long as they reflect the principles and rules set out in CSMC. The principles in CSMC cover, among other things, the need for civil servants to be seen to be honest and impartial in the discharge of their duties. In particular, civil servants must not misuse official information; must not do anything which compromises their political impartiality; and must not use their official position to further their own interests. CSMC also contains the rules on business appointments and on political activity.

59. The detailed departmental and agency regulations which derive from these principles are held to form part of a civil servant's contract of employment, and breaches can be the subject of disciplinary action. The process of delegation creates the possibility that, over time, detailed rules on conduct might diverge, depending on the circumstances of the department or agency making them. The Cabinet Office has therefore recently carried out a survey and discussion of the operation of these rules, intended to promote best practice.

We recommend that the Cabinet Office should continue to survey and disseminate best practice on maintaining standards of conduct to ensure that basic principles of conduct are being properly observed.

60. Central statistics on disciplinary cases in the civil service are no longer collected. We therefore carried out a survey of our own, to which 82 departments and agencies responded, covering disciplinary cases between 1989 and 1994. The results did not demonstrate any significant increase in any category of disciplinary case over the period. We are however concerned to note that comparatively few departments or agencies felt it worthwhile to draw the attention of their staff to the rules on conduct, other than by issuing an annual circular or office notice. Even fewer bodies had attempted to survey their staff to determine what awareness existed of their codes and what understanding there was of the principles underlying them.

61. We find this regrettable. Commercial organisations which have gone through what is called 'de-layering' have recognised that increased management responsibility at lower levels may confront junior staff with ethical issues of which they have had no previous experience. They may need support which is no longer provided by the line management hierarchy. The civil service is increasingly in the same position and at the same time is being asked to become more flexible and entrepreneurial in its provision of services.

We recommend that there should be regular surveys in departments and agencies of the knowledge and understanding staff have of ethical standards which apply to them; and that where such surveys indicate problem areas, guidance should be reinforced and disseminated appropriately, particularly by way of additional training.

The Business Appointment Rules

62. In paragraph 28 above, we summarised the salient features of the business appointment rules. We suggested how they might be applied to Ministers. We now turn to their operation in respect of civil servants. About 1,000 applications a year are examined by the advisory committee, the Cabinet Office, or departments. The advisory committee deals with applications made by civil servants in Grades 1 and 2. The Cabinet Office deals with all cases at grade 3, or at more junior grades where the applicant has had significant dealings with the prospective employer and conditions are likely to be required. The remainder are handled by departments. Of the 1,000, about 300 are handled centrally, and waiting periods or conditions

are recommended for some 30% of these. The comparable figure for waiting periods or conditions for the 700 or so cases handled in departments is about 20%.

63. The Treasury and Civil Service Select Committee has examined the operation of the business appointment rules in detail on a number of occasions, most recently in 1991*. It is their view that on the whole the system works well and achieves the appropriate balance between reassuring the public and permitting civil servants (and other Crown servants) to move freely into the private sector where there is no perception of impropriety. Sir Robin Butler described the system to us as offering 'a reasonable balance'.

64. We have recommended for Ministers that a maximum two-year restraint on taking up outside appointments is normally adequate. We believe that the same applies to the civil service. We have however recommended in paragraph 34 above that the advisory committee should have the power to recommend to applicants—whether Ministers or civil servants—that they should not proceed with an unwise application.

65. At present, applications under the business appointments system remain confidential. We have recommended in the case of Ministers that the system should become open (except in the case of applications which are not followed up) and that the advisory committee should give reasons for its decisions. The Government has consistently argued in the past that openness would not be appropriate for the present system and said in written evidence to this Committee that 'if it was known that details of all applications and the decisions made on them were routinely made public, it is likely that employers would be inhibited from opening discussions with those affected and employees would be reluctant to make applications'.

66. We agree that there is no reason based on public confidence why speculative applications made by civil servants should be made public. We do not, however, accept that the disclosure of decisions in individual cases is wrong in principle once the appointment has been taken up. The system is designed to maintain public confidence in the conduct of individual public servants. It is contradictory to keep details secret and to expect the public to take on trust the application of the rules. We were reinforced in that view by our witnesses Elizabeth Symons, Lord Armstrong, and Lord Carlisle, none of whom saw any objection to openness about applications after the employment has been taken up. If a civil service union leader, the former head

---

* Fourth Report 1990–91, 'The Acceptance of Outside Appointments by Crown Servants'.

of the civil service, and the chairman of the advisory committee are of one mind, we find their testimony very persuasive.

We recommend that the Advisory Committee on Business Appointments should, when an appointment has been taken up, give the reasons for its decision in that particular case.

It would be unnecessarily time-consuming for cases at lower grades routinely to be published in that way. However, departments and agencies (and the Cabinet Office, for centrally determined applications) should be ready to give such information on demand.

67. In order to comply with our recommendation, those who administer the system will need to be in a position to know whether the applicant has taken up a post. Applicants to the advisory committee should therefore be asked to notify it when they take up an appointment which has been the subject of an application.

68. It is a striking weakness of the existing system that there is at present no monitoring of its effectiveness. Although the rules are considered binding on all civil servants, no attempt is made to track, even on a sample basis, conformity with decisions taken by departments, by the Cabinet Office, or by the advisory committee. We have been made aware during our work of cases of failure to apply under the rules although the proposed employment fell well within their scope. From time to time departments become aware by chance of failures to apply and retrospective applications may then be made. Although we accept that in the vast majority of cases the rules are complied with and the decisions which flow from it are observed, it is damaging to public confidence in the system for this state of affairs to continue. It would however be unrealistic and unjustified to expect all movements out of the civil service to be monitored.

We recommend that the operation, observance and objectives of the civil service business appointment rules should be reviewed.

This would be a suitable subject for an inter-departmental efficiency scrutiny team, which can build on the work that is currently being done on the operation of the rules in the light of the changing pattern of civil service employment. Thereafter, occasional sampling of compliance with the rules should be undertaken.

69. One group of civil servants remain entirely outside the scope of the existing rules: special advisers. Special advisers are civil servants but, like Ministers, may lose their posts with little or no warning. Because in theory they are not permitted to have access to details of individual companies or to become involved in the placing of contracts or other work that requires an application under the rules, they have been exempted. However, the rules are not limited to these circumstances. Applications have to be made 'to avoid the risk that a particular firm might gain an improper advantage over its competitors by employing someone who, in the course of their official duties, has had access ... to information relating to proposed developments in Government policy which may affect that firm or its competitors'*.

70. Special advisers probably have a better knowledge of proposed developments in Government policy than most other civil servants in their departments, and it is not easy to see why they should be exempt from the rules. If Ministers are brought within the system, as we recommend, then the anomaly is even more obvious.

We recommend that special advisers should be subject to the business appointment rules.

The Acceptance of Gifts and Hospitality

71. We are satisfied that the rules relating to the acceptance of gifts by officials are sufficiently strict and rather tighter than those which apply to Ministers. In most departments, officials are not allowed to accept more than trivial gifts, while Ministers can accept gifts up to a current value of £125 so long as they are declared. Although there might be a logical case made for relaxing the civil service rules in respect of officials who are not involved in the award of contracts, on balance we consider that the present strict rules on gifts should continue.

72. As for hospitality, for officials generally we see advantages in their continuing to be free to accept invitations to working lunches and dinners, and for those with a representational role to attend other events. We understand that in most departments either a central or local record is kept of such invitations and acceptances, and it is specified that management must be consulted about hospitality which is in any way disproportionate, frequently repeated, or otherwise unusual.

---

* Civil Service Management Code 4.3 Annex A, paragraph 3(b).

We recommend that a central or local record of invitations and offers of hospitality accepted is kept in all departments and agencies. There should be clear rules specifying the circumstances in which staff should seek management advice about the advisability of accepting invitations and offers of hospitality.

Appendix 2 Rebuilding Trust

Extracts from the Report of the sub-committee on Bill C-43 of the Standing Committee On Industry (Canada)

Pages vii, 3–7, 9–12, 13–19, 28–34, 45–53

ORDER OF REFERENCE

Extract from the Minutes of Proceedings and Evidence of the Standing Committee on Industry of Wednesday, June 15, 1994:

On motion of David Iftody, it was agreed,—That without anticipating a decision of the House, if the Lobbyists Registration legislation is referred to the Committee, that pursuant to Standing Order 108 (1), a Sub-Committee of the Standing Committee on Industry be established, to be composed of Paul Zed as Chair, and five other Members after the usual consultations with the Whips and the Coordinator of the different parties, as the remaining members to study the Lobbyists Registration legislation and to report thereon to the Committee; that on presentation of the said report it be deemed adopted; and that the Chairman of the Committee present it to the House on behalf of the Committee.

On motion of David Iftody, it was agreed,—That the Sub-Committee be empowered, except when the House otherwise orders, to send for persons, papers and records, to sit while the House is sitting, to sit during periods when the House stands adjourned, to print from day to day such papers and evidence as may be ordered by it and to authorize the Chair to hold meetings to receive evidence when a quorum is not present and to authorize the printing thereof.

On motion of David Iftody, it was agreed,—That a Research Officer be provided to the Sub-Committee, by the Library of Parliament.

On motion of David Iftody, it was agreed,—That when the Chair of the Sub-Committee is unable to act in that capacity at or during a meeting of the Sub-Committee, he shall designate a member of the Sub-Committee to act as Chair at or during the said meeting.

Extract from the Minutes of Proceedings and Evidence of the Standing Committee on Industry of Tuesday, November 15, 1994:

Paul Zed moved,—That in regard to its Order of reference of Wednesday, June 15, 1994, and to the subject-matter thereof, for Sub-Committee on Bill C-43, An Act to amend the Lobbyists Registration Act and to make related amendments to other Acts, be deemed to have the same powers as those granted to the Standing Committee pursuant to Standing Order 108(2), and be authorized to report on the subject-matter in the same manner as before.

After debate thereon, the question being put on the motion, it was agreed to.

ATTEST

J.M. Robert Normand
Clerk of the Sub-Committee

CHAPTER I – LOBBYING AND THE DEVELOPMENT OF A REGISTRATION SYSTEM

The Evolution of Lobbying in Canada

Before discussing our study of Bill C-43 and setting forth the amendments we are making to this Bill, we believe it is first worthwhile to establish the context within which our review took place. In doing so, we think that readers will share the appreciation we have developed for the complexity of contemporary lobbying for the work done in this area by others before us.

Lobbying has long been an integral part of the democratic life of our society. Indeed, lobbying has so long been deeply imbedded in the Canadian political landscape, that until recently its presence has largely escaped notice. In the past, this activity was conducted discretely by a small number of well-placed individuals who could exert influence on government away from public view. The scope of government was restrained, and the number of decision makers accordingly few. Thus lobbying had little public prominence and its impact was felt by few. Lobbying was perceived by most Canadians as something in which their neighbours to the South engaged and the notion that this form of political activity did not exist in this country became a part of our political mythology.[1]

During and after the Second World War, the nature of government began to change radically and lobbying changed with it. For reasons linked to the war, and societal and economic changes, the Canadian federal government became directly involved in a widening circle of activities previously considered the exclusive domain of private interests. As the boundaries between what was considered private and public were either broken down or blurred, the government apparatus burgeoned. Citizens began to discover that there was very little touching their daily lives that was not affected by government; the need to know what government was up to and have to have some active say in influencing its decisions became more acute than ever.

---

[1] A. Paul Pross, "The Rise of the Lobbying Issue in Canada: 'The Business Card Bill'", in Grant Jordan, editor, *The Commercial Lobbyists: Politics for Profit in Britain*, Aberdeen University Press, 1991, p. 76.

Interactions between citizens and the state underwent a profound change, and so did lobbying. What was once an activity involving a small circle of practitioners began to attract greater numbers. These individuals possessed specialized knowledge in fields as diverse as law, economics, and political science. Often they were joined by former public servants who had developed an intimate understanding of government and could offer expert guidance through an increasingly complex maze of state regulations and institutions. New methods were added to the mix of personal contacts and persuasive abilities traditionally relied upon by lobbyists to exert influence on government. Contemporary lobbyists make full use of advanced polling techniques, media advertising, in-depth research, and detailed policy analysis.

Lobbying's enhanced sophistication and a perceived need to engage lobbyists to deal with government led to the rapid growth of the profession. As one of our witnesses, Dr. John Chenier, publisher of the *Lobby Monitor*, told us, "government relations is a growing business in Canada. It grows every year, even through the recession, even through the tough times" (19:28). This growth has been accompanied by an increasing suspicion that lobbying was beginning to exercise disproportionate influence over public policy, threatening to erode more traditional democratic forms of representation.

Members of Parliament and the Registration of Paid Lobbyists

Members of Parliament were among the first to understand the full implications of lobbying's growing influence, and to see the need for a legislative response. While lobbying's fundamental legitimacy was never in question, parliamentarians were concerned about its secretive nature: public policy, they reasoned, should be publicly conducted. MPs had to ensure that lobbying was subjected to greater public scrutiny but without damage as a legitimate form of expression in a democratic society. The solutions they identified have formed the basis for Canada's current system of lobbyists' registration.

Beginning in 1969—more than two decades ago—backbench Members of Parliament began to introduce a series of private members' bills on lobbying. These 20 bills, proposed at various times by Members from all parties, had two principal features in common: they called for the registration of paid lobbyists and for some form of disclosure regarding their activities. The words of one of the leading proponents of a registration scheme, the Hon. Walter Baker, express the goal of all these proposals. Speaking to his colleagues in the House of Commons, he argued that the purpose of registration was to ensure that lobbying, as much as possible, is conducted in the open so that people can see who is trying to influence what, and if necessary respond. Where lobbying is done with the knowledge of everyone concerned, there is a better chance that it will be done openly and that improper practices will have a smaller chance of survival or success.[2]

As Professor Paul Pross, who appeared as a witness before our Committee, points out, from the time the first Private Member's bill was tabled until 1985 when the notion was finally endorsed by government, "the idea of regulating lobbyists through registration was very much a private members' scheme."[3] Thus, the importance of the contribution made by Members of Parliament cannot be underestimated. As Dr. Pross recognized,

> The private member's debates helped to define the major issues surrounding the lobbying question and articulated an approach to the regulation of lobbyists that influenced subsequent action.[4]

The Creation of a Registration System

In September 1985, in the context of a statement on public sector ethics, it was announced that the government intended to establish a registration system for lobbyists. Following the announcement, a discussion paper on registration was released by the then Department of Consumer and Corporate Affairs. Among other things, this discussion paper proposed four guiding principles that have since provided the foundation for the registration system. These principles consisted of:

> Openness: There should be a publicly available record of paid lobbyists, their clients and any other additional information desirable to "... demonstrate the government's commitment to transparency and integrity in its relations with the public."[5]

> Clarity: Registration requirements should be clear, concise, and leave no doubt as to who should register and who should not.

> Access to Government: Registration requirements should not hinder access to public office holders.

---

[2] House of Commons, *Debates*, 28 January 1977, p. 2516.
[3] Pross (1991), p. 79.
[4] *Ibid.*, p. 81.
[5] Canada, Department of Consumer and Corporate Affairs, *Lobbying and the Registration of Paid Lobbyists*, Ottawa, 1985, p. 4.

Administrative Simplicity: Administrative requirements should be kept to a minimum and should not be so onerous as to discourage registration. Creation of a large bureaucracy to administer the registration system should be avoided.

The discussion paper was referred to the House of Commons Standing Committee on Election, Privileges and Procedure (Cooper Committee) which reported its endorsement of registration for paid lobbyists at the end of January 1987. Several months afterward, the government tabled Bill C-82 to enact the *Lobbyists Registration Act*.

The main features of the proposal included the division of lobbyists into two categories or tiers, each with its own set of registration and information disclosure requirements. Tier I (professional lobbyists) consisted of those who work for clients on a fee basis. This group would be required to register each undertaking that involved direct contact with government or arranging a meeting with an office holder. Disclosure of certain information regarding the nature of the undertaking, such as its proposed subject-matter and information on the lobbyist's client would also be required. A second category of lobbyists (Tier II) was designated for those employed by persons or organizations to communicate with public office holders with the aim of influencing government. Lobbyists in this latter category would have to disclose only their names and the name and address of the person or organization that employed them.

Only minor changes were made to the legislation as it passed through committee stages in the Senate and the House of Commons. In September 1988 it was given Royal Assent and came into force on 30 September 1989.

Despite valid criticisms of the existing *Lobbyists Registration Act*, its importance as a first step cannot be denied. As another of our witnesses, Professor Michael Atkinson, commented:

> Before 1988, before there was any legislation at all, it might have been plausibly inferred that what went on behind closed doors between lobbyists and politicians and bureaucrats was really no one else's business, ... The introduction of the disclosure provisions in 1988, even disclosure provisions that a lot of people regard as toothless, have had the symbolic affect of introducing the citizen into the process. The citizen's interest is in the room somewhere, even if the citizen isn't there and even if the citizen cannot reasonably participate (14:8).

Previous Parliamentary Review of the Lobbyists Registration Act

One of the provisions in the *Lobbyists Registration Act* called for its review by a committee of the House of Commons three years after coming into force. Accordingly, the Act was referred for review to the Standing Committee on Consumer and Corporate Affairs and Government Operations (Holtmann Committee) in November 1992.

Most witnesses before the Holtmann Committee agreed that the LRA was a step in the right direction; many, however, argued that its provisions were insufficient. In particular, criticism was directed at the dual registration and disclosure regimes as failing to provide the desired degree of transparency with respect to paid lobbying activities.

The Holtmann Committee generally agreed with these observations and issued a unanimous report in June 1993 (*A Blueprint for Transparency*) in which it called for enhanced registration and disclosure requirements for all paid lobbyists. In particular, committee members recommended that lobbyists disclose more detail on the subject-matter of their lobbying activities, including the name of the bills, legislation, amendments to current Acts, grants, contributions, regulations, policies, programs, contracts and legislative proposals they were trying to influence. In addition, the Committee determined that lobbyists should name the government department, parliamentary office, or agency of government with which they had communicated and the kinds of activities in which they engage when seeking to influence public policy. Other recommendations called for registration of professionally organized grass roots lobbying efforts that exceeded a specified expenditure threshold and a strengthening of the Act's administrative provisions. To deal with its concerns regarding ethical standards in the lobbying industry, the Committee urged lobbyists to establish a professional association with a code of ethics for its members.

Before government could issue a formal response to the Holtmann Committee's recommendations, Parliament dissolved for a general election. The report was timely, however, in that it coincided with rising levels of public concern over the state of public sector ethics. Most major political parties participating in the 1993 general election sensed this concern and committed themselves to implementing elements of the Holtmann Report should they be elected to form a government.

The Liberal Government, elected in October 1993, outlined its approach to enhancing the registration system for lobbyists in the chapter on governing with integrity in its campaign document, *Creating Opportunity: The Liberal Plan for Canada*. The Party proposed to implement the Holtmann Report and promised that it would create the position of Ethics Counsellor to develop a Code of Conduct for Lobbyists. The Ethics Counsellor would monitor compliance with the Code and would have "the power both to require reporting of lobbying fees in relation to government procurement contracts and to disclose publicly any contract, fee, or activity" that contravened the Code.[6] The new government subsequently acted on its commitments, tabling amendments to the *Lobbyists Registration Act* on 16 June 1994. In keeping with another electoral commitment, a decision was made to refer the Bill (*Bill C-43, An Act to Amend the Lobbyists Registration Act*) to a committee of the House immediately following first reading. In so doing, the government accorded recognition to the important role played by Members of Parliament in laying the foundations for the present lobbyists' registration system.

Concluding Comments

As a Committee and as individual Members of Parliament, we have approached our review of this Bill with awareness of both the goals registration is meant to achieve and the principles that the registration system is meant to respect. These goals and principles were first identified by past Members of Parliament and have not changed. We have also measured Bill C-43's amendments against the recommendations made by previous parliamentary committees.

Finally, we have undertaken our review with a deep sense of appreciation for the work and unwavering commitment of our predecessors. It is our hope that our own deliberations and refinements to this important piece of legislation honour their effort and help achieve the goals we hold in common.

---

[6] Liberal Party of Canada, *Creating Opportunity: The Liberal Plan for Canada*, 1993, p. 95.

CHAPTER II – THE FUNDAMENTALS

Bill C-43 would make two major changes to the *Lobbyists Registration Act*, both intended to enhance the achievement of its fundamental purpose — helping to restore trust in government. First, the Bill would substantially strengthen the disclosure requirements of the Act, to make more information about lobbyists and what they do available to Canadians. Second, it would provide for the creation and implementation of a code of ethics for lobbyists, which would help to ensure high standards of behaviour across the industry.

In this section, we set out our interpretation of the principles that underlie this legislation. This provides a basis for consistency in the examination of the Bill undertaken in following sections, and for the changes we are proposing.

Principles of Disclosure

The Preamble of the current LRA reflects four basic principles: (1) the importance of open access to government; (2) the legitimacy of lobbying; (3) the need for public awareness of the various influences upon government; and (4) that the requirements of a registration process for lobbyists should not impede access to government.

Bill C-43 would not amend these principles. Nor, on the basis of what we have heard from our witnesses, do we think they need to be changed. Properly balanced, they can guide us in enhancing the central objective of Bill C-43: the restoration of public trust in government.

The first principle — the importance of free and open access to government in a democratic society — is self-evident. The fourth principle makes it clear that lobbyists must be included in a commitment to accessible government. It also is self-evident, when understood as a requirement that access by lobbyists should not be impeded more than is made necessary by the other principles. The key issue, to which we return below, is what these principles mean in practice.

The second principle, the legitimacy of lobbying as a part of the democratic process of accessing government, may not be self-evident but it is hard to deny on reflection. First, the right of corporations or groups to engage specialists to help them understand and communicate with government is one dimension of the principle of free and open access. Second, modern government works in partnership with the whole range of organizations in society; without a two-way flow of information and explanation, decisions would be less well-informed and the public interest could be jeopardized. Most lobbying enhances this exchange of information and, in our view, most Canadians have no objection to this.

The need for public awareness of lobbying is the result of its importance. The business of providing specialized representation to corporations (either through hired consultants or employees), along with the full-time representation of groups and associations before the federal government, employs literally thousands of people and is the source of pervasive influence on the actions of the government. Ordinary Canadians need to know about this influence. Only when there is public knowledge of who is influencing whom and on whose behalf can the effect of organized interests on government be properly balanced in the interest of the unorganized public. Ensuring this balance is a vital part of our job as Members of Parliament; without it we cannot have a healthy democracy.

Seeking a Balance

The need to ensure a balance, within our political system, between the influence of those who can afford specialized assistance and the influence of other Canadians is a central challenge in applying the principles of the LRA. As we were reminded by Professor Atkinson, of McMaster University, equality of access to government is one element of free and open access. There is only so much access available: if it is monopolized by those with the financial and organizational means to do so, it will be denied to others. A system which permits this to happen does not achieve real openness of government, and does not earn the trust of the public.

We therefore reject the view, expressed by a number of our witnesses, that the public's need to know (and the need for lobbyists to invest time and money in disclosing information) is necessarily opposed to the principle of free and open access to government. In our view, the requirements which Bill C-43 would establish for lobbyists are, instead, a necessary part of preserving the accessibility of government to all Canadians. Here, as elsewhere in a democratic society, there must be a balance between the freedom of particular interests, and the freedom of other citizens.

Where disclosure of information by lobbyists is needed to achieve this balance, the fact that providing it may present an inconvenience to lobbyists, or even discourage their activity, is not a valid objection. The only valid objection would be that the information is not genuinely needed.

In examining the various disclosure proposals in Bill C-43, or placed before us by witnesses, we have therefore continually relied upon this basic test: is the information being requested from lobbyists genuinely needed to satisfy Canadians that lobbyists' activity is compatible with the public interests, and to help parliamentarians counterbalance the efforts of individual lobbyists with efforts on behalf of ordinary Canadians?

In general, this approach leads us to endorse the new disclosure requirements set out in Bill C-43, and to add some further requirements which we believe are necessary if the Bill is to achieve its fundamental objective. Some have challenged us to demonstrate any public desire for more information about lobbying; we can only respond that the current LRA has not significantly dispelled apprehensions among Canadians about the role of lobbyists in the political process. Like the members of our predecessor committee in the last Parliament, whose unanimous recommendations provided an important basis for Bill C-43, we believe that making more information about lobbying available is part of the solution. More information is needed, especially from corporation and association lobbyists, from whom the current Act requires little more than what is provided on a business card.

Keeping Bill C-43 in Perspective

The question of genuine need that we apply to the various disclosure options considered in this report challenges us to make difficult judgements. As we have found in our discussions with witnesses and among ourselves, there is plenty of room for sincere disagreement about some of the answers.

In making these judgements, we have found it helpful to remember that Bill C-43 is by no means the only initiative being launched for the purpose of restoring trust in government. At the time Bill C-43 was placed before the House, the government released a strengthened *Conflict of Interest and Post-Employment Code for Public Office Holders* which, among other things, requires senior officials to make decisions on the merits of each case and in the public interest, and to refrain from giving preferential treatment to any person or group because of the person hired to represent their concerns. As well, an Ethics Counsellor position was created for the purpose of administering this Code, advising public officials and performing new functions created by Bill C-43 (discussed below). It was indicated, furthermore, that Parliament would be asked to develop a formalized code of conduct for MPs and Senators. Finally, policies governing contracts were altered so as to prohibit suppliers from engaging lobbyists on a contingency fee basis to help them obtain contracts.

In considering the issues addressed in this report, we have attempted to ensure that Bill C-43 and our amendments would not duplicate other initiatives. The role of a strengthened LRA is to supplement and complement changes which, in our view, are already having beneficial effects on the way in which Canadians view their government. Our approach recognizes that lobbying is not the only source of public mistrust in government, and that it is necessary to keep the issue of lobbying in perspective.

We believe, in addition, that this approach minimizes a danger identified by Mr. Norm Stewart, of the Ford Motor Company of Canada (12:29): the possibility that our work would only generate new expectations and that four years from now a future parliamentary committee would be busily engaged in adding still more disclosure requirements to the LRA. This danger is created, in our view, by a tendency apparent in many of the submissions we received to take the "transparency" of the lobbying process as the ultimate objective of this legislation. Once "transparency" is adopted as an objective, attention naturally focuses on things we do not yet know about lobbying and, by an entirely logical progression, expectations about what should be disclosed take flight.

In our approach, the transparency of lobbying is not an ultimate objective. Rather, it is recognized as a means to the restoration of public trust in government, having value only as it serves that end. We believe the detailed proposals provided below meet the requirements of this approach. We also invite Canadians to adopt this approach in weighing the merits of Bill C-43.

Enhancing Ethics

Bill C-43 moves well beyond the recommendations of the Holtmann Committee in providing for the appointment of an Ethics Counsellor, charged with (in addition to duties mentioned above) developing a code of ethics for lobbyists, and authorized to investigate failures to comply with this code and report them directly to Parliament.

This proposal is an extremely important component of Bill C-43. Indeed, one of our consultant lobbyists — SAMCI (Susan A. Murray Consultants

Inc.) — described it as "the most important most progressive new change to the LRA" (brief, p. 6).

While we have some detailed recommendations concerning this proposal, it is appropriate here to consider the underlying issue of principle it raises: should government be in the business of supervising the ethics of lobbyists at all? There are two arguments which we believe support an affirmative answer to this question.

First of all, the ethics proposals forge the link between the information disclosure requirements in the Bill and the objective of improving public trust. Unless we can be sure that lobbyists are adhering to acceptable ethical standards, the disclosure of information about their activity need not increase public trust in government. If disclosure were to reveal ethically dubious behaviour it would, on the contrary, simply fuel suspicion and distrust.

The Code of Conduct will provide lobbyists with the clarified standards which they need in order to ensure that heightened information disclosure will have a positive effect on public trust in government. These standards also provide members of the interested public with a basis for evaluating the information produced by the new disclosure requirements.

None of our witnesses denied the need for ethical standards which, after all, are in the long term interests of the lobbying industry itself, aside from any considerations of trust in government. A number of witnesses argued, however, that standards already in use, such as the Code of Conduct of the Canadian Society of Association Executives (CSAE), are sufficient for the purpose, removing the need for intervention by government.

This brings us to our second point. The industry as a whole has not developed a code (or codes) of ethics that we believe satisfies public concerns about lobbyists' influence on government, even though these concerns have been evident at least since the mid-eighties. Indeed, the category of consultant lobbyists, which is probably the focus of public concern, has no code at all, although we are advised that efforts to develop one are under way within the recently established association, the Government Relations Institute of Canada (GRIC), and some individual firms such as the Ottawa-based SAMCI supplied us with corporate codes which provide a clear basis for conduct of a high standard. Furthermore, the CSAE code, which applies to participating association lobbyists, only goes part of the way towards fully addressing the need for ethical standards. While it sets out standards which are commendable as part of the business culture of lobbying, it remains a voluntary code without a defined enforcement mechanism or record of enforcement, despite having been in effect for some 20 years.

In our view, government is justified in filling the gap left by lobbyists in the development of industry-wide codes because of the proximity of lobbying activity to the political process. Lobbying behaviour that does not meet prevailing ethical standards reflects on the lobbyist engaging in it, and on the industry as a whole. It also casts a pall over the broader political process, and reducing the level of trust Canadians can place in their governments. This has a corrosive effect on the health of our democracy, and creates a corresponding public interest in its correction.

Taken together these considerations supply a strong affirmative answer to our basic 'is the information genuinely needed?' question when we apply it to the new Ethics Counsellor position and proposed Code of Conduct for Lobbyists. Clear standards and credible enforcement are important. Without them, we have serious doubts about the impact of increased disclosure, taken by itself, on public trust in government.

CHAPTER III – WHO SHOULD BE COVERED BY THE ACT?

The LRA currently requires registration by any person who, for payment, attempts to influence the Government of Canada on behalf of a range of specified organizations or individuals. While Bill C-43 substantially retains this definition, it would close a significant loophole, and witnesses have suggested to us that there are others which should also be closed.

Coalitions

Bill C-43 would address an important gap in existing legislation by adding coalitions to the list of organizations on behalf of which lobbying must be registered. This reflects the recognition, shared by our predecessor committee in the previous Parliament, that coalitions of business and interest groups have become an important means of coordinating attempts to influence government. Our hearings are consistent with this recognition as well. None of our witnesses objected in principle to the requirement that coalition lobbying be disclosed and several, unaware that Bill C-43 incorporates such a requirement, specifically called for it. We therefore endorse:

The provisions of Bill C-43 relating to coalitions.

These provisions include the addition of "coalitions" to the list of groups enumerated in the definition of "organization" at 1(1) of the Act. This provides the basis for requirements that lobbyists register who employs them (in the case of lobbyists employed by coalitions), or on whose behalf they are working. We therefore endorse:

5(2)(*e*) of Bill C-43, which would require disclosure of the membership of a coalition for which a consultant lobbyist is working.

Grass Roots Lobbying Campaigns

In the widest sense, lobbying consists of actions whose central objective is to influence the decisions of government; these actions may be either direct or indirect. As currently worded, the LRA does not require the registration of indirect lobbying efforts only those efforts that involve direct communication with office holders. Thus, an important form of lobbying — grass roots lobbying — is not an activity that would require registration.

Grass roots lobbying is intended to suggest to government the impression that there is a significant community of interest that either advocates or opposes a particular policy. In order to communicate this message, grass roots lobbies typically rely on mass letter writing and fax campaigns, phone calls to office holders, media advertising, and public demonstrations. The organization of a grass roots lobbying campaign often requires considerable skill, effort, and financial resources.

In most instances, expressions of grass roots preferences regarding policy choices are genuine, a constitutional right, and useful to government. Citizens who feel strongly about certain issues organize to convey their feelings to government. Unlike other kinds of lobbying, these efforts are clearly public. Like other forms of lobbying, however, grass roots campaigns can provide valuable information for office holders as they examine various options during the decision-making process. In summary, grass roots lobbying is an important element in the democratic life of this country and is worthy of encouragement. Perhaps this is why the current Act makes no reference to it.

There are good reasons however why grass roots lobbying should be subject to some degree of disclosure. It is one of the most powerful means available for transmitting policy preferences to office holders, not only because it provides evidence of public support or opposition to certain policies, but also because it is an inherently legitimate exercise in a democratic society. Thus, grass roots lobbying campaigns are an attractive instrument for influencing government policy and may be a preferred way for an individual or group to persuade government to adopt or reject certain courses of action. Indeed, the fact that grass roots lobbying is not addressed by the current Act, may make it additionally attractive. The Committee was told by a witness that grass roots lobbying is the most rapidly growing form of lobbying in Canada.

Very little is known about grass roots lobbying. As Professor Ian Lee pointed out, "what is not public is the orchestration, organization, planning and financing of a grass roots campaign" (13:19). Yet Bill C-43 does not propose to close this gap in the legislation. As a consequence, the Committee believes that the major objective of the Act — the promotion of transparency surrounding lobbying efforts — cannot be achieved fully. Indeed some may be attracted to engage in this form of lobbying in order to circumvent the need to register; thus the goal of transparency may even be defeated.

Some argue that grass roots lobbying is aimed at the general public, not at government. As such, they point out, this form of lobbying involves communication between individuals: an attempt to register grass roots lobbying would infringe on the rights of citizens and would lead to a challenge under the *Canadian Charter of Rights and Freedoms*. The Committee understands fully the basic premise underlying this assertion; taken literally, grass roots lobbying implies an effort to organize people around a particular issue. Thus the initial communication that takes place occurs between individuals and not between individuals and government. However, we also accept the view of one of our witnesses who stated that "the entire and sole purpose of a grass roots campaign is to influence government" (13:19). We note, as well, that paid lobbyists often organize grass roots lobbying in order to lend additional weight to their other lobbying efforts.

Thus, the challenge to us as a Committee was to suggest a means by which fuller transparency regarding grass roots lobbying campaigns organized by paid lobbyists could be achieved without infringing on the rights of average Canadians. After careful and lengthy consideration, we believe that we have found a solution. Bill C-43 proposes to amend to the LRA is to require paid lobbyists to disclose the techniques they use when they communicate with office holders. Given that generating a grass roots campaign is a method that paid lobbyists use in conjunction with other efforts in order to convey a message to office holders, we propose that this activity be treated as a communication technique. This should achieve the desired level of disclosure with respect to professionally organized grass roots lobbying without interfering with the grass roots activities of citizens. This conclusion is reflected in our recommendation on communications techniques.

Volunteer Lobbying

A number of our witnesses argued that lobbying activity by volunteers can be a significant element within paid lobbying initiatives, and that the failure of existing legislation to capture this should be remedied. In the words of one witness:

> Does it (the LRA) only require information about those who are paid to lobby either as an employee or on a fee-for-service basis? Or, is the *Lobbyists Registration Act* supposed to help Canadians understand which interest groups are

making how much effort to influence what program policy, grant, contract, amendment or regulation?... (Is an) extensive effort by an unpaid volunteer ... inherently benign and thus requires no disclosure? (Stanbury, brief, p. 19).

A number of our association witnesses confirmed that volunteers play an important role in their lobbying efforts. The Canadian Dental Association, for example, estimated that some 80% of Association lobbying is carried out by volunteers. While witnesses did not oppose a registration requirement for volunteers, this is likely because Bill C-43 does not propose one. Had it done so, we expect that witnesses who pointed with pride to their "volunteer-driven" organizations would have expressed strong objections on the grounds of additional administrative burden.

On balance, we do not think that registration by volunteers is genuinely needed at this time, given the ultimate purpose of disclosure. It is not suspicion about the role of volunteers that has made lobbying a focus of public concern, and the disclosure of information on their use by associations will not provide information needed to address trust issues. Indeed, volunteers are typically used by association lobbyists precisely because they lack the advantages of money or personal contacts that have fostered public suspicions, or because the volunteers may have technical expertise related to a specific initiative. We therefore endorse:

The exclusive focus of Bill C-43 on those who are paid to attempt to influence government.

Information and Advice to Clients

Several witnesses argued that activities such as obtaining specialized government information for clients, and providing strategic advice to clients based on this information, are important functions of lobbyists, and should be covered by the Act. They are not covered by existing legislation or by Bill C-43, both of which focus on attempts to communicate with public officials.

Witnesses who argued that people providing these services should be deemed to be lobbyists for the purposes of the Act saw the issue as one of achieving the needed degree of transparency. One witness described the failure to capture such activity in these terms: "That means people can escape detection even though they may be providing inside access" (10:11).

Bill C-43 does not propose that activities such as information gathering, research, and the provision of strategic advice to clients should be registrable.

It is, however, predictable that such a proposal would prompt concerns about burdening lobbyists with additional disclosure duties and attendant costs, and raise questions about the need for this information.

In line with our general approach to disclosure, we think that the creation of additional burdens on lobbyists obliges us to consider a proposal with extra care, but the decisive consideration is whether or not the information is genuinely needed by Canadians and their representatives in Parliament.

In this regard, we note that a number of consultant lobbyists, along with other witnesses, stressed the importance of aspects of their work that do not involve direct lobbying of public officials, and that rather function to help clients develop policy positions and communicate effectively with government. The importance to clients of this aspect of lobbying does not, however, necessarily create an issue of public trust. In our view, the fact that the clients of lobbyists may receive expert advice does not, in itself, cast doubt on the fairness of public decisions; a good portion of the content of this expert advice is available to any citizen who takes the time to become informed about government and the policy process. When the clients of a lobbyist put this knowledge to work by communicating with government, or engaging a consultant to do so on their behalf, they become subject to existing registration requirements. We think this achieves what is really needed. We therefore endorse:

The absence, in Bill C-43, of disclosure requirements relating to the provision of information or advice to clients.

Consultations Initiated by Government

A large number of our witnesses stated that the present Act requires them to file information on virtually all contacts with public officials, including those initiated by public officials soliciting information or advice in order to perform their duties more effectively. There was a widespread perception that this requirement makes unfair demands on lobbyists, imposing on them the full administrative burden of disclosure when public officials, and the public interest, may be the sole beneficiaries of a consultation. Objections by in-house lobbyists were particularly heated, reflecting that fact that Bill C-43 would replace the minimal disclosure requirements for them contained in existing legislation with requirements closely approaching those now applied to consultant lobbyists. The concern was that the administrative burden of the new disclosure requirements would discourage communications and information exchange between government and the experts within associations, to the detriment of good decision-making. In the words of a representative of the Shipping Federation of Canada:

> I think the second point we need to make is rather than do anything that could close up the communications conduits between communities of interest such as ours and the federal public service in particular — the administrators of the state — I think it's important to open up the windows as wide as possible (11:11).

The concern expressed in such comments is valid, in our view, both because of the danger of impeded communications and, as well, because the registration of every exchange of technical information or advice would burden the registry with information that contributes little to attaining the broad objectives of lobbyist registration. At the same time, legitimate concerns about impeding information exchange should not, in our view, lead to the exemption of consultations used as an opportunity for lobbying.

Bill C-43 and the LRA already go some distance towards addressing concerns about the registration of government-initiated consultations. First of all, Bill C-43 would not amend provisions of existing legislation which base registration requirements on attempts to influence government. If, for example, an association is contacted by a public servant requesting technical information for purposes that may not even be disclosed in detail, registration of the communication would not be required. In general, if there is no attempt to influence legislation or the other items set out in the Act, there is no requirement to register. An interpretation bulletin from the Registrar would be useful as a source of more specific guidance, here, and any remaining grey areas may ultimately have to be resolved by the courts which will, we are confident, give due weight to the fact where a communication is initiated by a public office holder.

Secondly, Bill C-43 would not alter section 4(2) of the current Act, which sets out certain varieties of attempts to influence which need not be registered. These include public appearances before parliamentary committees, appearances before tribunals and the like which exercise jurisdiction given by legislation and whose deliberations are a matter of public record, and representations to public office holders regarding their authority to enforce, interpret and apply legislation or regulations.

We believe, however, that existing legislation could further reduce the burden on (especially) associations and organizations with respect to purely consultative contacts with government. Improvements in this area are timely because of the emphasis by the present government on a consultative style of policy development, as reflected in major ministerial and/or bureaucratic consultative initiatives in a number of policy sectors. This consultative style, we believe, is increasingly important for technically superior policy-making, and the enhancement of disclosure requirements for lobbyists should not impede its use.

Exempting participation in government-initiated consultations from registration would do three things. It would help to address concerns about burdensome reporting requirements mentioned by witnesses, and help the registry achieve its fundamental objectives by minimizing the collection of unneeded information. Most fundamentally, it would ensure that government and outside groups work in partnership as much as possible, to meet the policy challenges of the nineties. We are therefore amending Bill C-43 so as to provide:

That 4(2) of the LRA be amended by the addition of a subsection (c) which would exempt from registration participation in a consultation with a public office holder initiated by that public office holder, or an employee working on behalf of that public officer.

We recognize that this amendment will require an interpretation bulletin from the Registrar, in order to ensure that the exemption is precisely defined and narrowly limited, so that only kinds of information which are entirely irrelevant to the purposes of the LRA will not have to be filed.

Levels of Disclosure: The Tiers

The present LRA establishes two classes or "tiers" of lobbyists, and applies differing disclosure requirements to each. The Holtmann Committee recommended that these tiers be eliminated, thus subjecting all lobbyists to uniform disclosure requirements.

Bill C-43 would retain a formal distinction between types of lobbyist. It reflects the Holtmann Committee recommendation, however, by making the disclosure requirements much more uniform than those of the current Act. The Bill thus responds to critics who have nicknamed the LRA the "business card bill" because it requires little more from corporate and association employees than the information on their business cards.

The fact that Bill C-43 would reduce what is at stake in the distinction between tiers of lobbyist was recognized by a number of our witnesses. Simon Reisman, for example, after questioning the need for a distinction declared: "... I don't see a great deal of harm in the distinction that is drawn, so it's nothing that I would go to war about" (15:8).

Organizations such as the Government Relations Institute of Canada (GRIC) and the Public Affairs Association of Canada (PAAC), which represent memberships consisting of both consultant and in-house lobbyists, indicated that no consensus was discernible within their memberships on this issue. In our hearings, the major advocates of the distinction were association lobbyists, who repeatedly stressed that their influence upon government is achieved through openness and public support, and consists substantially of the provision of technical information and advice to government officials rather than more political pressures. While several indicated that the convergence in disclosure requirements for the two tiers would reduce the practical importance of a distinction, virtually all commended the government for the recognition, however formal, that their work differs from that of consultant lobbyists. Thus, in the words of representatives of the Canadian Chemical Producers' Association: "CCPA is pleased that Bill C-43 continues the distinction between individuals who lobby for clients and in-house lobbyists. In our view, this is a valid distinction to make" (letter, p. 2).

Witnesses making the countercase argued, in essence, that a lobbyist is a lobbyist. After noting that Canada is the only jurisdiction regulating lobbying which employs different reporting requirements for "people who do essentially the same thing," Dr. John Chenier, Editor and Publisher of *The Lobby Monitor*, argued that

> While the internal roles of corporate, association and consultant government relations people might vary considerably, there is very little difference in the external roles and goals of these people (19:29).

The concern, aside from the principle, is that each tier includes large, well-resourced lobbying enterprises as well as small, more modestly resourced efforts. Thus, for example, consulting lobbyists may be small themselves, or represent smaller firms that cannot afford internal government relations departments, while association lobbyists range from minuscule one-person outfits to well-financed and highly professional organizations such as the Chamber of Commerce. Lighter disclosure requirements for one category would inevitably give an additional advantage to some organizations whose resources already give them substantial leverage, and by definition limit public knowledge precisely where it should be most complete.

Academics and others have developed a wide variety of classifications of lobbyists for research purposes. Our approach to the issue of tiers, as to the issues discussed elsewhere in this report, is based on whether or not they contribute to the effectiveness of legislation in ensuring the disclosure of genuinely needed information. If they do this, they have a place in the Bill. If the tiers impede effectiveness, they ought not to be retained, irrespective of our convictions about differences among organizations involved in lobbying.

In our view, one of the most significant changes that Bill C-43 would bring about would be substantially consistent disclosure requirements across the lobbying categories. Bill C-43 thus reflects the "lobbying is lobbying" argument where it counts, in the actual disclosure requirements to which lobbyists would be subjected. Substantial differences in requirements applying to different types of lobbyists are likely, we believe, to dilute otherwise positive effects on levels of public trust, because they impose "information needed" standards on one aspect of lobbying only to refrain from imposing them on another. As well, they create an uneven playing field for the different types of lobbyist, to no apparent public benefit.

At the same time, Bill C-43's proposed retention of a formal distinction between the tiers, and between corporation and organization lobbyists within Tier II, would enable some fine-tuning of disclosure requirements to increase their potential effectiveness. Thus, for example, it would permit consultant lobbyists to be required to disclose information on a "by undertaking" basis, reflecting the fact that they do business differently from in-house lobbyists.

Furthermore, we think that the classification system provides useful information to users of the registry. It enables them to determine easily the status of a lobbyist, and to limit information searches to specific types of lobbyist. This is useful, given that the public concerns that led to the LRA focused on a limited number of consultant lobbyists and are likely to be addressed, primarily, through information about this group. We therefore endorse:

The tripartite structure of Bill C-43, which enables separate attention to disclosure requirements for consultant lobbyists, corporation lobbyists and organization lobbyists.

...

Bill C-43 would not provide for the disclosure of spending, and only a small number of witnesses raised the issue. In our own deliberations, however, we concluded that similar considerations apply to the desirability of disclosing spending as to the disclosure of fees. Subjecting lobbyists to such a requirement, alone among the players in the policy process, seems arbitrary. In addition, such a requirement would not capture direct spending by the clients of lobbyists on items such as public opinion research. It could therefore provide an inaccurate picture of such spending or, worse, drive spending into channels outside the application of the present Act. We therefore endorse:

The omission from Bill C-43 of a general requirement for the disclosure of lobbyist's disbursements (although we are elsewhere empowering the Ethics Counsellor to deal with special cases).

With respect to requiring disclosure of fees and disbursements, we concluded that public interest in these areas properly focuses upon a small number of cases in which grossly excessive fees or spending prompt concern about the integrity of the policy process. For example, media stories alleging substantial lobbying fees in connection with arrangements entered into by the previous government are well known.

Our conclusion is that we do not need to burden the Registry with volumes of routine fee and disbursement data in order to deal with problems created by exceptional incidents. A more efficient approach would be to enhance the powers of the Ethics Counsellor, in order to ensure that such incidents are investigated and that needed information (including fee and spending figures) is disclosed to Parliament and the public. Specific proposals are presented later in this report.

Political and Government Connections

For some, the suspicion that lobbyists use personal connections with office holders to obtain special favours from government lies at the heart of what disturbs them most about lobbying. Lobbyists develop these personal connections in two ways: through participation in partisan politics and through previous service with government.

The issue of lobbyists' involvement in partisan political activities is most contentious because it puts two fundamental principles against one another. On one side lies the right of all Canadians to participate in the political life of their community; on the other, the belief that for lobbyists, who influence the ways in which government allocates public resources, to engage in partisan activities seems to prejudice the outcome of decision-making processes.

During the hearings, we heard both points of view expressed. One witness asserted that the political activities of lobbyists should be restricted. Consultant lobbyists, on the other hand, told Committee members that such a restriction would be unreasonable. Susan A. Murray of SAMCI was particularly persuasive in this regard, arguing that "lobbyists should have the same civil rights as other citizens — including, for example, civil servants — to belong to political parties and participate in their affairs" (10:58).

The use of connections built up through former employment in government is less contentious, in part because this area is already regulated. The *Conflict of Interest and Post-Employment Code for Public Office Holders* prohibits senior office holders from lobbying their former departments for one year after having left office. Other provisions mentioned above require office holders to base their decisions on the merits of an argument rather than on who is presenting it.

After having listened to the arguments of witnesses, the Committee — is sympathetic to the concerns of Canadians that the potential for abuse exists, and is exacerbated when the political or other ties between lobbyists and those they lobby are not known publicly.

However, there are several important reasons why disclosure of this sort of information is neither necessary — nor indeed wise. We begin by presenting our reasons why a lobbyist's political activities do not constitute suitable information to be listed in the Lobbyists Registry. First we doubt that simple registration of political affiliations will eliminate opportunities to abuse connections. More appropriate instruments already address this problem. Provisions in the *Criminal Code* provide sanctions against influence peddling and the *Conflict of Interest and Post-Employment Code for Public Office Holders* obliges office holders to base decisions on the merits of a case. Second, transparency is a central goal of this Act. From the Committee's point of view, information concerning past or present political involvement is already publicly known. Many of our lobbyist witnesses made no secret of their involvement in partisan politics, and the political ties of lobbyists are prominently featured in media coverage of the profession. Consequently, we have no fears that this information needs formal disclosure mandated by the Act. Last of all, we are concerned that placing a disclosure requirement for political involvement in the Act would imply that such involvement is illegitimate. At a time when Canadians should be encouraged to participate in the public life of their community, we feel that sending such a message would be wrong.

In terms of registering past service with government, we consider that the post-employment codes and other measures already in place are sufficient guarantee against potential wrong-doing. Past service with government does not constitute a secret that needs "disclosure". Indeed, we believe that the public policy process — and the public — are benefited by the continued involvement in public life of former office holders who can provide expert knowledge regarding the complexities of government. Consequently, after careful examination, the Committee has decided not to amend Bill C-43 to require lobbyists to disclose past or present political activities or past service with government.

ISSUES APPLYING ONLY TO CONSULTANT LOBBYISTS

Before discussing the proposals in Bill C-43 as they would affect consultant lobbyists, the Committee must express its strong disappointment that so few of these lobbyists were willing to appear before us. The Committee Chairman took the unusual step of writing to invite consultant lobbyists to appear as witnesses; very few responded — fewer still accepted the invitation. A surprisingly large number cited the formation of a professional lobbyists' association as a reason for declining the invitation. This attitude is particularly regrettable in light of lobbyists' repeated claims that they are valuable contributors to the making of good public policy in this country; when offered an opportunity to make a concrete contribution to a piece of legislation that affects them directly, many of them refused. On the other hand, the Committee wishes to commend those consultant lobbyists who helped in our work by submitting briefs and appearing as witnesses. Although they and the Committee did not always agree, their participation illustrates their true professionalism.

One consultant lobbyist who appeared before the Committee argued that Canadians do not care about them; he said:

> The common guy out in the street doesn't really care that I represent some little firm in northern New Brunswick that is having problems with the Public Works department (5:16).

The Committee could not disagree more. Canadians do care deeply about the activities of consultant lobbyists, activities that often have a profound impact on how their tax dollars are spent. This concern is reflected in the terms of the LRA and, indeed, is the principal reason why a registration system for lobbyists was created in the first place. The conclusions reached by the Holtmann Committee indicated that the LRA did not go far enough in meeting these concerns. Bill C-43 is a response to those conclusions and to the legitimate concerns of Canadians regarding the role and influence of lobbying in a system of government which, by definition, is theirs.

On the whole, the Committee believes that the proposed changes to the registration requirements for consultant lobbyists respond to both the Holtmann Committee proposals and the needs of Canadians with commendable accuracy. When these changes are implemented, consultant lobbyists will have to disclose greater detail concerning their lobbying undertakings. We are confident that transparency will thus be enhanced substantially and that Canadians' trust in government — the ultimate goal of this Bill — will be strengthened.

Despite our general approval for this section of the Bill, we believe that an additional improvement is called for.

Contingency Fees

Contingency fees, as noted earlier, are those fees charged by lobbyists in exchange for success for lobbying. The practice of charging these fees is particularly disturbing when government contracts are involved. We believe that this concern has been met in an appropriate and timely fashion by the government when it included a clause in all of its contracts forbidding suppliers to hire lobbyists on this basis. This prohibition also covers situations in which lobbyists have been hired by clients to help obtain government grants and/or subsidies. The ability of consultant lobbyists to charge contingency fees with regard to other efforts undertaken for their clients has not however been impeded in the least.

At first glance it may seem reasonable that a successful lobbyist be rewarded by his/her client in this fashion. As the Committee was frequently told, other professions often charge such fees and as in such cases, contingency fees should be an exclusive matter between lobbyists and their clients. Other witnesses — including several consultant lobbyists — were less sanguine. Contingency billing, Simon Reisman told us, "encourages the wrong kind of people into the business" (15:19). A good lobbyist, he argued, ought to get paid for services provided, regardless of whether the desired outcome is achieved. Susan A. Murray of SAMCI told the Committee that "contingency fees perpetuate the perception of cronyism and backdoor access to government insiders" (10:59). For this reason, Ms. Murray argued that the Act should ban contingency fees, a sentiment that was echoed by another witness, Democracy Watch.

The Committee agrees that there are reasons to be concerned about this form of billing. Although it has been banned with regard to government contracts, grants, and subsidies, successful lobbying directed towards other areas of government policy — regulatory change for example — may result in considerable profit to clients of which lobbyists would earn a share. While the connection between the additional reward and taxpayers' dollars is not as straightforward as it is in the case of procurement, it exists nonetheless.

The Committee, however, does not propose to ban the charging of contingency fees as some witnesses suggested. Several reasons lie behind our decision. A measure of this nature would involve contract law which is beyond the jurisdictional powers of the federal government. Furthermore, we believe that this form of billing does nothing to improve the public image of lobbyists or their profession; if there is to be a decision to end this practice, it is in their own interest to make this change themselves as some consultant lobbyist, to their credit, have already done. Lastly, we recognize that unscrupulous lobbyists could, if they wished, find a way to disguise their contingency billing.

When contingency fees are charged, however, we believe that Canadians do have a right to know this, since this practice does have a bearing on the public policies constructed in their name and paid for out of their pockets. Lastly, the availability of such information in the Lobbyists' Registry should assist the Ethics Counsellor when suspected transgressions of the Lobbyists' Code of Conduct are investigated. Accordingly, and in conformity with the direction taken by the *Lobbyists Registration Act*, the Committee is amending Bill C-43 to:

Require consultant lobbyists to disclose when they undertake a lobbying effort on a contingency-fee basis.

ISSUES APPLYING ONLY TO IN-HOUSE LOBBYISTS (CORPORATE)

a. Parent/Subsidiaries Who Benefit From Lobbying

The LRA requires consultant lobbyists to disclose parents and subsidiaries of corporate clients, in order to clarify the true beneficiary of a lobbying initiative. The Holtmann Committee argued convincingly, in our view, that the same logic applies to in-house (corporate) lobbyists, whose corporate employers may be linked to subsidiaries and/or parent companies who benefit from corporate lobbying activities and may ultimately control or direct them.

Bill C-43 would require corporate lobbyists to disclose the parent and subsidiary companies of their employer, limiting the disclosure of subsidiaries to those having a direct interest in the lobbying activities being undertaken. This limit was also recommended by the Holtmann Committee, which recognized that multiple subsidiary relationships in some companies might be hard for corporate lobbyists to keep track of, and could burden the registry with information of little real use.

A number of witnesses supported this requirement. In its brief, Democracy Watch treated it as a self-evident element of acceptable disclosure. None, including witnesses from the in-house (corporate) lobbying community, opposed it. We believe its inclusion within the LRA is necessary if disclosure requirements are to inform people adequately about who is lobbying government. As in the case with consultant lobbyists and for the same reasons, "who" includes the beneficiaries of lobbying initiatives, not merely those employed for the purpose of lobbying. We therefore endorse:

The provisions of Bill C-43 relating to the disclosure by in-house (corporate) lobbyists of parent companies and interested subsidiaries.

b. **Employer's Business Activities**

The only employer-related information required by the LRA of in-house lobbyists (corporate) is the name and address of the employer. Among the new disclosure requirements which Bill C-43 would impose is a requirement that in-house lobbyists provide a general description of the employers business activities (6(3)(*f*)).

This requirement was not addressed specifically by our witnesses, except in general comments referring to the increase which Bill C-43 would achieve in the amount of potentially useful information available through the register. A general understanding of the business activities of a corporation is necessary for those who use the registry to be able to understand the connection between an individual lobbying initiative and the corporate interests it serves. This information is directly relevant to the underlying objectives of the bill: only when one identifies the corporate interests of a lobbyist can one draw conclusions about whether they correspond with, serve or oppose the interests of the general public. We therefore endorse:

The provision at section 6(3)(f) of Bill C-43.

c. Proposed Subject-Matters

The LRA currently requires consultant lobbyists to disclose the subject-matter of lobbying. This is done by means of a 52 subject check-list provided by the Registrar. Bill C-43 would extend this requirement to corporate lobbyists (along with those for associations) in line with its general shift towards relatively uniform reporting requirements across the tiers.

The information provided by the check-list may have become less important as a result of other disclosure requirements, notably the requirement to identify bills, policies, and etc., that are the subject of lobbying. It continues to serve, however, as a bird's eye view of the lobbying activity of a registrant. We expect it will be particularly useful in relation to corporations having a broad span of interests and, as in result, listing an extensive number of bills, policies, regulations and so on. We therefore endorse:

The provision at section 6(3)(h) of Bill C-43.

ISSUES APPLYING ONLY TO IN-HOUSE LOBBYISTS (ORGANIZATION)

Bill C-43 proposes to establish a separate category for lobbyists who work for organizations or associations. Before reviewing the new registration requirements for such lobbyists, it is worth noting that its definition of organization includes:

> any business, trade, industry, professional or voluntary organization, trade union or labour organization, chamber of commerce or board of trade, partnership, association, charitable society, coalition, interest group and government.[7]

Thus all these entities would be required to adhere to the registration requirements that are set forth in the bill for in-house organizational lobbyists.

---

[7] The Government of Canada and corporations (which are covered by the section of the Bill dealing with in-house corporation lobbyists) are excluded from this definition.

As earlier stated, the Committee endorses the retention and refinement of the tier system as proposed by Bill C-43, largely because a recognition of the distinctions between lobbyists provides a needed degree of flexibility in terms of the kinds of information being solicited. This is particularly so for organizational lobbyists who, though their methods may be similar to other kinds of lobbyists, represent interests that are publicly known and consistent across time. We are pleased, therefore, to note that the Bill acknowledges this difference through the reporting requirements it would establish for organizational lobbyists.

One of our witnesses, Professor Ian Lee, described lobbying as a three-legged stool made up of direct lobbying, grass roots lobbying and coalitions. The Committee thus welcomes the inclusion of one "third leg" — coalitions — under the Bill's definition of organization. This would subject coalitions, often created expressly for lobbying purposes, to the same disclosure requirements as apply to other kinds of organizations. The LRA's lack of any provision producing transparency for coalition lobbying was one of the leading concerns of the Holtmann Committee; we are gratified to see that this concern has been answered and a major gap in the legislation closed.

Other aspects of this section of the Bill meet with our approval as well. The proposal to make the senior paid officer of an organization the one responsible for filing information seems to us sensible and intelligent. The Committee also believes that the proposed subject-matters that organizations would have to report and the requirement that they describe their membership are suitable and meet the test of needed information.

We note, however, the concerns expressed by many organizations that the requirements proposed for them in the Bill may be excessive as well as administratively and financially burdensome. We feel that it is only natural that organizations faced with a series of registration requirements that are new and unfamiliar would harbour such reservations. Other witnesses, however, told us that organizations should have no great difficulty complying with the proposed measures which Professor Paul Pross had studied and concluded should not be onerous. The ability to submit information to the Registry in electronic form, in particular, he stressed, should lighten any potential burden. The Canadian Construction Association's (CCA) fear of overzealous reporting requirements has long been a matter of public record. During our hearings, the CCA stated that it found the Bill's requirements acceptable, repeating what it said in a letter to the Committee:

While more information will be required from organizations like CCA under the proposed legislation, the new reporting requirements recognize the administrative burden we face and are certainly manageable (7.26.94).

We agree with the CCA that the new disclosure requirements for organizations should not impose an undue burden yet generate greatly needed information about the lobbying activities of an important sector. We therefore endorse:

The disclosure requirements for in-house lobbyists (organization) as set forth in Bill C-43.

While we think that the disclosure requirements for in-house lobbyists (organization) are appropriate, we do have some concern about the frequency with which they would have report information to the Registry. We have addressed this concern elsewhere in the report by proposing to reduce the frequency with which these lobbyists would have to file updates of information.

Disclosure of Funding Sources

The funding received by some organizations that lobby government was of particular concern to some committee members and witnesses. It was noted that governments currently supply funding to a wide range of groups. When these groups lobby the federal government, it is plausible to suggest that part of the monies supplied them to governments is used to underwrite the costs of this activity.

Most organizational witnesses did not attempt to disguise their funding arrangements with government, information which is already part of the public record. Many argue that government in a pluralist society such as ours, government needs input from many sources in order to make informed choices. Yet not all groups in our society, they pointed out, possess the resources to convey their views to government. Were all voices not heard, the policy-making process would be impoverished. As the Hon. Mitchell Sharp told us, "if a group of people who would otherwise not be in a position to make the representations are silent, then it's a pretty one sided picture that appears before government" (3:17).

The Committee tends to support the general view that some government assistance to groups may be warranted. We disagree with suggestions that such funding be banned altogether, a measure we feel would do serious harm to both the democratic and policy processes in this country. Instead, we agree with another witness, Professor William Stanbury, that disclosure of the amount of government funding received by organizations that lobby is called for:

> What is important ... is disclosure. You ought to know what part of taxpayers' dollars are being used to make a representation to you as a public office holder. This doesn't mean it's nefarious. It just means that you ought to know that (8:22).

Disclosure, as we have pointed out elsewhere in this report, is consistent with the LRA's overall approach to the misgivings held by many regarding the activities of lobbyists. Accordingly, the Committee is amending Bill C-43 so that:

Senior officers of organizations that lobby the federal government and receive funding from any level of government, be required to disclose that information, along with the amounts received, as part of the registration process.

...

CHAPTER IV – THE ETHICS COUNSELLOR AND LOBBYISTS' CODE OF CONDUCT

In the section of this report reviewing fundamental issues, we affirm our support in principle for Bill C-43's proposal to establish an Ethics Counsellor position. The Ethics Counsellor would have authority to develop a code of conduct for lobbyists, monitor compliance, investigate questionable behaviour, and report findings to Parliament.

The proposed responsibilities and powers, reporting relationships and mode of appointment of the Ethics Counsellor attracted extensive attention from our witnesses. In considering the range of views expressed, we begin with a discussion of the responsibilities of the office. This is the logical starting point for a discussion of particulars, shedding light on appropriate powers, methods of appointment and reporting relationships.

Responsibilities

The central responsibilities Bill C-43 would give to the person designated Ethics Counsellor for purposes of the Act are:

(1) developing a code of conduct for lobbyists, in consultation with interested persons, and relating to the various types of influence upon government enumerated in 5(1), 6(1) and 7(1) of the Bill; and

(2) administering the code, through the exercise of powers to investigate and report findings to Parliament.

Only witnesses who disagreed in principle with government involvement in the area of lobbyists' ethics questioned these responsibilities. Otherwise, it was generally recognized that once such a role is created, it involves these responsibilities virtually by definition.

If it is agreed that the responsibilities to be assigned to the Ethics Counsellor reflect the purpose of the office, a second and equally important question remains. Are the responsibilities of the Ethics Counsellor with respect to lobbyists compatible with the responsibilities of the office?

The responsibilities Bill C-43 would confer upon the Ethics Counsellor are additional to powers which will be exercised as a result of revisions to the *Conflict of Interest and Post-Employment Code for Public Office Holders*. Section 5(1) of that code charges the Ethics Counsellor with its administration and the application of sanctions, under the general direction of the Clerk of the Privy Council. In this capacity, as well, the Ethics Counsellor will provide advice to the Prime Minister and ministers on issues of interpretation and appropriate behaviour in the area of conflict of interest.

As set out in the Prime Minister's press release of June 1994, the appointment of the Ethics Counsellor is designed to strengthen and broaden the advisory capacity within the Government of Canada on all ethical issues.

Several witnesses expressed concern about this combination of responsibilities. Reflecting on the scope, importance and powers of the office, Mr. Simon Reisman declared: "In fact, this Ethics Counsellor is going to have to be, if not a god, a demi-god ..." (15:10). He went on to indicate concern about the combination of responsibilities relating to advising government and lobbyists: "It strikes me that these are rather different kinds of things ...". Another witness went so far as to argue that the Ethics Counsellor position itself would involve a conflict of interest.

Most witnesses did not express concerns about conflicting responsibilities. We also note that Mr. Robert Boyle, whose experience as Assistant Deputy Registrar General prior to 1987 puts him in an excellent position to comment (his role involved the conflict of interest duties to be performed by the Ethics Counsellor), saw no problems of compatibility. As well, it is instructive to remember that when he originally presented the government's series of ethics initiatives in the House, Prime Minister Chrétien argued that combining these functions would create a stronger and more unified oversight role, and avoid the overlap and possible costs involved in creating separate offices. This argument drew immediate support from the Leader of the Official Opposition, M. Lucien Bouchard:

> We are also fully in favour of the proposed combining of the duties and responsibilities of the Ethics Counsellor. It seems to me that the government is right to want to avoid duplication and to safeguard consistency and greater effectiveness in the implementation of provisions ensuring respect for ethical standards, especially as regards lobbyists (*Debates*, June 16, 1994, p. 5397).

We do not see how combining responsibilities relating to lobbyists' ethics and responsibilities relating to conflicts of interest on the part of office holders would create, in itself, a conflict of interest. In fact, these two responsibilities fit well together. The Ethics Counsellor will help to keep order inside the government in the areas covered by the Conflict of Interest Code, and he would also deal with lobbying from outside in, under the powers proposed in C-43. Moreover, the usefulness of coordinated implementation is clearly suggested by the fact that a significant number of office holders find employment as lobbyists following their departure from public office. These people would be subject, simultaneously, to the post-employment provisions of the conflict of interest code and ethical provisions of the lobbyists' code during the transition period. To be effective, administration of each code would have to mesh closely with administration of the other.

More broadly, the trustworthiness of government can only be enhanced by addressing both the conduct of public office holders and the conduct of lobbyists. It is necessary to take a holistic view of the decision-making process, which involves various stakeholders including public office holders, the public and lobbyists. It makes sense to combine responsibilities for both areas in the hands of a single official, who would thus be in a position to take issues systematically and channel resources and effort to the areas where they will achieve the greatest benefits.

The Starr-Sharp Report of May 1984 recommended that the Assistant Deputy Registrar General's function be elevated "into a new entity, a body or office which would have a clearer mandate, broader powers, and a higher public profile." The Report also recommended that the head of this new body be called the "Ethics Counsellor." In June 1994, the Prime Minister created the function of the Ethics Counsellor precisely to meet these objectives. In fact, the Ethics Counsellor's new powers are broadened, particularly in the areas of lobbyists' registration and the lobbyists' code of conduct.

We suspect that concerns about combining responsibilities may arise from confusion about the role of advising the Prime Minister and ministers. Several witnesses seemed to envision an extremely close relationship, which would inevitably implicate the Ethics Counsellor in prime ministerial decisions.

While there are excellent functional reasons for the new position, it is important to recognize that one of its challenges would be to avoid being drawn into realms of ethical counselling beyond those envisioned in the Conflict of Interest Code or the LRA, and to communicate clearly to the public the difference between Ethics Counsellor roles relating to lobbyists and those relating to public officials.

We are confident that Mr. Howard Wilson's discharge of the duties of Ethics Counsellor will respond to these concerns. Amendment of the Act in this regard is thus not needed at this time, and would needlessly sacrifice the advantages of combined responsibilities. In the event that public concerns about the political neutrality of the Ethics Counsellor in dealings with lobbyists do emerge in the future, a reconsideration to the decision to combine lobbying and conflict of interest responsibilities may be appropriate. We therefore endorse:

Bill C-43 as proposed with respect to the responsibilities of the Ethics Counsellor.

Powers

Bill C-43 would provide the Ethics Counsellor with the investigatory powers of a superior court, including the power to summon and enforce the attendance of person, and to compel the giving of evidence and the production of documents and payment records. As well, the Bill would confer a power to administer oaths and receive information, whether or not it would be acceptable as evidence in a court of law.

These investigatory powers would enable the Ethics Counsellor to investigate questionable behaviour by lobbyists, with a view to exercising the sole sanction envisaged by Bill C-43 for failure to abide by the lobbyists' code of conduct: such a report to both Houses of Parliament which may include details of payments received by a lobbyist for assistance given to a client in obtaining any government contract.

The creation of a position equipped with these powers would represent a substantial change from the LRA, which does not specifically provide for the investigation of lobbyists. (Investigation is left to the RCMP, where there are allegations of a failure to comply with the Act.)

None of our witnesses argued that the powers proposed for the Ethics Counsellor are excessive. Rather, the central issue was whether they are extensive enough. In particular, witnesses differed over whether the sanction created by publicizing a breach of the lobbyists' code of conduct would be sufficient. One argument in favour of its sufficiency was made by Mr. Resnick of the Government Relations Institute of Canada:

If the ethics counsellor conducts an investigation and in his report, which is made public, finds someone in some way breached the Act or breached the code, then the marketplace would perforce blacklist that person (10:41).

More generally, the submission provided by SAMCI declared:

The powers granted by Bill C-43 to the Ethics Counsellor are extensive and suitable for the purposes of overseeing the activities of lobbyists (brief, p. 6).

A number of our witnesses called for more extensive sanctions. While these views most frequently took the form of arguments that the code of ethics should have the status of law and be enforceable through the courts, in some cases they addressed the enforcement powers of the Ethics Counsellor. Professor Michael Atkinson, of McMaster University, expressed concern that the reports of the Ethics Counsellor to Parliament could not be supplemented with further measures, and wondered if some means might be found of obliging organizations to take action in respect of members reported upon by the Counsellor. Mr. Duff Conacher of Democracy Watch expressed the same concern:

Because he doesn't have investigation or enforcement powers that are significant, he is currently like a traffic cop without the ability to give anyone a ticket (10:12).

In discussing this question, we have found two considerations to be decisive. First, the consistent focus of the LRA, along with the amendments proposed in Bill C-43, is on the disclosure of information about lobbying to Canadians. The Ethics Counsellor envisioned in Bill C-43 would reflect this focus, by advising Parliament of infractions of the Code of Conduct rather than undertaking the direct regulation of lobbyists. This underlying approach recognizes that an informed public, represented by an informed Parliament, provides stronger guarantees of the ultimate integrity of the political process than could be achieved by additional regulation, given that influence peddling and other criminal offences are already included within the *Criminal Code*.

Second, caution is required by the fact that, for reasons explored below, the Code of Conduct will not have the force of law. Actions relating to it will thus not involve the protections against abuse provided by the courts. Providing the Ethics Counsellor with significantly increased powers to enforce the Code of Conduct would create a need for expanded procedural protections, and result in the establishment of an enforcement bureaucracy. It would thus inevitably involve increased costs. Alternatively, in the absence of expanded protections, an increase in powers could create significant dangers of abuse. We therefore endorse:

The general approach taken in Bill C-43 to defining the powers of the Ethics Counsellor.

We note, however, that section 10.3 of Bill C-43 as referred to us would leave the Ethics Counsellor with discretion as to whether or not to investigate when it is believed on reasonable grounds that a breach of the Lobbyists' Code of Conduct has occurred. Given that consistent application will play an important role in fulfilling the objectives of this legislation, we think that investigation should be made mandatory in such a case. We are therefore amending Bill C-43 in order to:

Provide that the Ethics Counsellor "shall" investigate possible breaches of the Code when the conditions set out in section 10.3 are met.

We note, furthermore, that Bill C-43 does not specify the content of the reports to Parliament the Ethics Counsellor would be required to prepare in relation to possible breaches of the Lobbyists' Code of Conduct. It refers only to "results," which could provide a rationale for limiting the content of reports to the conclusions of the Ethics Counsellor. Given that these reports would provide the public with its sole source of information about possible breaches, we think it is important that they include the evidence and rationale behind conclusions the Ethics Counsellor may have drawn. This legislation will achieve its fundamental objectives only if the level of disclosure it achieves is sufficient to answer the important questions, not only about the conclusions of the Ethics Counsellor but about what lobbyists have actually done and how the conclusions have been reached. We are therefore amending section 10.4(1) of Bill C-43 to:

Replace the reference to "results" of investigations by the Ethics Counsellor with a reference to "full investigatory findings, conclusions reached and reasons therefor."

We have argued, in a previous section of this report, that Canadians do not normally need to know the details of lobbyists' fees or salaries, and spending. The exceptions are those rare occasions when extremely large amounts are paid, or expensive campaigns undertaken, the costs of which clients must then recover through increased charges to governments or consumers. The paying of fees on a contingency basis suggests a direct link between whatever a lobbyist is being paid to obtain and the client's ability to pay, and thus provides a special basis for public suspicion when payments are exceptionally large. The magnitude of spending becomes an issue of special public concern when spending on behalf of one side of a policy controversy so greatly exceeds spending on the other side as to threaten to distort public debate and decision-making.

Section 10.4(2) of Bill C-43 would give the Ethics Counsellor authority to report to Parliament the fees a consultant lobbyist has received in relation to the award of a government contract, where the Ethics Counsellor feels this is in the public interest. In our view, an expanded version of this provision could provide the basis for the kind of monitoring of lobbyists' fees and disbursements needed to address the problem situations identified in our discussions.

In order to do the job, however, section 10.4(2) needs to enable the Ethics Counsellor to obtain and publicize fee or salary information on lobbying for any purpose, not just lobbying for government contracts, and to obtain and publicize information on spending. The Bill also needs to enable the Ethics Counsellor to obtain and disclose information about payment arrangements, including the use of contingency fees, where this is seen to be in the public interest. We are therefore amending section 10.4(2) of Bill C-43 to:

Authorize the Ethics Counsellor to obtain as evidence and include in the report of an investigation any payment received, disbursement made or expense incurred by a lobbyist, where this is seen to be in the public interest.

Appointment and Reporting Relationships

Bill C-43 provides that the Ethics Counsellor be appointed by the Governor in Council (i.e. by the government). The Registrar General would be the minister responsible for the Ethics Counsellor, with respect to the duties set out in Bill C-43. Reflecting this, the Ethics Counsellor would participate with the Registrar in preparing an Annual Report on the administration of the Registry and lobbyists' Code of Ethics for submission to the Minister. The other (conflict of interest-related) duties of the Ethics Counsellor would be carried out under the general direction of the Clerk of the Privy Council, for whom the responsible minister is the Prime Minister.

Our witnesses were sharply divided over who should appoint the Ethics Counsellor, and to whom he or she should report. A number argued that appointment by the government compromises what should be the neutrality of the position. Democracy Watch, for example, called for the Ethics Counsellor position to be replaced by an independent ethics commission appointed by and reporting to Parliament (10:15). Failing this, it called for a position modelled on that of the Auditor General, reporting directly to Parliament. This position was supported by Ms. Nancy Riche of the Canadian Labour Congress:

> We see that (transparency of lobbying activities) as the fundamental purpose of lobbyist registration. So in that respect, we would want the Ethics Counsellor appointed by Parliament and reporting to Parliament (6:12).

Professor Pross, of Dalhousie University, likened the situation of the government with respect to lobbying to its earlier situation with respect to filling positions in the public service, and compared the advantages of an autonomous ethics commission to those of the Public Service Commission:

> It is possible that an ethics counsellor appointed by Parliament could perform a similar function relieving the government of the day of the burden of coping with the demands for special favours and also the burden of an embarrassment of explaining lapses of ministers and supporters (8:29).

On the other hand, many of our witnesses expressed no concerns about proposed appointing and reporting arrangements, and a number made a point of affirming their appropriateness. A central argument was that, within our Westminster model of government, the Prime Minister is ultimately responsible for the behaviour of public office holders, and that the appointment by Parliament of an official with responsibilities in this area could cloud this line of responsibility. Thus, in the words of Professor Michael Atkinson of McMaster University.

> In the final analysis, however, we would have to re-invent the parliamentary system in order to create a situation where the Prime Minister was not responsible for the dismissal of his or her ministers, for example .... I would urge you not to contemplate changes to legislation that would in some respects run against the grain of that (14:18).

Many of our witnesses seemed to focus more on the role of the Ethics Counsellor as an advisor to the Prime Minister than as a counsellor to lobbyists. If a single official performs a dual role these considerations, of course, become relevant, and we accept the advice of Mr. Robert Boyle, retired Assistant Deputy Registrar General, that it would be extremely anomalous to have an official providing advice on sensitive matters to the Prime Minister, but appointed by and answerable to Parliament.

In fact, we do not think the duties of the Ethics Counsellor involve requirements for impartiality and good judgement radically different from those applying to a host of duties presently conducted, to the apparent satisfaction of the public, by members of the public service.

We are thus left with only a relatively minor concern about the appointment and reporting provisions of the bill. The fact that the annual report of the Ethics Counsellor would be combined with that for the Registry could blur public perceptions of the distinctiveness of this role and its duties. We are therefore amending Bill C-43 to:

Provide for separate annual reports by the Ethics Counsellor and Registrar, while otherwise affirming the provisions of the Bill relating to the method of appointment and reporting relationships of the Ethics Counsellor.

The Code

Bill C-43 would mandate the Ethics Counsellor to develop a Code of Conduct for lobbyists, on the basis of consultations with interested persons and organizations. Our hearings have raised issues relating to the legal status of this code, its content, and the process by which it would be developed.

a. **Status and Content**

The aspect of the code that received the most substantial attention during our hearings was the legal status proposed for it by Bill C-43. Views differed considerably over whether the code should be a set of prescriptions whose violation would result only in negative publicity, as proposed in Bill C-43, or a statutory instrument containing offences that could be enforced by the courts in the same manner as other *Criminal Code* offences.

Those, such as representatives of Democracy Watch, who favoured the latter approach argued that the code proposed in Bill C-43 is essentially toothless, and that the possibility of negative publicity alone would be insufficient to bring about compliance.

Most witnesses, however, recommended caution on this issue, calling for a step-by-step approach which would see the development of a code, some experience with its application, and then the consideration of whether it might be appropriate to endow it with legislative status. This incremental approach was recommended, in part, because of concerns about prescribing legislative status for an instrument yet to be developed. In the words of Mr. Simon Reisman: "Whether it's suitable to be law or not really depends on what's in it" (15:9).

As was noted by a representative of the Public Affairs Association, the *Criminal Code* already provides sanctions against offences such as bribery, corruption and influence-peddling (10:26). A further concern, raised by representatives of the Canadian Society of Association Executives, was that if a code of this kind functioned to regulate a profession, it could intrude on a provincial jurisdiction.

More broadly, several witnesses suggested that an emphasis on sanctions and enforcement does not magically foster acceptable conduct. Mr. Brian Grainger, of Grainger and Associates, shared with us an extensive knowledge of American practices, which have resulted in a detailed 200-page book of ethical instructions for public servants and an enforcement program with a full-time staff of some 100 people. His judgement of the results:

> At the present time there is little evidence to suggest ethical behaviour is more likely to occur only because a compliance-based code is in place. Under a compliance-based approach, the formalities are often respected but the workplace behaviour may not necessarily change (14:5).

On balance, we do not think that a code focused on the definition of offences and penalties is needed at this time. The concerns raised by our witnesses are, we believe, persuasive on this issue. More broadly, the code envisioned in Bill C-43 is consistent with the approach to lobbying taken elsewhere in the Bill: it would result in the disclosure of questionable behaviour rather than direct sanctions, and leaves members of the public, their representatives, and prospective employers of lobbyists free to respond according to the particulars of the situation.

We are, furthermore, concerned that amendment of Bill C-43 to give the code the status of a law could result in a tendency to restrict its content to offences that could be proven before the courts, and preclude more judgmental provisions which may be needed to define acceptable conduct by lobbyists. It would be preferable, we believe, to establish a code setting out standards that respond to public expectations about how the various types of lobbyist should behave, and leave the possibility that its effectiveness would be enhanced by being made a statutory instrument for consideration by the parliamentary committee which will review all aspects of the Act in four years' time. This is the approach taken in Bill C-43. We therefore endorse:

Bill C-43 as it relates to the legal status and prospective content of the Lobbyists' Code of Conduct.

The only code-related area in which we are amending the Bill concerns the need for an explicit provision obliging lobbyists to comply with the code. As the Hon. John Manley, Minister of Industry, pointed out to us during his appearance early in our hearing process, in the absence of such a provision a lobbyist might not recognize an obligation to comply, or at least profess not to recognize one. We are therefore amending Bill C-43 so as to:

Specify that lobbyists shall comply with the Code of Conduct following its publication in the *Canada Gazette*.

b. Parliamentary Review of the Code

Bill C-43 would make it mandatory for the Ethics Counsellor to consult to interested persons and organizations in developing a Code of Conduct for lobbyists. A number of witnesses singled out this provision for applause, and we believe there is a widespread willingness within the lobbying community to participate in developing a code.

We too, applaud the inclusion of a consultation requirement within the Bill. This recognizes that the objectives of the Bill can be realized only through collaboration among government, lobbyists and others, reflecting a shared interest in effective measures responding to public concerns about the place of lobbying in the political process. It also reflects a consultative approach to government, which will benefit all Canadians.

Our only concern is the absence of a specified role for Parliament in this process. We have argued throughout this report that parliamentarians have a special interest in the LRA, reflecting their role in counterbalancing the representation provided by lobbyists. This role, in our view, provides clear justification for the direct involvement of Parliament in reviewing a draft code of conduct, prior to its publication in the *Canada Gazette*. Parliamentary involvement at this stage would enable the code to be scrutinized in a public forum in order to determine its adequacy in meeting public expectations and responding to the public interest. Scrutiny of this kind is important so that the process of developing a lobbyists' code of conduct will, itself, foster public trust in government and live up to the ideal of openness which the Act in other respects affirms. We are therefore amending Bill C-43, section 10.2(2) to:

Require that the Ethics Counsellor provide a draft code for review by the House of Commons Standing Committee on Industry, before publication of the Code in the *Canada Gazette*.

As we have argued above, the establishment of an Ethics Counsellor mandated to develop a Code of Conduct for lobbyists would represent a major change from the status quo, and a major enhancement of previous proposals relating to lobbying. Recognizing that lobbying represents only one aspect of the political process, and that the restoration of public trust in government requires decisive action in other areas as well, we do not think that the heightening of standards should be restricted to lobbyists. We therefore applaud the commitment made by Prime Minister Chrétien when he outlined the Government's integrity measures before the House on June 16, 1994, and announced that a parliamentary committee would be asked to develop a Code of Conduct for Members of Parliament and Senators. In order to emphasize our support for this initiative, we recommend that:

A joint committee of the Senate and House of Commons be established immediately, and be referred the task of developing a Code of Conduct for Members of Parliament and Senators.

Appendix 3   Committee Systems

Chairman: Hon. Peter Caruana, MHA Leader of the Opposition, Gibraltar
Opener: Senator the Hon. Gerald R. Ottenheimer (Deputy Speaker of the Senate, Canada)
Rapporteur: Andrew Imlach (Editor, CPA Secretariat)

The widely held theory that committee systems offer parliaments an effective solution to many perceived deficiencies in the democratic process dominated the proceedings in Discussion Group A. But the exchange of views chaired by Hon. Peter Caruana of Gibraltar and opened by Senator the Hon. Gerry Ottenheimer of Canada produced a preliminary set of criteria which, it was argued, must be satisfied if committees are to be effective in making parliaments more representative, responsible and relevant.

Principal among those criteria was the basic premise that committees must operate independently from party discipline. Functioning as autonomous, specialized investigators, they should be freed from the constraints of party lines so points of agreement can be identified and legitimate differences of opinion can be expressed in less provocative terms. Working together, it was felt that individual members could reach the truth of a matter if both government and opposition parties were not whipping their members towards preconceived positions. A rational examination of issues and alternatives would be possible.

This was seen as a way to meet public demands for parliamentarians to be less adversarial and more constructive in developing solutions for the problems facing their society. The cooperative approach to politics would enhance public confidence in the ability of parliaments to resolve community problems.

While it was accepted that committee membership should follow party standings in the House, and that adversarial politics was necessary to give people a real choice of governments, there was said to be no need to duplicate this clash of ideas within committees.

It was suggested that the non-partisan nature of committee work could be reinforced by spreading chairmanships among the various parties represented in parliament rather than allowing government members to dominate these crucial positions. In Canada, the secret ballot election of the Speaker had elevated the stature of that office, so similar elections could be held for committee chairmen.

However, as a corollary to freeing members from the constraints of party policy, the public must accept that members will also be free to use their own judgement and experience to reach responsible decisions in the national interest. As representatives rather than delegates, parliamentarians should not be freed from the party whip only to be held captive to public opinion.

Nonetheless, committees were seen as an ideal vehicle for the expansion of public participation in policy-making. Instead of excluding the electorate after voting, ongoing public involvement in the parliamentary process could be directed through the less formal and less forbidding atmosphere of committee hearings. But it was emphasized that committees must not simply hear lobbyists, interest groups and the articulate and organized minorities; provisions must be made so that ordinary citizens can also express their views to committees.

It was noted that public input in New Zealand has been formalized through the committee system. All legislation in the New Zealand House of Representatives must be referred to a committee and the public must be given at least one month to comment. Legislation is now therefore substantially changed in committee on a regular basis. Some bills have even been stopped completely.

Allegations that parliamentarians become aloof and divorced from their electorates could be countered by enabling committees to hold public meetings throughout the country rather than just at the seat of parliament.

Once formed, committees must be armed with the facilities and services to conduct their enquiries. Support staff, the right to summon witnesses and the funds to hire non-departmental advisers were identified as key elements in an effective committee structure.

Examples were cited of ministers and senior officials refusing to appear before committees, of former civil servants refusing to appear because they had become MPs and of governments ignoring reports from important committee investigations. These stonewalling tactics could be dealt with through standing orders compelling ministers to appear and requiring governments to respond to committee reports. Measures to compel appearances should not, however, rely on the executive for enforcement.

In the United States, committee powers to reduce the future budgets of an uncooperative department or minister were seen as an effective deterrent to government obstruction of committees.

Public and media opinion could be mobilized behind a committee and parliamentary business could be disrupted until a proper response emanates from a reluctant executive. But a decision to establish effective committees must be accompanied by the recognition that all sides have to cooperate with each other and respect the role of committees.

Parliaments in Canada, New Zealand and Jamaica have moved committee review of legislation into the early stages of parliamentary consideration. Committees now examine legislation prior to second reading so changes can be made before the House approves the intent of a bill in principle. Canadian committees also look ahead to comment on future spending and policy priorities.

The relationship between a House and its committees was a cause of some debate. Concern was expressed that the Chamber would lose its place in the political process and thus deny the opposition and backbenchers opportunities to disrupt government plans and generate publicity. But it was argued that such opportunities would still exist when committees report their findings to parliament.

It was in fact suggested that time spent in the Chamber could be reduced to enable members to devote more time to committees. Committees in New Zealand were already having trouble finding the time to scrutinize legislation and oversee the executive. In India, more time is made available as the House does not sit at all while its committees are examining the budget.

A significant problem in the application of committee systems surfaced early in the discussion. Many parliaments, such as those in small Caribbean islands, lack sufficient members to serve on committees. Furthermore, when they do hold committee enquiries, their members often know witnesses personally, thus making it difficult for them to reach dispassionate decisions.

Although it was suggested that small parliaments may already be so close to their people that they don't need committees, it was acknowledged that this is a problem which needs further study. The inclusion of non-parliamentarians on committees was proposed as a possible solution, as was using appointed senators to represent particular interests.

Another problem identified in the group was in the handling of broad policy questions. An issue may cut across the activities of several committees, so that no single committee can examine the matter as a whole. A proliferation of special issue-oriented committees was not recommended.

While it was clearly the view of the group that committees are, in principle, valuable additions to the parliamentary process, it was also evident that parliaments need comparative information on various practices so that committee systems actually do make parliaments more representative, responsible and relevant.

Appendix 4   Making Laws Make Sense

Chair: Elizabeth Smith (SG, Commonwealth Broadcasting Association)
Opener: Sen. Margaret Reynolds (Commonwealth of Australia)
Rapporteur: Diana Reynolds (CPA)

Sensible legislation must be able to stand up in Court, should fit in with existing domestic legislation and global standards, and be accessible, both in terms of its readability and availability.

These ideals are not totally compatible or necessarily achievable, but new legislation where possible should aim to obtain a balance between comprehensibility, yet still address all necessary legal complexities.

It was noted that there often exists a gap between the original legislative ideal and the Act which is finally promulgated and implemented. Reasons for this breakdown in the original legislative goal, the actual legislative interpretation and the final implementation of the law include:

- the fact that many Members do not fully understand the role and practice of the parliamentary draftspersons in translating an idea into law (especially true of new MPs), or lack familiarity with the practical environment of bureaucracy which must implement the legislation (especially true of MPs who have been a long time in opposition).
- the fact that the original policy defining the need for a piece of legislation is unclear – the policy was developed in a near vacuum with little outside consultation, and unclear instructions have been given to the legislative draftspersons.
- the fact that, during the course of its parliamentary journey, a proposed piece of legislation is revised and amended, pieces of subordinate legislation or subordinate clauses added; steps are taken to ensure that it is compatible with existing domestic and international laws,

and possible loopholes closed. This process can result in the original legislative intention being compromised. In addition, during the course of this precarious journey, the Bill can fall victim to the guillotine, with the result that, whilst the initial parts of a Bill are thoroughly examined and revised, later sections of it are not so thoroughly perused. It was suggested that this could be resolved by introducing timetabling for bills.

Possible means of addressing some of the other problems identified include: the experience of Australia, where a Parliamentary Committee on Legal and Constitutional Affairs recently investigated the question of making laws more easily understood. It concluded that one of the keys to defining clearer policy (which would lead to clearer legislation) is consultation with those who will be affected by legislative change, and went so far as to recommend rewriting the 'Cabinet Handbook' so as to include a requirement that Cabinet submissions dealing with proposed legislation record whether consultation has already taken place outside Government, and if not why not, along with details of suggested further consultation should Cabinet approve the proposed legislation.

Further, this report identified the preparation of drafting instructions as being critical in the effective drafting of more coherent legislation and suggested that a uniform format of drafting instructions be adopted, which would include

- written (rather than verbal) instructions
- the use of a narrative format (rather than a lay draft)
- and the use of a standardised text, including a statement of legislative purpose.

It was further proposed that training should be provided for government officers to enable them to give effective instructions to the legislative draftspersons.

As regards the committee stages of a Bill, in the Australian Senate these are not necessarily debated in depth in the whole parliament – instead, a bill's committee stages may be referred direct to the relevant standing parliamentary committee. Such committees can call the relevant Minister for a face-to-face discussion at their Friday meeting, and make their report the following Monday. Less typically, and more time-consuming, the committee can invite key interest groups to participate with written and/or verbal submissions. The final option is that the committee will advertise the terms of reference of a bill, and hold public consultations around the country in major population centres (a very lengthy process).

It was agreed that explanatory notes at the start of a piece of legislation were a useful tool for parliamentarian and public alike. Many pieces of Australian legislation include reader's guides, explanatory notes, tables of provisions and an index.

It was felt that, if possible, bills should not be too large or wide-ranging, but it was acknowledged that very tight drafting (with an attendant increase in size) was necessary if Acts were to be free of loopholes and challenges in Court.

Other means of making legislation more accessible were suggested, including the use of linear language to replace the current practice of clauses hanging from subordinate clauses in legislation.

Legislation needs not only to be comprehensible, it also needs to be easily accessible. The prohibitive costs of government documents were identified as a major barrier to accessibility. In Australia, efforts are underway to place summaries of new legislation on to the Internet.

Finally, it was noted that whilst the population is more informed than ever on political issues, the actual process of legislation is still shrouded in mystery. Education initiatives to overcome this are essential – Parliamentary Education Units focusing particularly on disillusioned youth were seen by some as an essential component in the process of making laws make sense.

Index

accountable government 5, 64–5
adversarial system 83
'affirmative action' 6
Africa, civil services 65–6
Arthur, Owen 26
Association of Secretaries-General of Parliaments 23
Australia 2, 70
   making laws make sense 217–19
   see also New South Wales

Bangladesh 58–9
Barbados 25, 49–50
   see also Miller, Billie
Blake, Lord 43
bribery 78
Britain/United Kingdom 2, 42–3, 60
   and European legislation 13
   lobbying 78–80
   role of parties 55–7
   standards of public life 42, 43
   see also Nolan Committee
Burke, Edmund 9, 22, 56
   on representation 5, 55

California, referenda 70–1, 72, 73, 74, 75
Canada
   civil service 65, 66, 67, 68
   ethical standards 47, 49, 50
   lobbying 79, 80, 173–215
   referenda 74–5
   role of parties 57
   Standing Committee on Industry: report 171–215

   see also Charlottetown Accord; New Brunswick; Nova Scotia
Canadian Broadcasting Corporation (CBC) 38
cash for questions 44
Charlottetown Accord 74–5
Chile 75
'citizen' legislatures 31
'citizen-legislator relations' 53–6
Citizen's Charter 65
citizens initiated referenda 69, 70, 71, 72
civics education 8, 9–10, 28, 31
civil servants, former, employed in private sector 46–7
Civil Service: Continuity and Change, The 26–7, 62
civil service
   evolving 61–8
   five key principles 62
   Nolan Committee on 94–5, 160–70
codes of conduct, general 48
Colorado state 74
Committee on Standards of Conduct in Public Life see Nolan Committee
committees and committee systems 32, 82, 83, 221–3
Commonwealth countries 18, 21
Commonwealth Parliamentary Association see CPA
congressional and parliamentary systems 60
'conscience' party model 53, 55, 56
constitutional referenda 70
contracting-out 64

CPA (Commonwealth Parliamentary Association) 1, 17–21, 27

democracy and democratic societies
  institutions underpinning 9
  see also direct democracy; MPs; parliaments
Denmark 13
direct democracy 60, 69–76
Disraeli, Benjamin 55
Donahoe, Arthur 17, 21, 22–3, 38

Economist 47
education, voter 8, 9–10, 28, 31
elected assemblies *see* parliaments
Election Observation Handbook 19
electoral systems, parliamentary associations and 19
ethical standards in public life 30, 41–51
European Commission 11, 12
European Council of Ministers 11, 12
European Parliament 11, 12, 16, 85
European Union (EU) 11–16, 85
  governing institutions 11
  and national parliaments 12–14
  second chamber concept 13
executive
  elected personnel 58
  Nolan Committee on 99–106, 146–70
  role 21
  see also civil servants; ministers

financing electoral campaigns 31
'first-past-the-post' system 2–3, 4
free votes 57, 58, 59

Gambia, The 1
Gandhi, Mahatma 36, 49
Germany 3, 22, 37, 58
Gibraltar 74
gifts for favours 42
Goff, Phil 69–71, 73, 75
'good constituency members' 4
government
  excessive 32

  increasing responsibilities 7
  referenda initiated by 70

Heath, Edward 67
Hewart, Lord, *The New Despotism* 26
human rights, IPU and 19

Imlach, Andrew 82
India 36, 49, 74
  civil service 65–6
  Lok Sabha 35, 38
  role of parties 54, 57, 58, 59
information, access to 10, 26, 32, 66, 83, 84
Inter-Parliamentary Union *see* IPU
International Monetary Fund 16, 86
international parliamentary activities, as justified? 22
IPU (Inter-Parliamentary Union) 17–21
Israel 4
Issues and Questions 43
Italy 59

Jennings, Sir Ivor 67
Jit, Inder 35–6, 38, 39
Johnsson, Anders 17, 21

Kenya 58–9
Kurtz, Karl 25, 29, 30, 31, 32

lobbying 4, 44–5, 50, 78–80
  Nolan Committee on 133
  and registration: Canada 173–215

Maastricht Treaty 12, 14, 16, 74
Major, John vii, 81
'Making Laws Make Sense' 82
Malta 3
'mandate' party model 53–4, 56, 57–8, 60
media 27, 43, 82–3
  political reporting 35–9
  and voter education 9–10
  see also press; television
Miller, Billie 25–7, 28, 29, 30, 32
Miller, Charles 77, 78

ministers
  former, employed in private sector 46–7
  Nolan Committee on 94–5, 147–60
minorities 2, 6
Mountfield, Robert 61–2, 63, 64, 65, 67
MPs (Members of Parliament)
  as following vocation or career? 32
  as 'lobby fodder' 4
  needs of 7–8, 28, 29
  Nolan Committee on 92–3, 97–9, 112–45
  outside interests 43–8, 85, 114–45
  potentially good candidates 28–9
  public perception of vii, 20, 25–33, 43, 82–3, 113–14
  qualities of good 28–9
  regulations proposed for 78–9
  remuneration 8, 43, 84–5
  as representing whom? 77–80
  workload 27–8, 85

'negative ballot box' 9
Nehru, Jawaharlal 36, 39, 49
New South Wales 48, 80
New Zealand
  proportional representation 3, 71
  referenda 69, 71–2, 73, 75
newly elected parliaments, parliamentary associations and 19–20
'Next Steps' programme 63
Nigeria 1
Nolan Committee 41–7, 50, 65, 77, 81, 86
Nolan Committee, first report 91–170
  introduction 107–11
  on MPs' outside financial interests 114–45
  recommendations 96–106
  summary 91–6
Nolan, Lord 41, 50
non-elected institutions 9, 13
non-governmental organizations 32
Northcote–Trevelyan Report 61
Norton, Prof. Philip 53–5, 56–7, 59
Nova Scotia 38, 49

Ombudsman 65
Ottenheimer, Gerald 82

parliamentarians *see* MPs
parliamentary associations 17–23
parliamentary procedure, reform of 27
parliamentary staff, and civil service 66
parliaments
  countries with 1
  fair operation of 6–7
  raison d'être 1
PARLINE 18
parties *see* political parties
Pinochet, General 75
Poland 74
political advisers 66, 67
political institutions, relevance to elected and those affected 5
political parties 2
  EU and 14–15
  internal discipline 4, 5
  Norton's models 53–5
  role 53–60
political summit, routes to 60
politicians
  pejorative overtones of term vii
  see also MPs
'populist' party model 53, 54–5, 56, 58
'positive discrimination ' 6
power-sharing 83–4
preferential voting system 2
presiding officers 6
press
  freedom of 35–9
  as 'unscrupulous' 48
pressure groups 59
Priestley, Julian 11–12
private members' bills 57, 59
private sector 28
privatization 64
professionalism
  constituents 22
  enhancing 17–23
'professionalized' legislatures 31
proportional representation 2, 3, 4